I0809968

IMAGES
of America

DOWNTOWN TACOMA

On the Cover: Early downtown Tacoma was a people place alive with the sights, sounds, and smells of a city fitting its stature as the terminus of the Northern Pacific Railroad. By around 1895, men, women, and children were ever present waiting to either catch an electric trolley on Pacific Avenue or return to the suburbs via horse and buggy. (Courtesy of Thomas R. Stenger.)

IMAGES
of America

DOWNTOWN TACOMA

Caroline Denyer Gallacci
and Ron Karabaich

ARCADIA
PUBLISHING

ISBN 978-0-7385-7002-0

Published by Arcadia Publishing
Charleston, South Carolina

Printed in the United States of America

Library of Congress Control Number: 2009921928

For all general information contact Arcadia Publishing at:
Telephone 843-853-2070
Fax 843-853-0044
E-mail sales@arcadiapublishing.com
For customer service and orders:
Toll-Free 1-888-313-2665

Visit us on the Internet at www.arcadiapublishing.com

To Thomas R. Stenger, whose dedication to Tacoma's history will always ensure the preservation of the past

Contents

ACKNOWLEDGMENTS

The authors of this *Downtown Tacoma* history are already bracing for the question as to why certain buildings were not included or conversely why others were. In anticipating such inquiries, we wish to acknowledge the many people living in Tacoma who take just as much interest in its history as the two of us and are inclined to ask such questions. Without the continuing interest of Tacomans over the years, neither the photographs nor the text would be possible.

Conversations with certain individuals helped shape how the story line progressed as captions were written for the various photographs in this work. Thomas R. Stenger is always a delight to talk to about Tacoma's past, and because of his continuing interest in what we do, this history is dedicated to him. We hope that this accolade will inspire him to write a history of the Hilltop neighborhood where he lives. Kathy Ursich, a neighbor of ours in Old Tacoma, reminded the authors as to how important downtown Tacoma was to earlier generations, who grew up at a time when going shopping downtown was a major event, and that going to the Tacoma Mall is simply not the same.

People at the Tacoma Public Library Northwest Room always deserve special praise for their willingness to respond to our many questions about some rather minute details related to the city's past. The library's online services were invaluable when researching the history of the various streets via the Building and Housing Index or looking for photographs through the Image Archives. The photographs provided by the library, or by Thomas R. Stenger, are acknowledged in the captions. Unless otherwise stated, the photographs come from the collection of coauthor Ron Karabaich.

To determine the focus of this work was a special challenge because we wanted to present a balanced story of how Tacoma's urban environment evolved over time. We hope the reader concludes that we met that goal.

INTRODUCTION

Tacoma had three beginnings. The first occurred in 1852 when Nicholas Delin established a sawmill near the head of present-day Thea Foss Waterway. He was soon joined by the Peter Judson family, who established a donation land claim on land that would later become the site of the Tacoma Hotel. The Judsons began logging the forested terrain, cutting the trees closest to the Commencement Bay shoreline so they could be easily transported to Delin's mill. As the pioneer loggers moved northward along the shoreline, they continued to fell trees and, although they did not know it at the time, began clearing the land for a future city. The Delin/Judson settlement ended three years later after territorial governor and superintendent of Indian Affairs Isaac I. Stevens's dealings with the Native Americans led to war in Washington.

In December 1864, Job Carr—after hearing that the U.S. Congress had incorporated the Northern Pacific Railroad with a mandate to construct a transcontinental line from Lake Superior to Puget Sound—arrived on Commencement Bay. According to his memoir, he perused the local waters and concluded that the terminus would be located northward from the former Judson claim near inlets of fresh water and a land already partially cleared. His dream was encouraged by land speculator Morton Matthew McCarver, who purchased a part of Carr's preemption claim and platted Tacoma City in 1869.

The Northern Pacific Railroad board took another four years to decide that its terminal wharves would be located not at Tacoma City, but 2 miles farther south along Commencement Bay closer to the original Judson donation land claim. While the railroad constructed terminal wharves along the shoreline, the Tacoma Land Company began to develop what at first was called New Tacoma. The attempts to create what some promoters called the "City of Destiny" began slowly, however, because of the collapse of Jay Cooke's bank in September 1873, just as the rails were inching their way toward Tacoma. Since this firm was financing the road construction, the city was born with a fear for its survival. Urban development was further hindered when Henry Villard assumed the presidency of the Northern Pacific. For the next 10 years, Portland, Oregon, was touted as the real headquarters for the railroad while Tacomans struggled to put life into the Puget Sound terminus.

The first chapter of *Downtown Tacoma* covers the period of time between 1873 and the late 1880s when Villard was forced to file for bankruptcy and control of the Northern Pacific Railroad reverted to Charles B. Wright, a Philadelphian who adopted Tacoma as his own personal project. The times were contentious politically as Northern Pacific and Tacoma Land Company managers fought for control of the city against Tacomans not wanting the two firms telling them what to do. This was also the time that Tacomans—businessmen, the political leadership, and laborers—forcibly expelled the Chinese from the city. While clearly racist in motivation, this action was also related to the development of the urban landscape, as well as the issues of law and order and controlling vice.

By 1888, Tacoma was indeed the center of the Puget Sound universe thanks to the completion of the Northern Pacific rail route across (and through) Stampede Pass. Building downtown blossomed as the older wood-framed walking city was replaced by brick business blocks, hotels, department stores, theaters, and government offices shown in chapter two. Creating this downtown was enabled by the introduction of electric trolleys and cable cars that allowed residents to move out of the downtown into Tacoma's first suburbs. This burst of growth was only to last a few years, however. By 1893, America was in the midst of a worldwide economic depression, and the City of Destiny never fully recovered from the ordeal.

The remaining chapters of *Downtown Tacoma* cover the urban growth and development that occurred throughout the 20th century, starting in the first decades when the city began to grow upward as well as outward. The demolition of the first generation of buildings continued with the introduction of many buildings still seen today. This was also the time that residents saw their first automobiles, an invention that prompted the *Tacoma Daily Ledger* to create an automobile section in its newspaper in 1906.

Major wars tend to slow development activity in cities, and downtown Tacoma was not an exception to this tendency during the five major ones that occurred during the 20th century. Even so, in spite of these ordeals and another major depression following the 1929 stock market crash, Tacomans continued to change the shape of the city through the demolition of the old and the construction of the new. What changed over time was the motivation for various acts of new construction, rehabilitation, and urban revitalization, especially after World War II, when it became clear that the automobile was not just a passing phase. Freeways and parking garages began to consume healthy portions of urban space. Suburban shopping malls drained the life out of central business districts as department stores and movie theaters departed. The opening of the Tacoma Mall in 1964 left portions of downtown deserted. Ever since that time, urban planners and developers have continued to seek new ways to bring life into the City of Destiny.

How Tacoma's downtown urban landscape grew and changed over time is the story told here through a portrait of its built environment. While reading the work, keep in mind that cities are living organisms that have evolved based on a wide array of factors. Urban planners, developers, and residents do not necessarily agree as to the appearance of a city, but what is seen when looking at these views of Tacoma is a representation of the life of the city covering over 100 years of its existence.

One

1873–1888

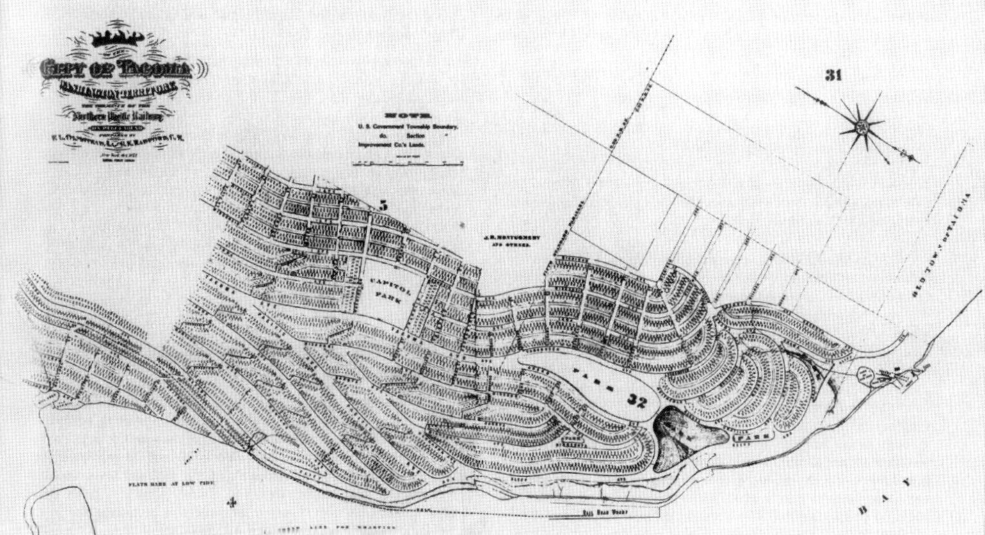

Figure 245. Frederick Law Olmsted's Plan for Tacoma, Washington: 1873

In July 1873, the board of the Northern Pacific Railroad selected the south shore of Commencement Bay as the terminus of its transcontinental line. The firm's board members then created the Tacoma Land Company to develop a city above the terminal wharves. The Tacoma Land Company retained Frederick Law Olmsted to create a plan for what came to be called "New Tacoma." The noted landscape architect's concept for the city, completed by September 1873, is shown in this illustration.

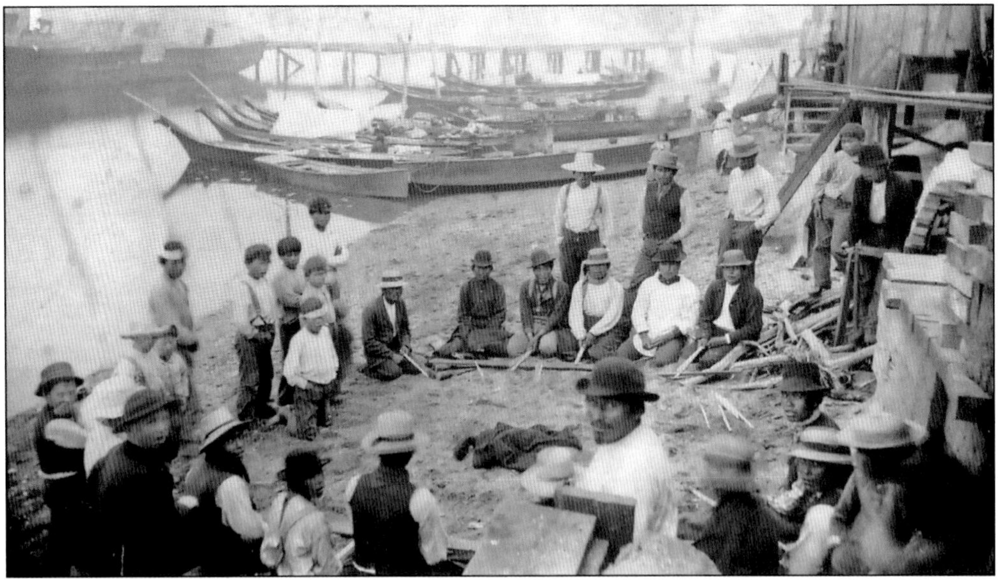

Those developing New Tacoma encountered a major Puyallup Indian village located within the area of present-day South Fifteenth Street. Even though by 1873 the Native Americans were to reside on a reservation established within the Puyallup River delta, members of the tribe would return to their customary places of settlement. In this view, taken around 1886, Puyallup natives have gathered to play their traditional bone game.

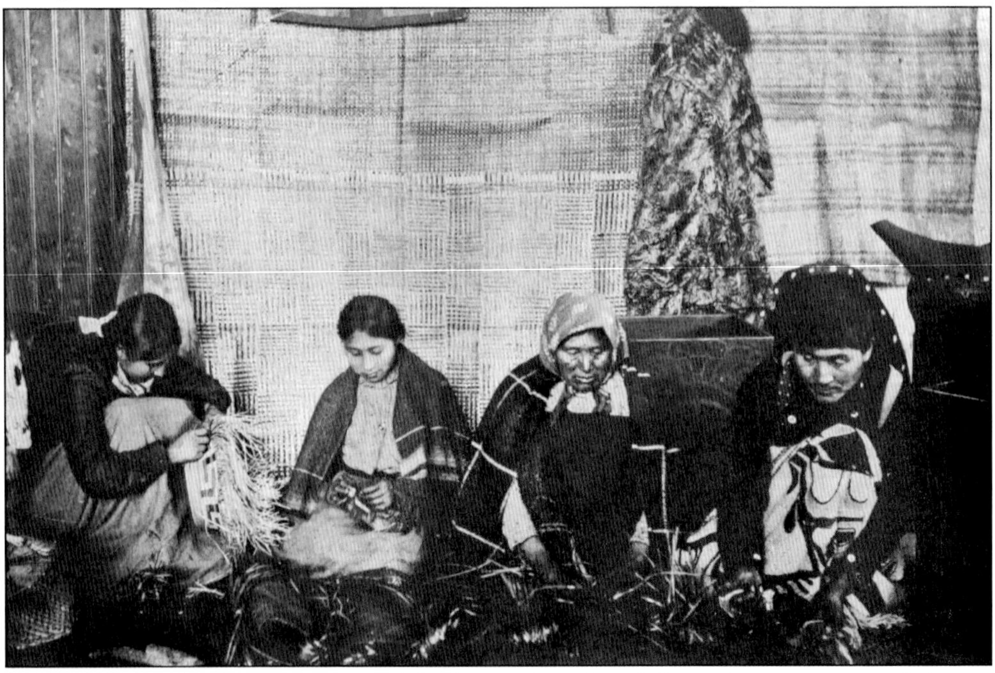

"Indians weaving baskets and mats and displaying them for sale," was the caption provided in an undated promotional booklet entitled *Tacoma: Where the Rails Meet the Sails*. The image serves as a reminder that throughout the history of the "City of Destiny," the Puyallup Indians were a clear and constant presence within the city. They would remain so throughout the history of downtown Tacoma. (Courtesy of Thomas R. Stenger.)

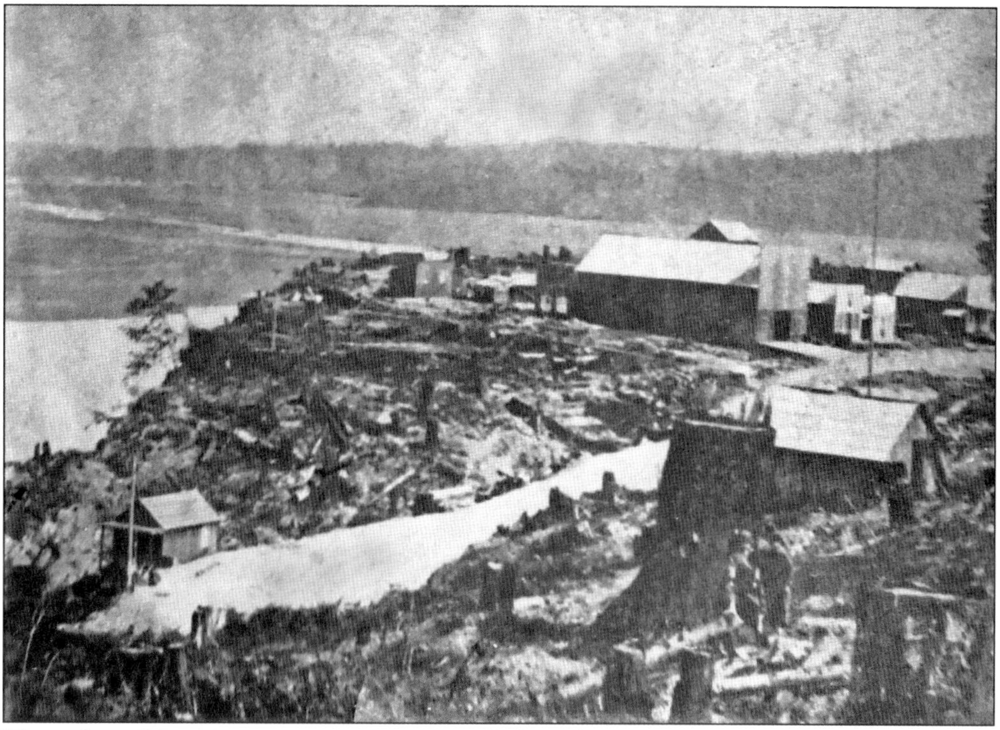

The reality of New Tacoma in 1874 was a partially logged terrain, tree stumps, and roughly graded streets. A resident of that year would have witnessed such a landscape when looking southeast from present-day South Seventh Street and Pacific Avenue toward the site where railroad officials would construct the Northern Pacific headquarters building a decade later.

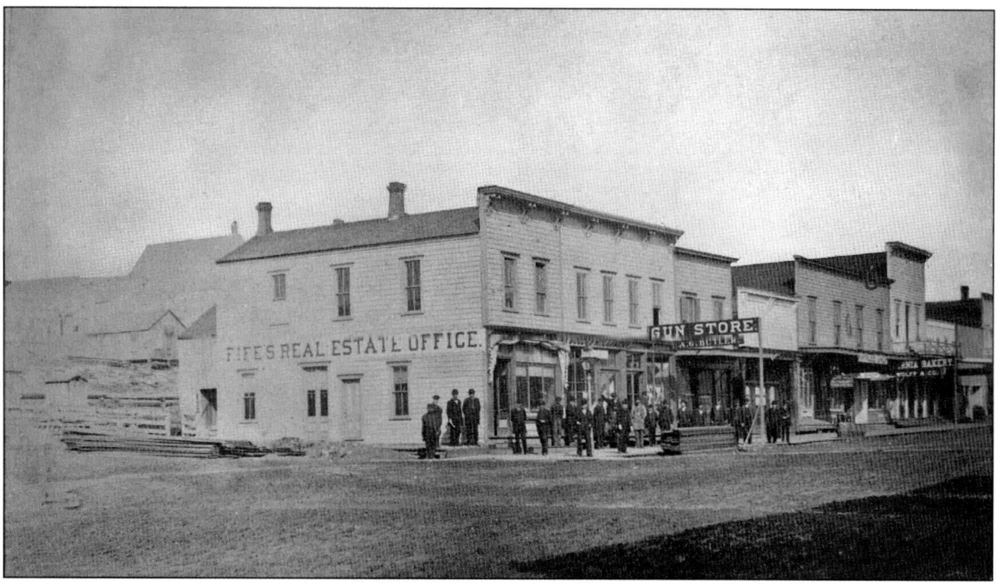

William H. Fife was one of the first to locate in New Tacoma, as this 1870s photograph shows. His real estate office and general store was located on the northwest corner of South Ninth Street and Pacific Avenue. His son William J. Fife also platted the city located east of Tacoma that bears the family name.

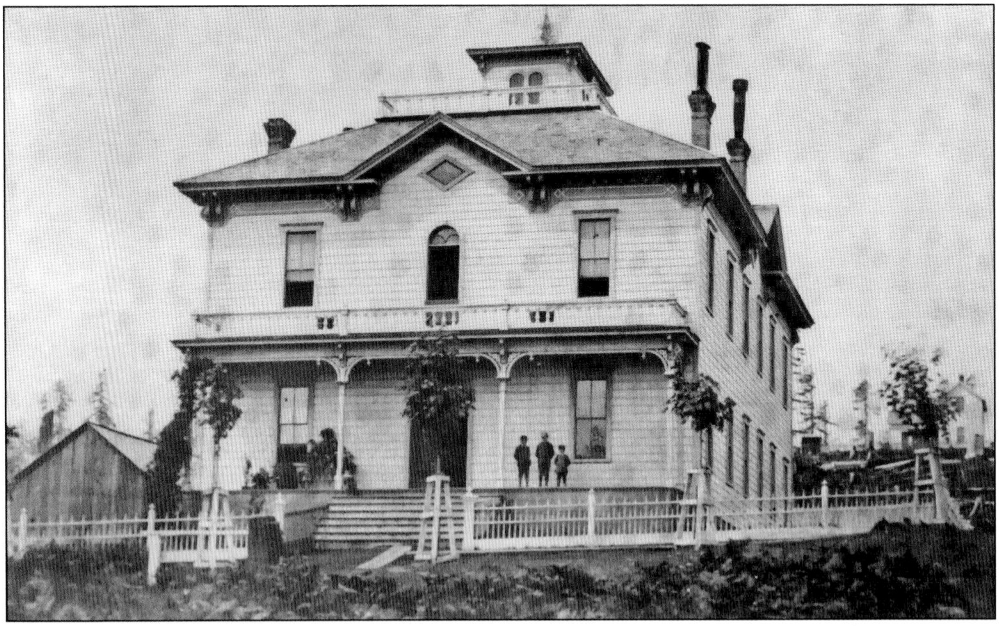

In 1874, Tacoma Land Company's general manager, Theodore Hosmer, authorized construction of its sales office on the southwest corner of South Ninth Street and Broadway. Following its completion in 1875, the sale of urban lots began. In most instances, sales were conditioned on the buyer clearing the lot before the deed was transferred. Other lots were donated at no cost provided the new owner built in the instance the *Tacoma Weekly Ledger*—the city's first permanent newspaper—reported favorably on the activities of the Tacoma Land Company and the Northern Pacific Railroad. (Courtesy of Tacoma Public Library.)

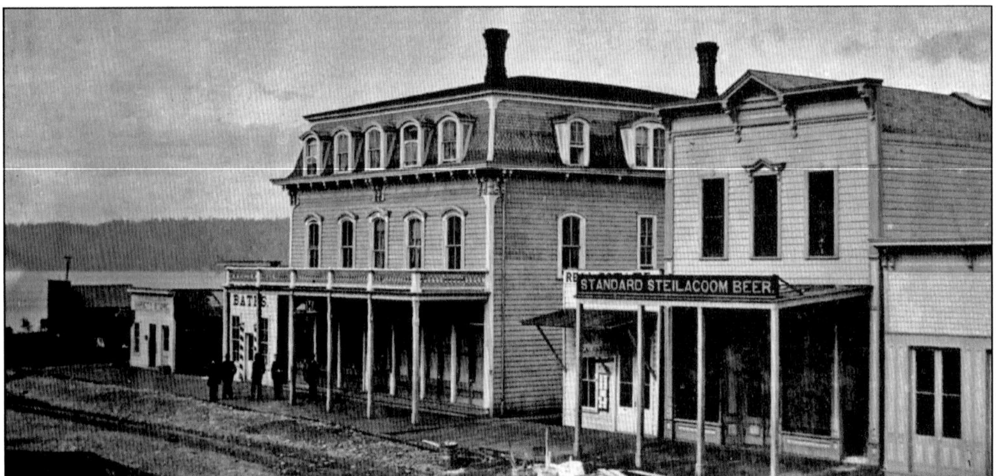

The first lots sold by Theodore Hosmer were situated on Pacific Avenue overlooking the Northern Pacific Railroad wharves. Jacob Halstead built his hotel at 707 Pacific Avenue in 1879. Fred Seger had built the Steilacoom Beer Hall by 1885, the year U. P. Hadley took this photograph. One block south, Harry Morgan built his Theater Comique in 1887. This combination saloon, gambling house, variety theater, and house of prostitution became the focus of a newspaper war between Morgan's *Morning Globe* and Ransom Foster Radebaugh's *Tacoma Weekly Ledger*. (Courtesy of Tacoma Public Library.)

When David S. Lister Sr. established his Tacoma Foundry and Machine Company in 1876, he became one of the city's earliest businessmen. The plant, located near present-day South Fifteenth Street and the shoreline, established the southern part of Pacific Avenue as an industrial zone that also saw the establishment of the Northern Pacific Railroad shops a decade later. Lister (shown at right) was also New Tacoma's first mayor when the city incorporated in 1881. And while little is known of his achievements in this position, it was his foundry whistle that called the workers together to begin the expulsion of the Chinese population in November 1885. Five years after this event, an unidentified photographer documented the foundry complex (below). (Both courtesy of Tacoma Public Library.)

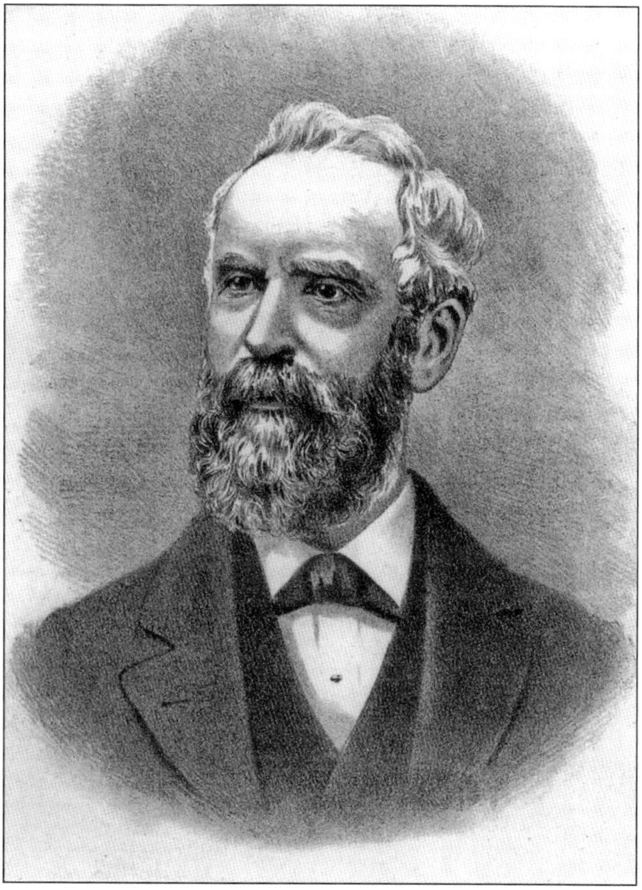

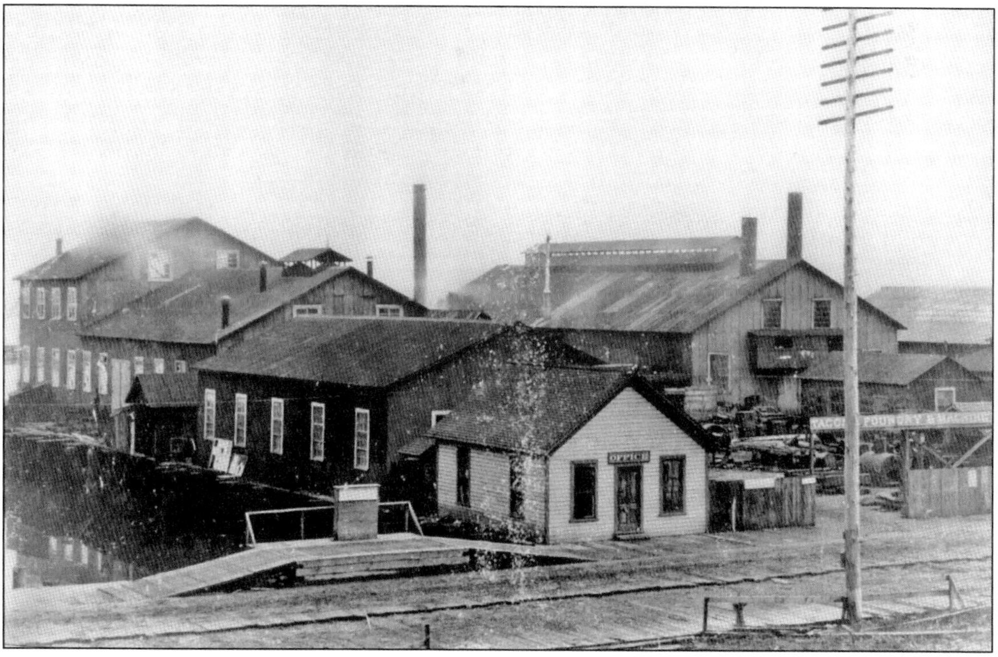

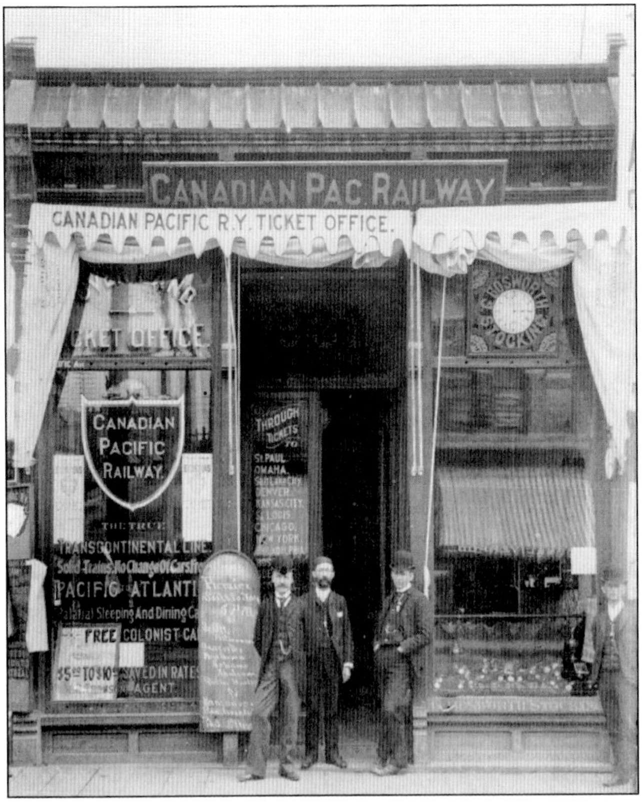

The corner of South Ninth Street and Pacific Avenue was a favored location for various transportation ticket sales offices, including the Northern Pacific, Great Northern, Union Pacific, and Chicago, Milwaukee, and St. Paul railroads. Northwest Airlines was selling plane tickets here by 1940. The Canadian Pacific Railway, photographed in 1880, might have been the first to use the space for ticket sales. (Courtesy of Tacoma Public Library.)

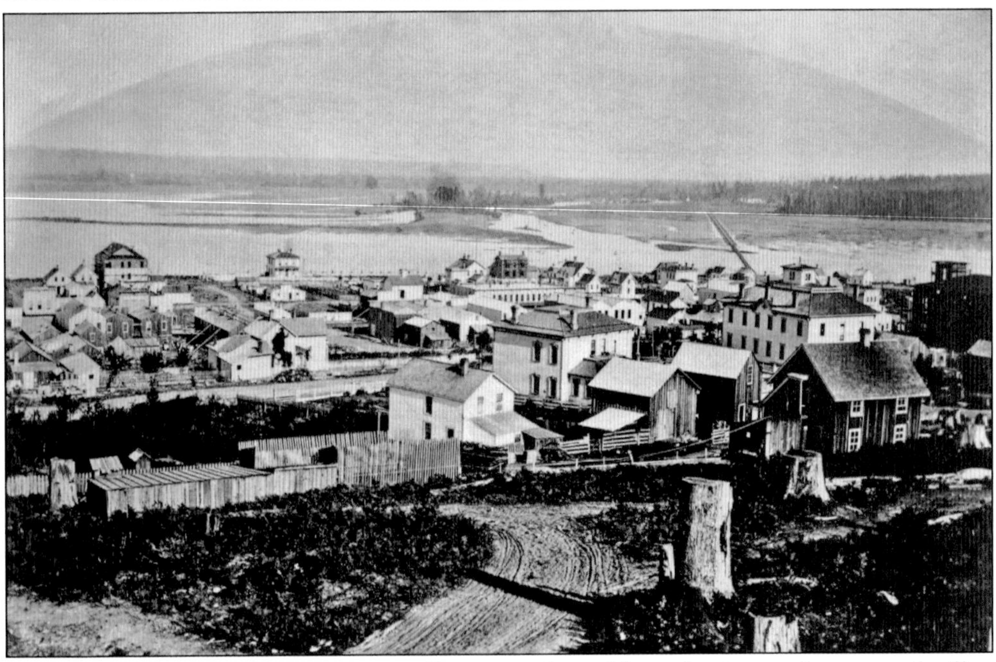

By the early 1880s, New Tacoma was a walking city of wood-frame businesses, houses, and still to be cleared tree stumps. A resident looking southeast from roughly Tacoma Avenue South would have seen the Tacoma Land Company office building as the center of the view.

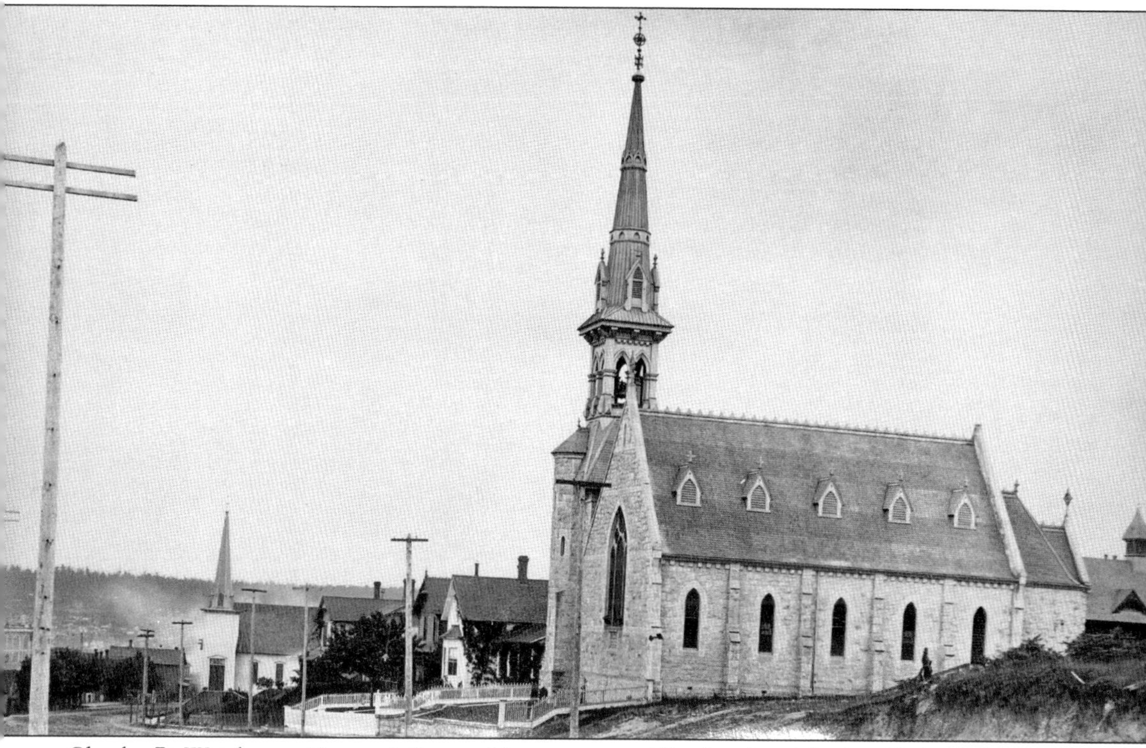

Charles B. Wright was Tacoma's first real booster, even if he lived and died in Philadelphia. He was dedicated to the creation of the city as a major Pacific Northwest metropolis and used his authority as both railroad and land company presidents to make sure that Tacoma was truly the "City of Destiny." He thought not just in terms of business blocks but also of private schools, churches, and parks. His land donations, however, always came with a condition. If the lands were not developed for the intended purpose, the deed would not be transferred to the new owner. Donations for parks specifically stated that the City of Tacoma had to create a park department to manage the sites. St. Luke's Episcopal Church, located at 602 Broadway, was completed in 1883 thanks to Wright's donation of the land. Other churches benefited as well during this time, and as this 1887 view shows, steeple spires became a visible scene upon the Tacoma urban landscape.

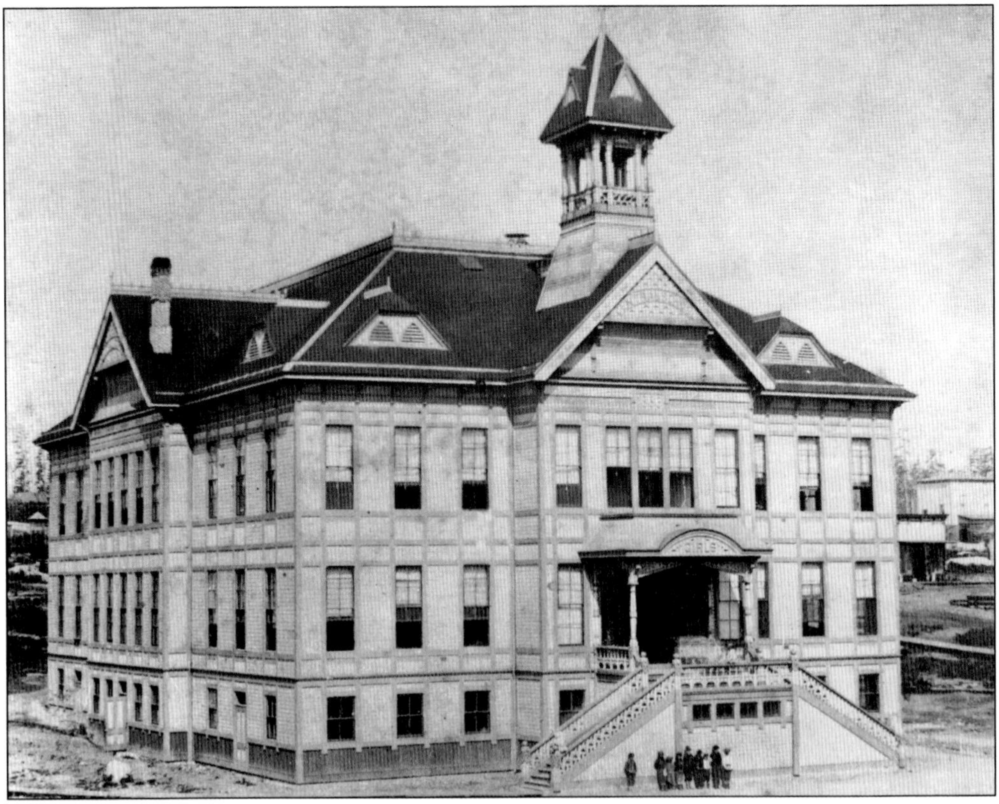

Portland, Oregon, architect Joseph Sherwin designed Central School in 1883. Located at South Twelfth and G (now Altheimer) Streets, this public school witnessed the first senior high school graduating class the next year. The school continued to educate both elementary and upper grades until its demolition in 1914. The site then became a sports field and playground.

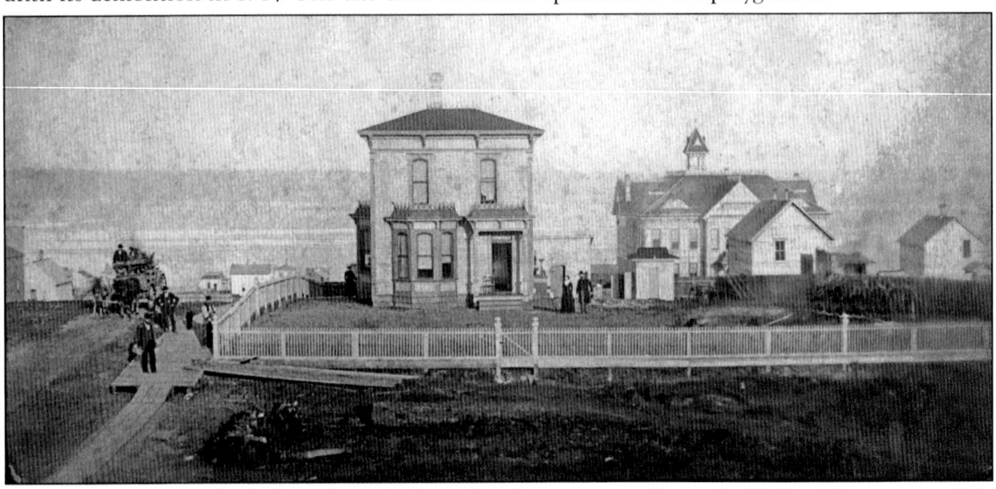

Central School marked the edge of urban development in the early 1880s. Houses, roughly graded roads, and board sidewalks characterized the surrounding area. Photographer U. P. Hadley documented this unidentified residence from present-day Yakima Avenue South and South Twelfth Street shortly after the dedication of Central School, seen here in the background. (Courtesy of Thomas R. Stenger.)

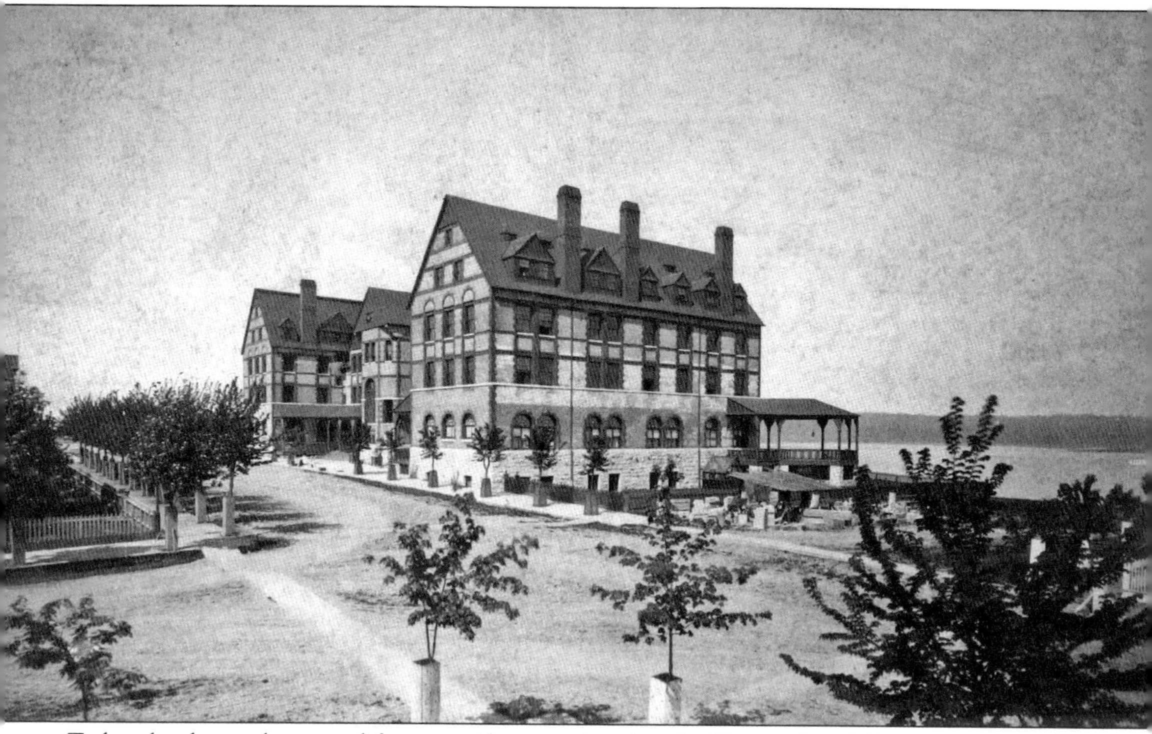

To lure land speculators and future residents to the city, the Tacoma Land Company retained the New York architectural firm McKim, Mead, and White to design a hotel to be prominently placed on South A and Ninth Streets overlooking Commencement Bay. Stanford White became the primary architect for the Tacoma Hotel that opened for business on August 8, 1884. Other architectural firms—including Spokane's Kirtland Cutter and Tacoma's Sutton, Whitney, and Dougan; Farrell and Darmer; and Proctor and Dennis—designed various additions and remodeling during the half century that the hostelry graced the urban landscape. Visitors expressed various opinions about the edifice. Rudyard Kipling saw it as pretentious. Fellow poet Joaquin Miller lauded its beauty. For Tacomans, it was the place where deals were made and commercial organizations met before constructing separate buildings for their functions. Besides a dining room, where one could eat in style, regulars kept their personally inscribed shaving mugs in African American Henry Asberry's barbershop.

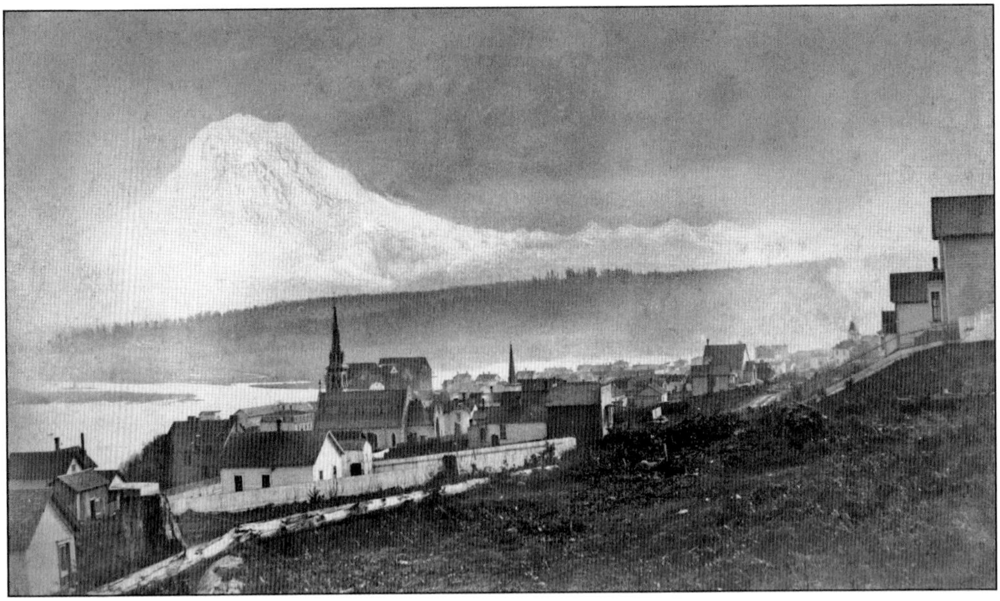

One landmark that Joaquin Miller noted while sitting on the veranda of the Tacoma Hotel was the beauty of Mount Rainier (or Tahoma as the Northern Pacific Railroad officially called it). An unidentified photographer in the above image clearly exaggerated the mountain's grandeur but points to the fact that Tacomans have always considered the mountain its own. This view was probably taken shortly after the opening of the hotel. The photograph below was taken later in the 1880s when a new hotel addition was under construction. Both images show, however, that at this time Tacoma was still in its infancy. (Above courtesy of Thomas R. Stenger; below courtesy of Tacoma Public Library.)

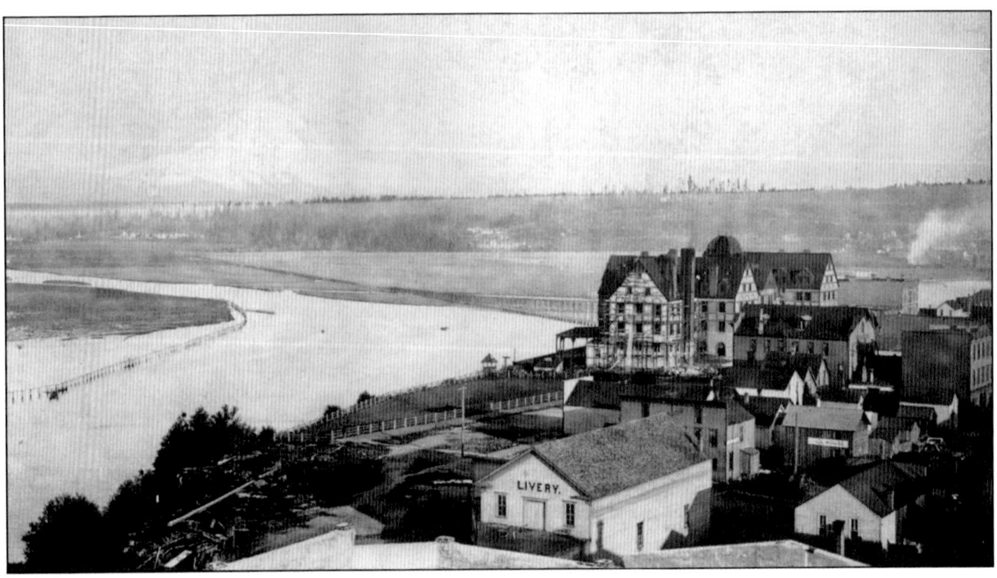

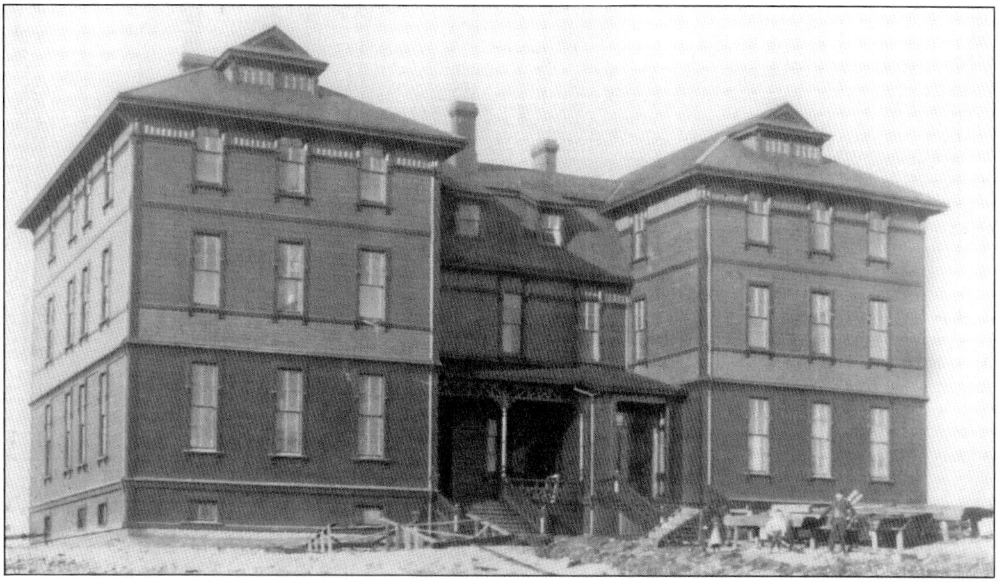

Charles B. Wright sponsored the construction of two private schools in Tacoma: Annie Wright Seminary for girls in 1884, located north of downtown, and Washington College for boys, located at 714 Tacoma Avenue South, in 1885. The architectural firm of Boone and Meeker designed the college building, shown above. The facility was not actually a college but an academy for men who had progressed beyond an elementary school education. By 1898, the building was Tacoma's first public high school. In 1912, it was demolished to make way for a new Central School on the same site. This building is now the administrative headquarters for the Tacoma School District. Photographer Hattie King captured both the school and the student group portrait (below) at an unknown time but most likely after the creation of Tacoma High School. (Both courtesy of Tacoma Public Library.)

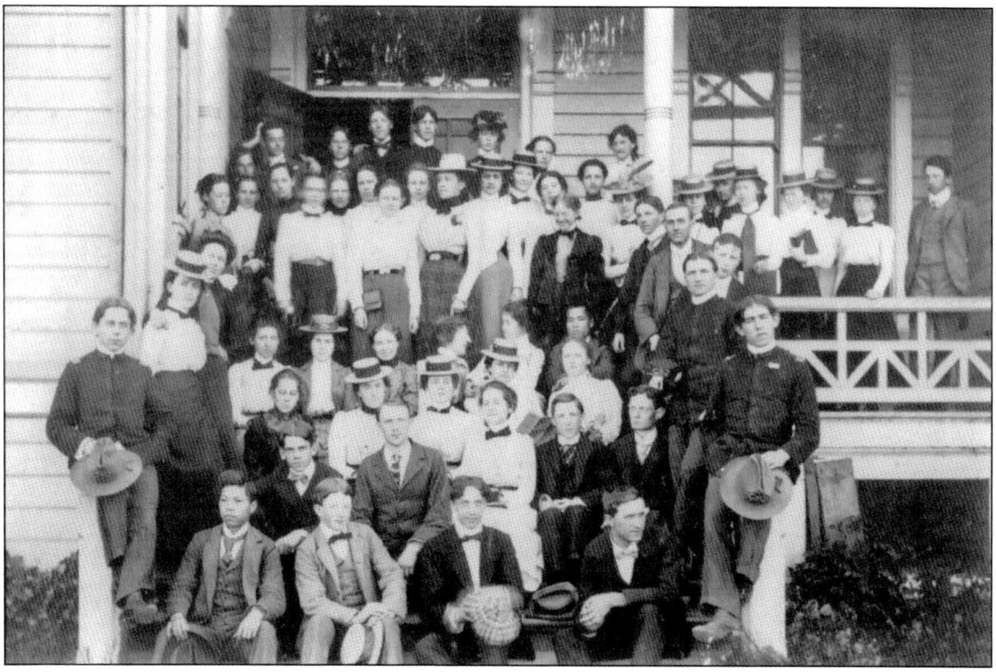

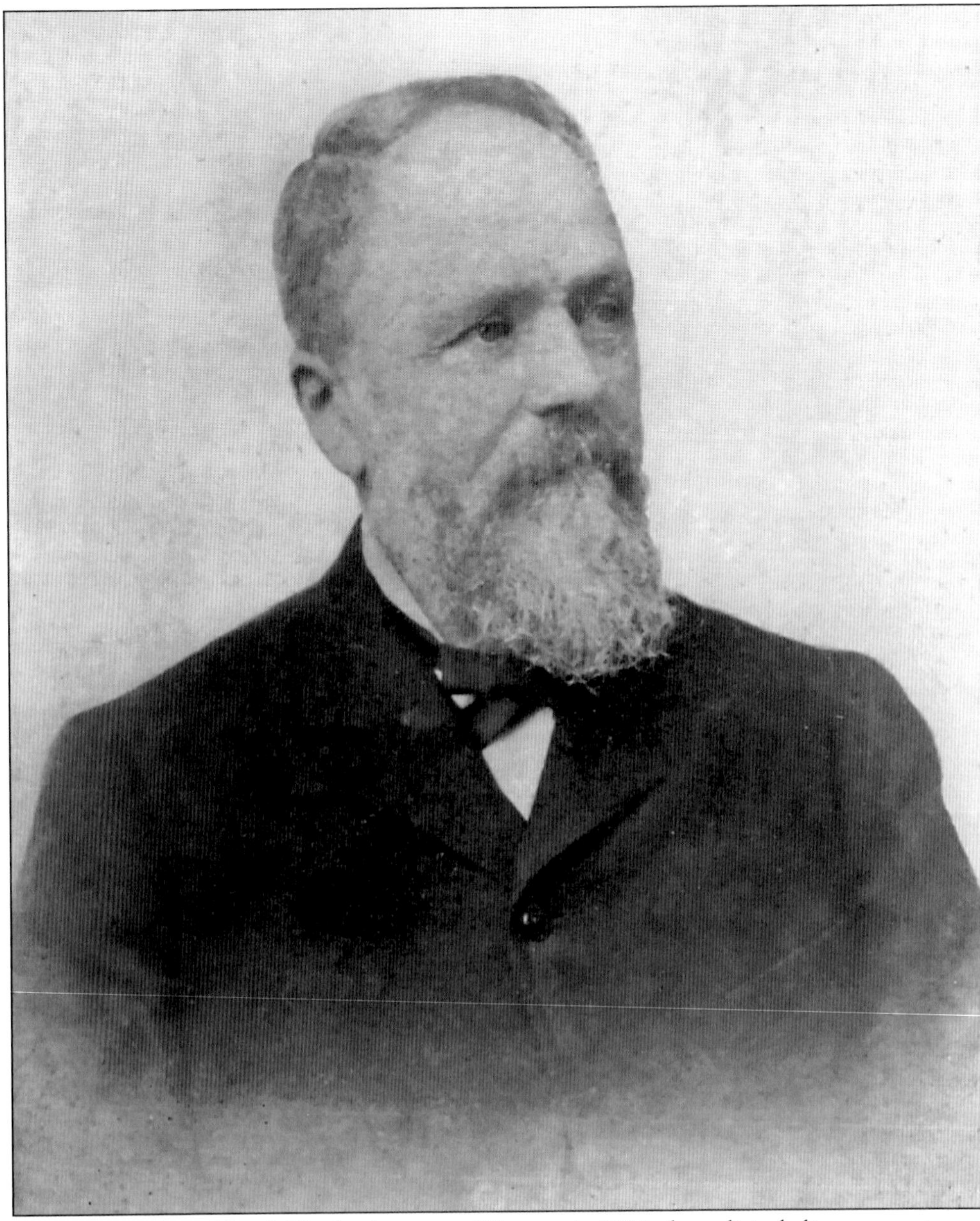

When voters elected Jacob Weisbach mayor of Tacoma in 1884, the political climate was stormy. Neither businessmen, managers of the Northern Pacific and Land Companies, realtors, nor laborers could agree on what the future of the city should be, especially when it came to how its downtown streets should be developed. Those arguing for law and order were pitted against those wanting an "open town." For most citizens, however, the greatest fear was that parts of the downtown area would become a "Chinatown." Weisbach was a German Socialist who sympathized with the various labor unions that proclaimed "the Chinese must go" because he believed, small as the Chinese population was, they were taking jobs away from white Americans. Businessmen thought the best solution was to create a Chinatown on land outside the city limits. No one, however, offered to donate the land. Both businessmen and laborers therefore joined forces to expel the Chinese from Tacoma, setting a deadline of November 3, 1885.

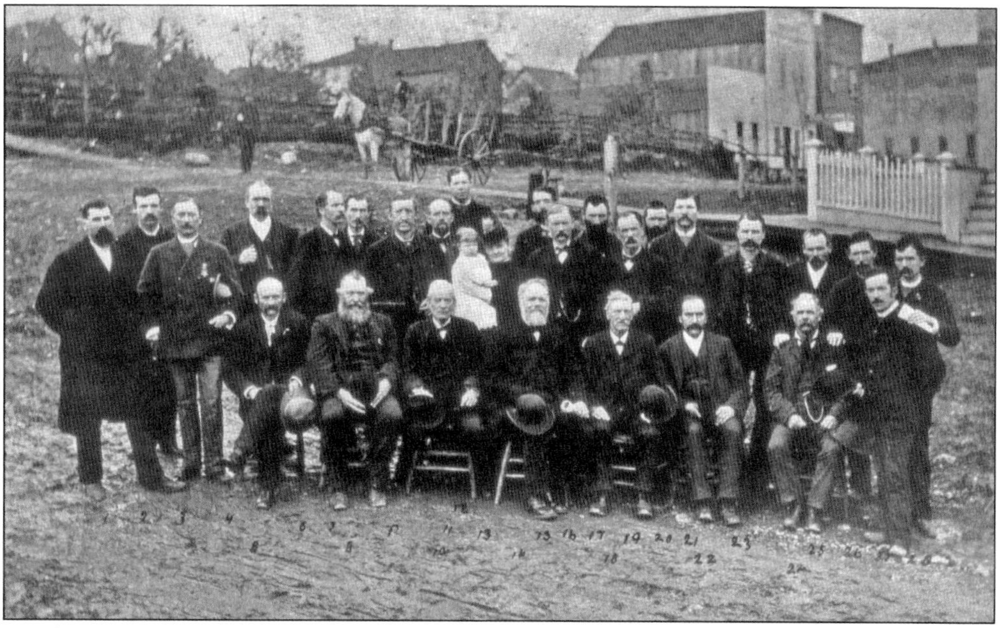

On the appointed day, the factory whistle at Lister's foundry announced the beginning of the expulsion. Men moved throughout Tacoma's downtown, forcing the Chinese out of their homes and places of business. They were gathered together and marched to a train station south of the city and placed on a freight train headed to Portland. While locals cheered, federal authorities viewed the action as a violation of treaties signed by the United States and China. Albert Whyte, shown at right in a 1935 photograph, obtained a grand jury indictment against those appearing above in a group portrait. No person was ever convicted for the crime. No Tacoman was willing to sit on a jury. (Below courtesy of Tacoma Public Library.)

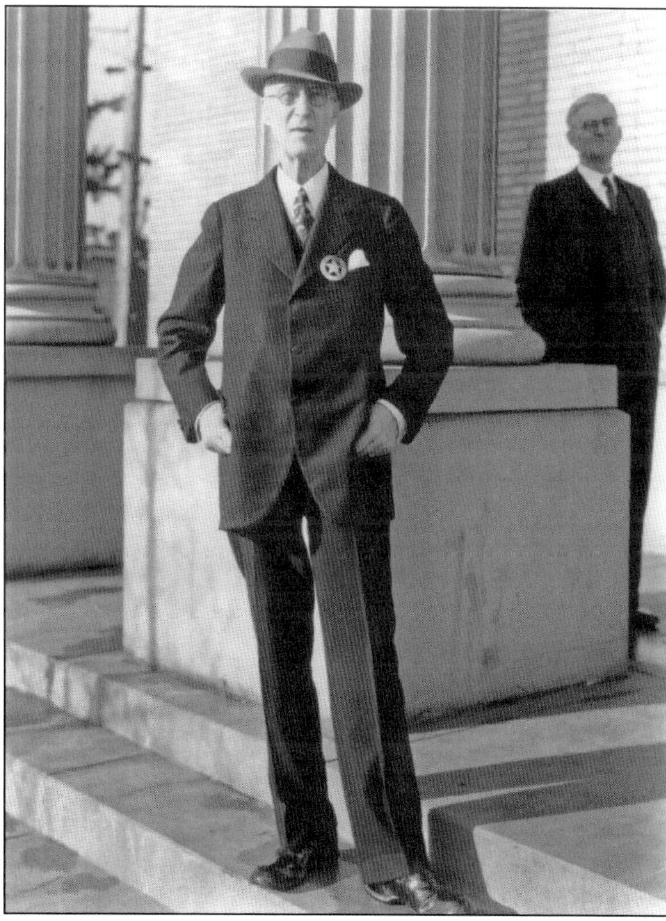

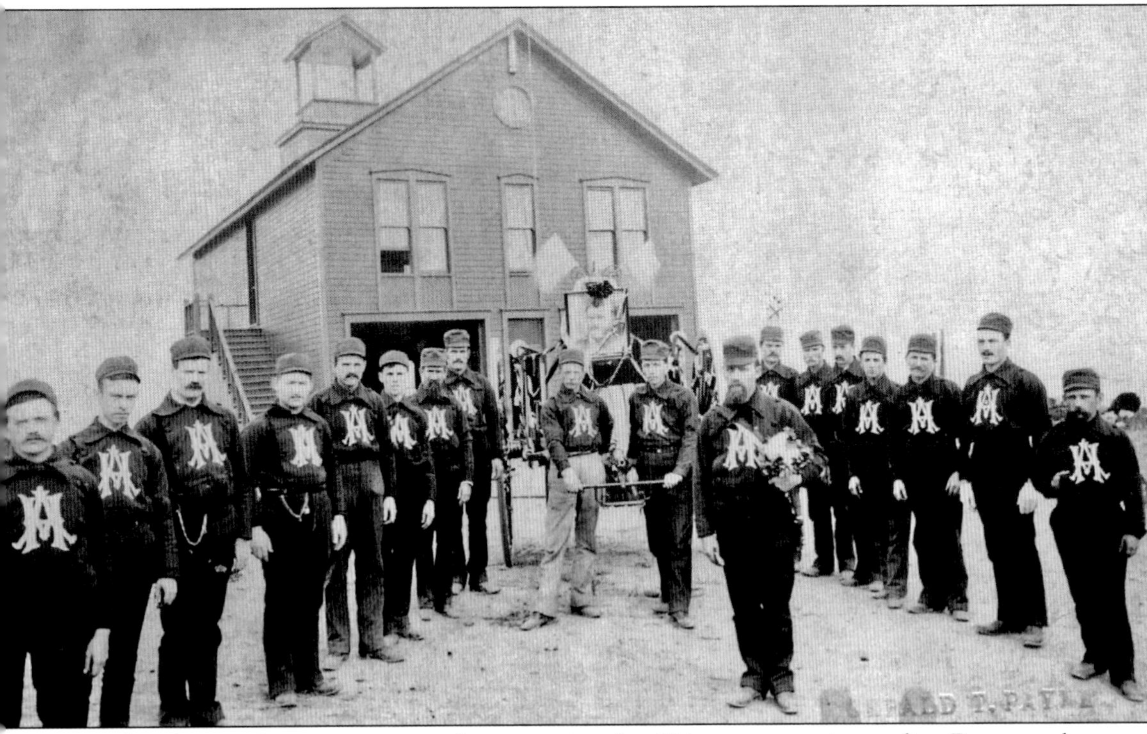

After the expulsion, perpetrators began setting the Chinese properties on fire. Firemen who responded found their hoses slashed. Were it not for the intervention of Fr. Peter Hylebos, the entire downtown area could have been reduced to ashes. The Catholic priest pointed out that the land and buildings being put to the torch belonged to whites, not the Chinese. Members of Tacoma's Alert Hose Company No. 2 volunteer unit probably were called to extinguish the fires. Here they are shown in an August 8, 1885, photograph before they join a parade honoring the memory of Pres. U. S. Grant, who had died in July. The company firehouse was located at the foot of South Thirteenth and A Streets at this time. Volunteer hose companies were located throughout Tacoma and remained the major firefighting units until the creation of the Tacoma Fire Department. (Courtesy of Tacoma Public Library.)

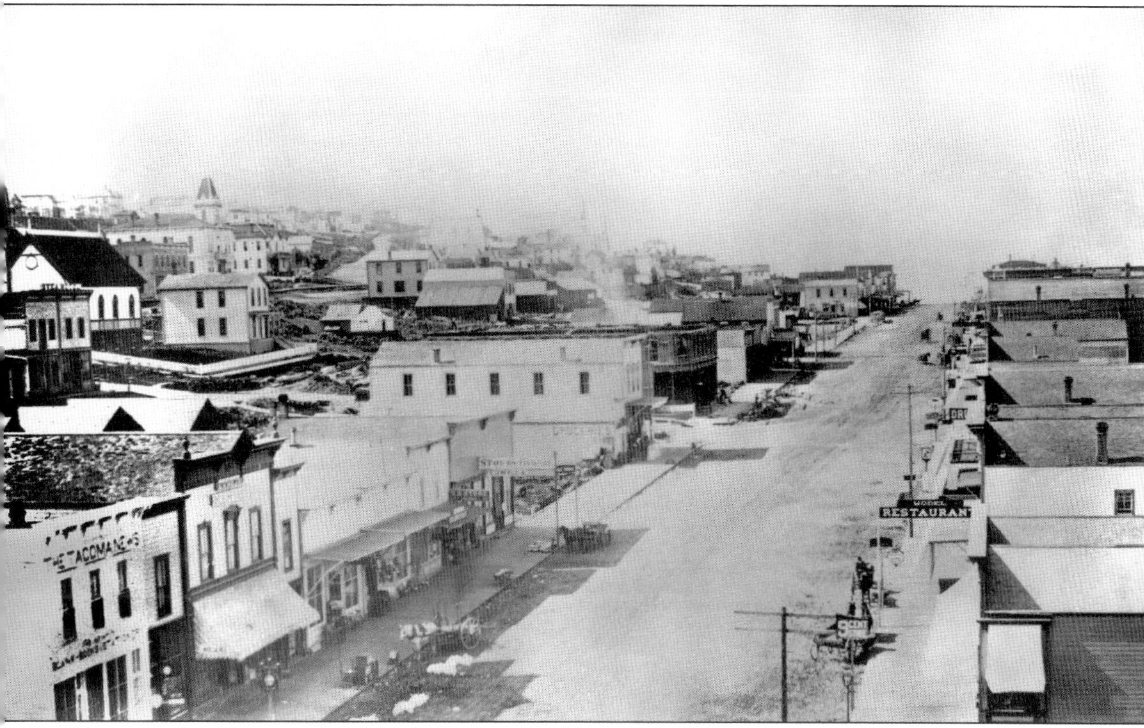

The year the Chinese were expelled, Pacific Avenue looking northward appeared as a frontier town of wood-frame buildings. The vacant land caused by a prior fire, shown in the upper left of the photograph and situated right across the street from Morgan's Theater Comique, was the point of debate. Chinese homes, gardens, and laundries were scattered throughout the landscape, but the fear was that more Chinese businesses would appear once the Northern Pacific began construction of its line across the Cascade Mountains. And even though railroad officials publicly said Chinese workers would not be used on the new project, local workers were taking no chances. Following the expulsion and as work began on the rails through Stampede Pass, Tacomans looked toward a future of economic prosperity and urban development. (Courtesy of the University of Washington Libraries Special Collections Division.)

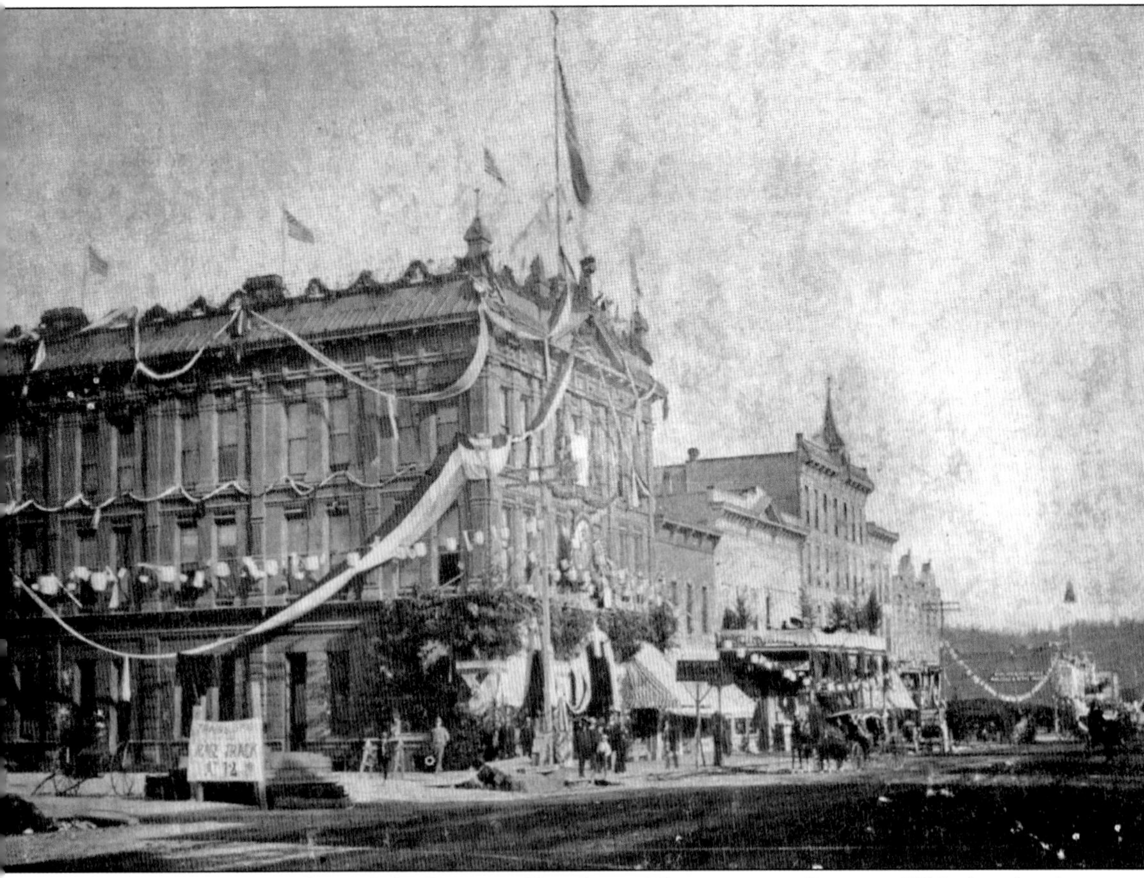

Local businessmen formed the Tacoma Chamber of Commerce in January 1884, shortly after Charles B. Wright became president of the Northern Pacific and ensured the city's future. The next year, the railroad board announced that construction had begun on the Stampede Pass route, and by 1887—traveling through a system of switchbacks—the first train over this route entered Tacoma. As the rails moved westward, the chamber of commerce began construction of its office building on South Twelfth Street and Pacific Avenue. To honor the first train to arrive via this route, chamber members decked the building with bunting and evergreens for a Fourth of July celebration. The railroad work was not done, however, as the switchbacks were only a temporary measure as Nelson Bennett engineered a tunnel through the mountains. By 1888, the project was completed, and Tacomans prepared themselves for the economic blessings that were to come. (Courtesy of Tacoma Public Library.)

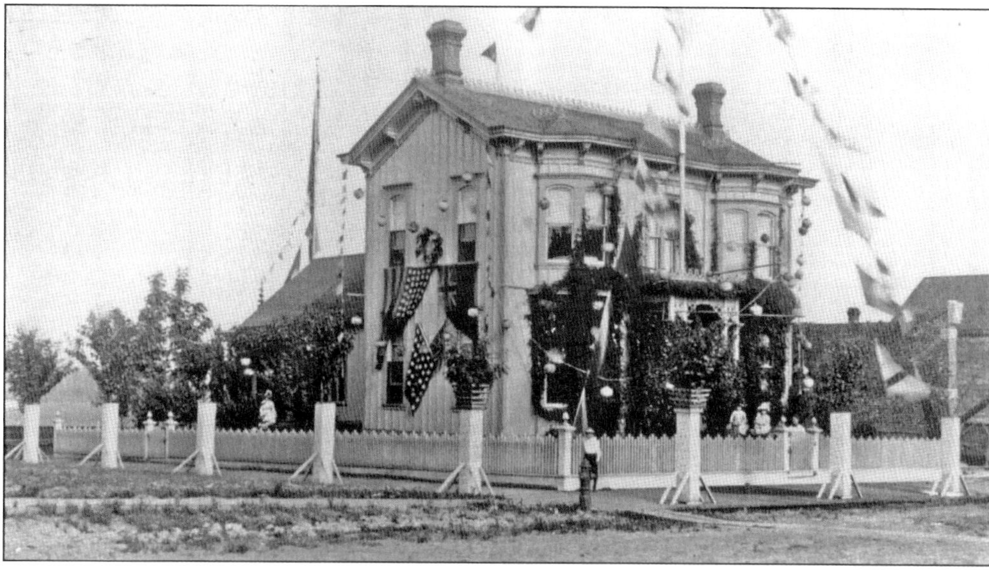

Following the arrival of trains via Stampede Pass, Tacoma's urban landscape began to change. As local developers moved toward creating the appearance of a permanent city, brick business blocks began to replace both older houses and businesses. The house of Capt. Charles E. Clancy (above) was constructed around 1883 at 1001 A Street. Family members would have been able to witness the construction of the Tacoma Hotel located out of view to the left. By 1887, the house had been moved so that Allen C. Mason could construct his business block (below) at the same location. Mason was a man of many talents who is best known for his development of streetcar lines that linked downtown Tacoma to its residential neighborhoods. (Above photograph by Isaac G. Davidson, courtesy of Tacoma Public Library.)

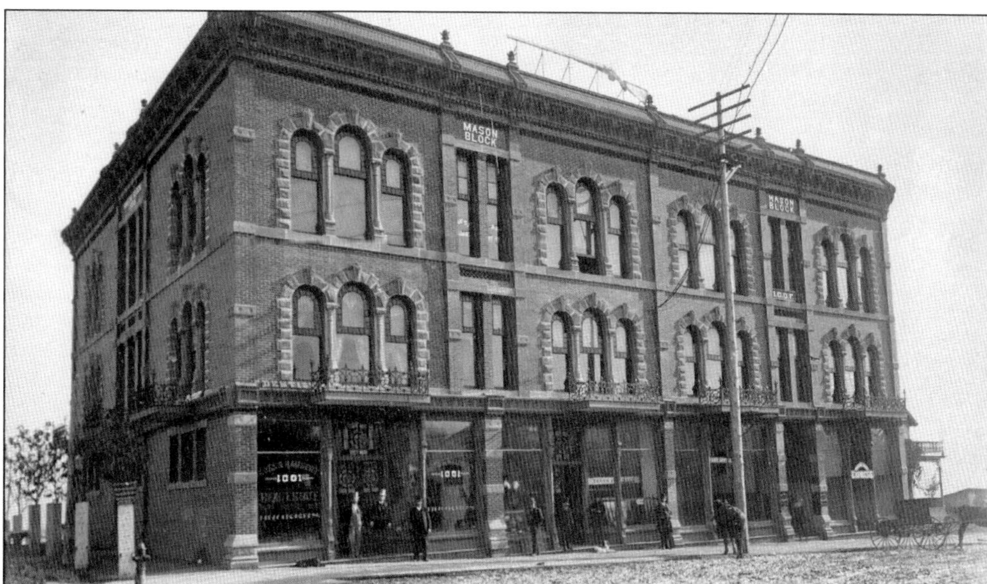

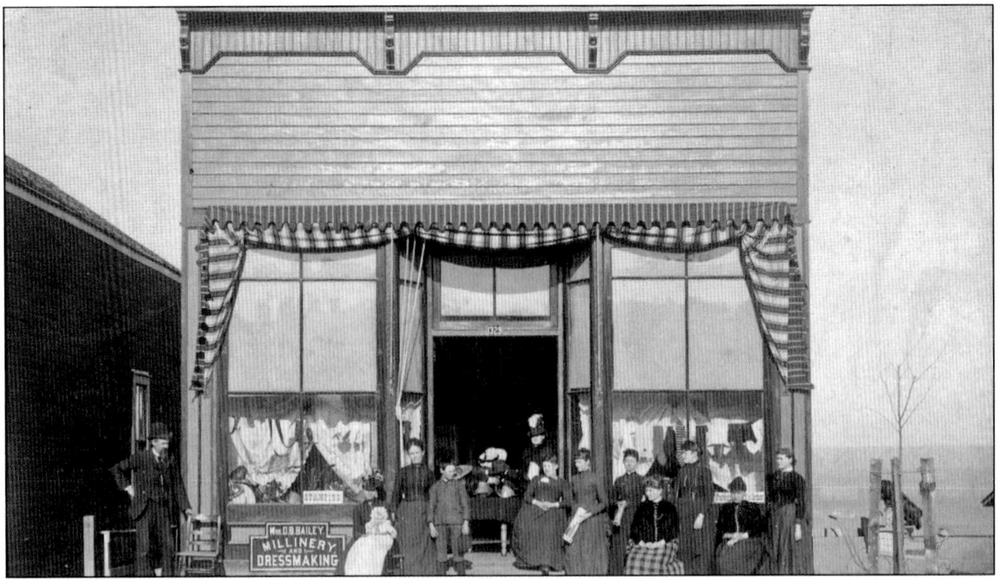

Downtown Tacoma was not transformed overnight. While brick business blocks began to line Pacific Avenue by the late 1880s, streets located to the west remained in a primitive state. Access was particularly difficult because of the steep and unkempt hillside that defined this part of the city. Even so, hearty entrepreneurs ventured into this part of the town as these two buildings illustrate. Mrs. Otis B. Bailey opened her millinery shop (above) at 1329 Tacoma Avenue South in 1888 and operated the business into the 1920s. The same year, the architectural firm of Farrell and Darmer designed the George H. Greer Building (below), located at 1102 Tacoma Avenue South. The drugstore firm of Lien and Selvig had been at this location for over a quarter century when Marvin D. Boland photographed the building in 1923. (Below courtesy of Tacoma Public Library.)

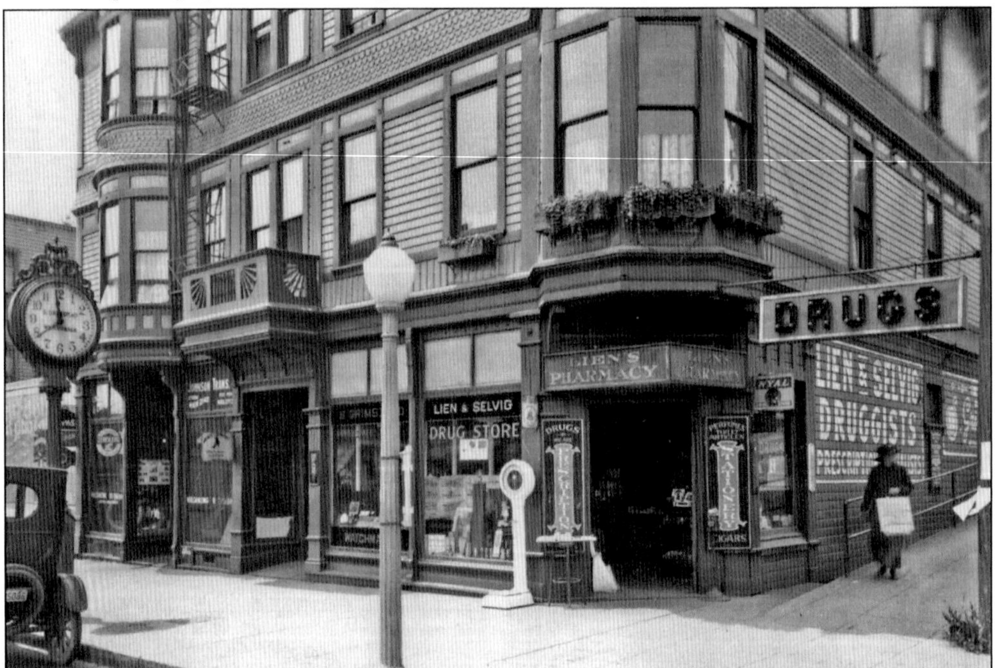

Two

1889–1900

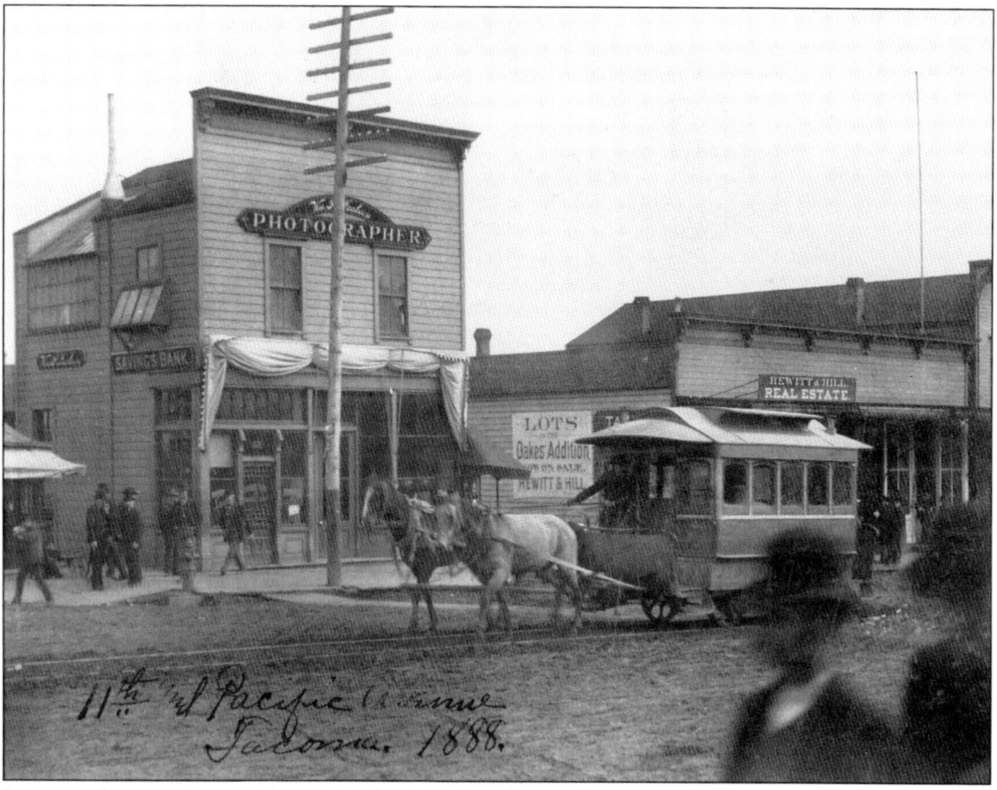

In 1888, photographer William P. Jackson captured one of Tacoma's earliest horse-drawn streetcars finding its way along Pacific Avenue. Little did he know that within a couple of years, the entire downtown area would be transformed by the introduction of electric trolleys and cable cars. The studio shown in this view was located at 1101 Pacific Avenue at an intersection that would ultimately become the hub of downtown Tacoma.

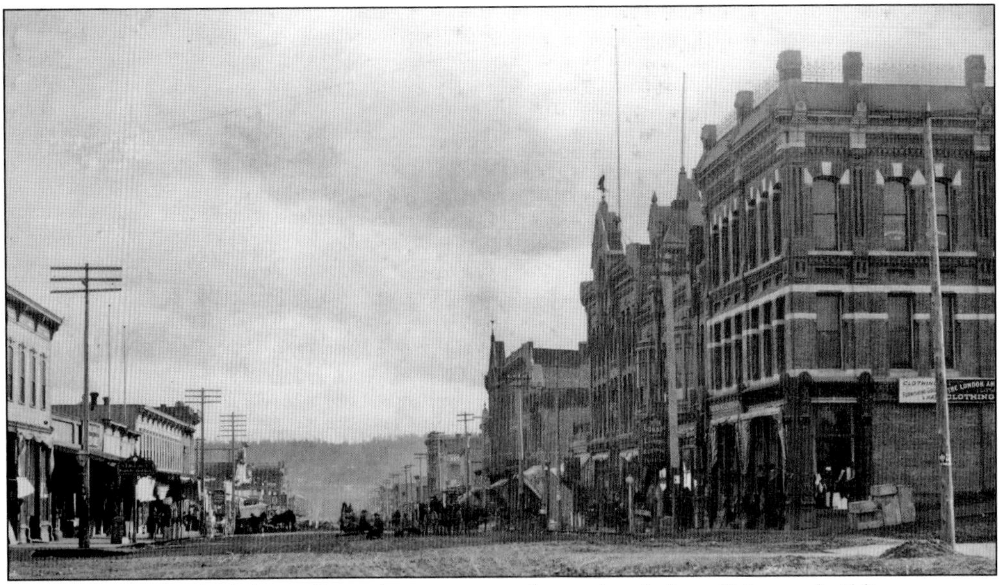

Prior to the arrival of the trolleys, the city council mandated that all future buildings were to be constructed of brick so as to avoid fires. In 1884, the Charles B. Wright building—located at 902 Pacific Avenue and seen at the right in this Isaac G. Davidson photograph—became one of the first substantial commercial buildings to appear. The change from wood storefronts to brick, however, was a slow and gradual process.

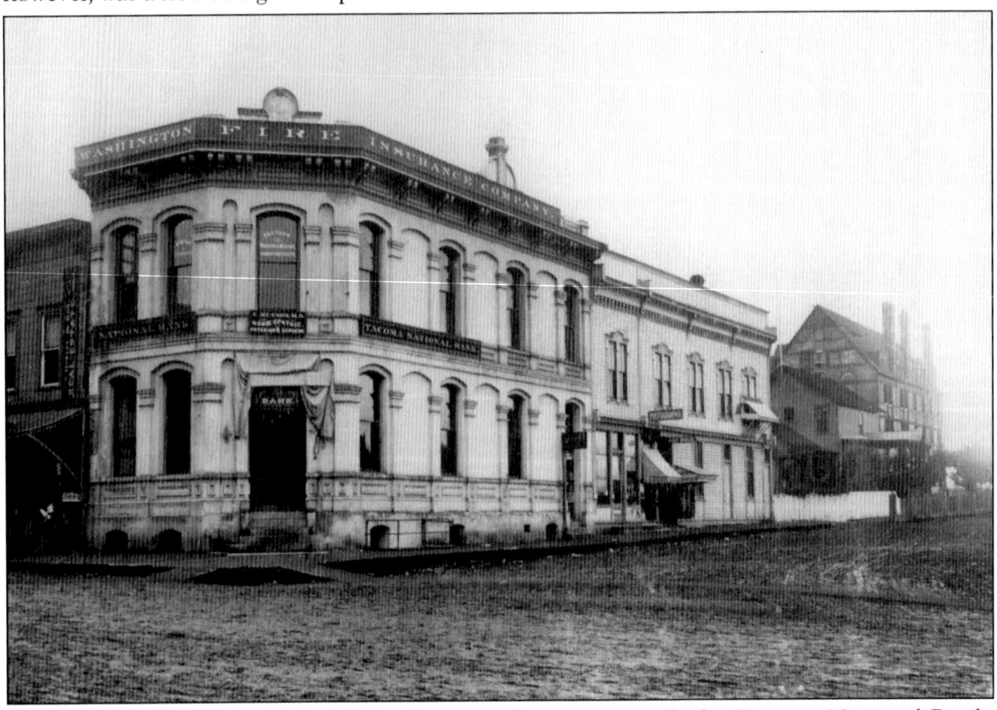

Banks were a necessary part of doing business downtown, with the Tacoma National Bank, completed by 1885 at 921 Pacific Avenue, one of the first. The firm of Farrell and Darmer designed an addition three years later. From this time forward, local professional architectural firms or individuals would design most of the city's buildings. (Courtesy of Tacoma Public Library.)

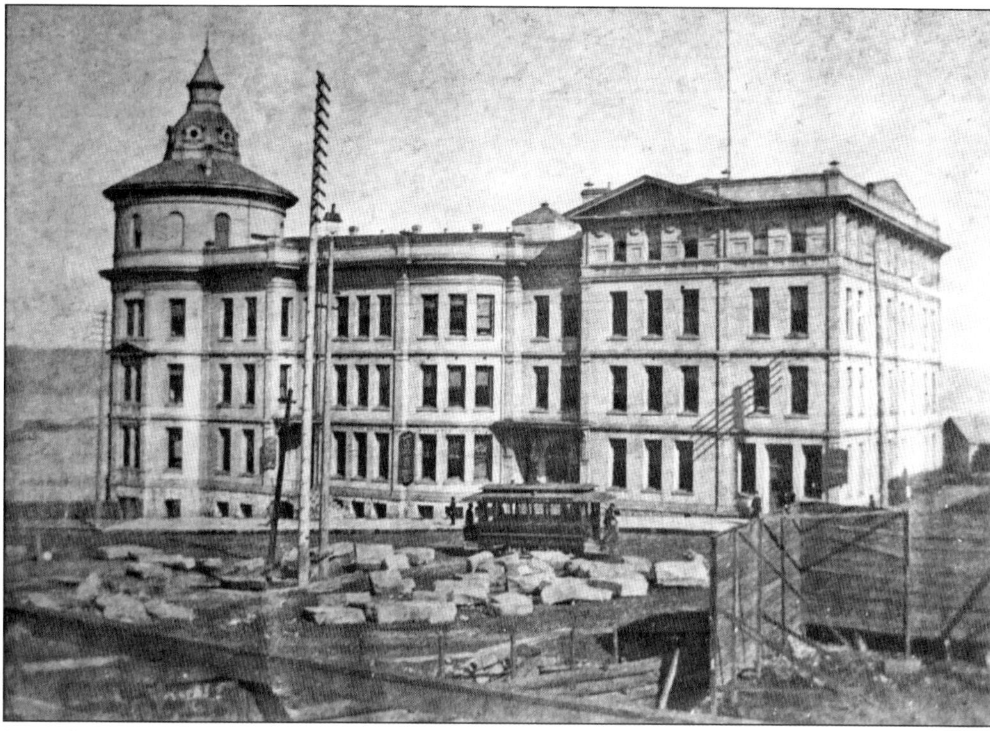

In 1887, construction began on the Northern Pacific Headquarters Building at 621 Pacific Avenue. Designed in-house by Charles B. Talbot, its appearance on the urban landscape meant that the railroad company was moving its official headquarters from Portland, Oregon, to the City of Destiny. Charles B. Wright through the Tacoma Land Company provided the funds.

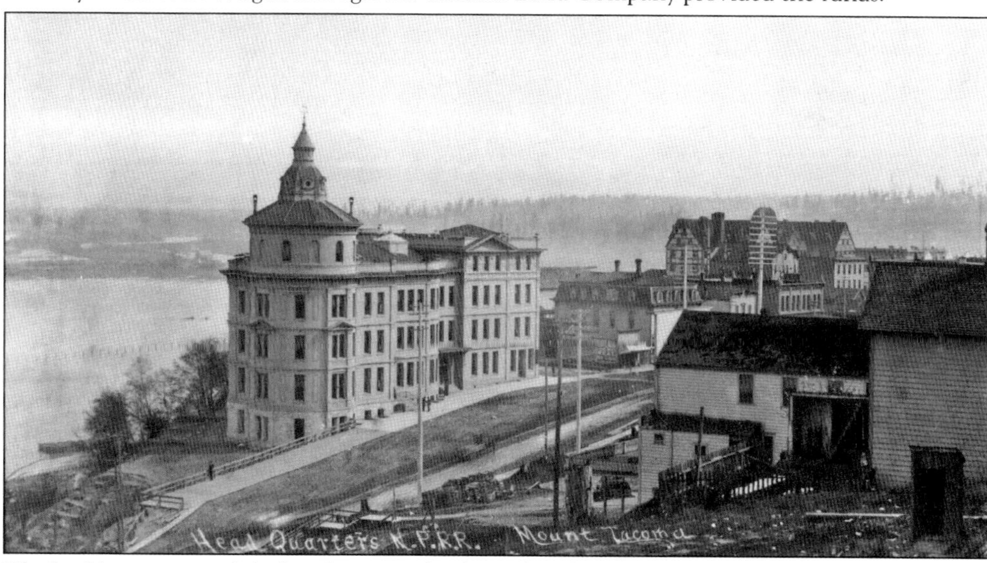

The building remained the headquarters for the railroad until the offices were moved to Seattle in the 1920s. Its isolated setting during the early years of the city must have provided a magnificent vista for residents and tourists. At the time this photograph was taken shortly after the building's completion, the only other competitor for visual attention would have been the Tacoma Hotel, seen in the background.

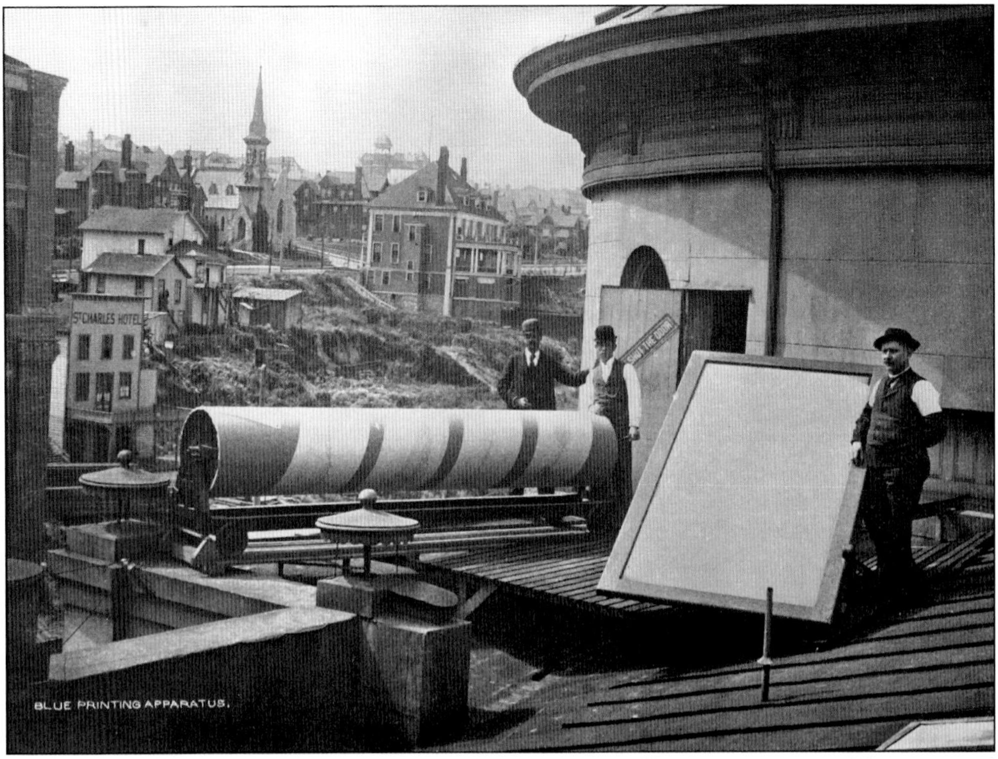

On the tower roof of the Northern Pacific Headquarters building, engineers could expose and produce the blueprints required for the construction of the rail line planned across and through Stampede Pass. Unfortunately, how long this process was used is unknown. However, subsequent images illustrate that the rooftop was a favored location for photographers wanting a bird's-eye view of the city.

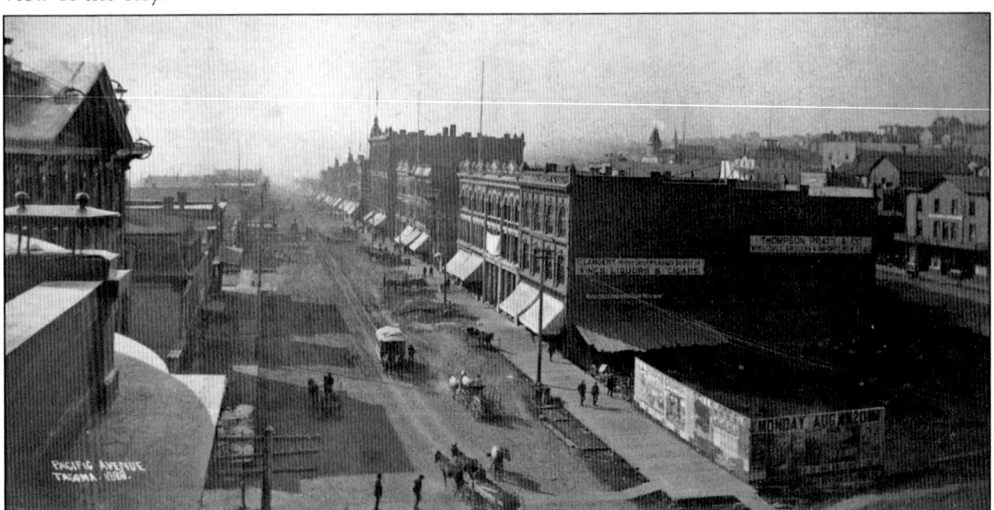

In 1888, Thomas H. Rutter made his way to the headquarters roof and photographed southward along Pacific Avenue. Horse-drawn streetcars and drays are still the primary mode of transportation. On the right in this view, however, brick buildings are sprouting along the street. This was also the block that was vacant, because of fire, at the time of the Chinese expulsion in 1885.

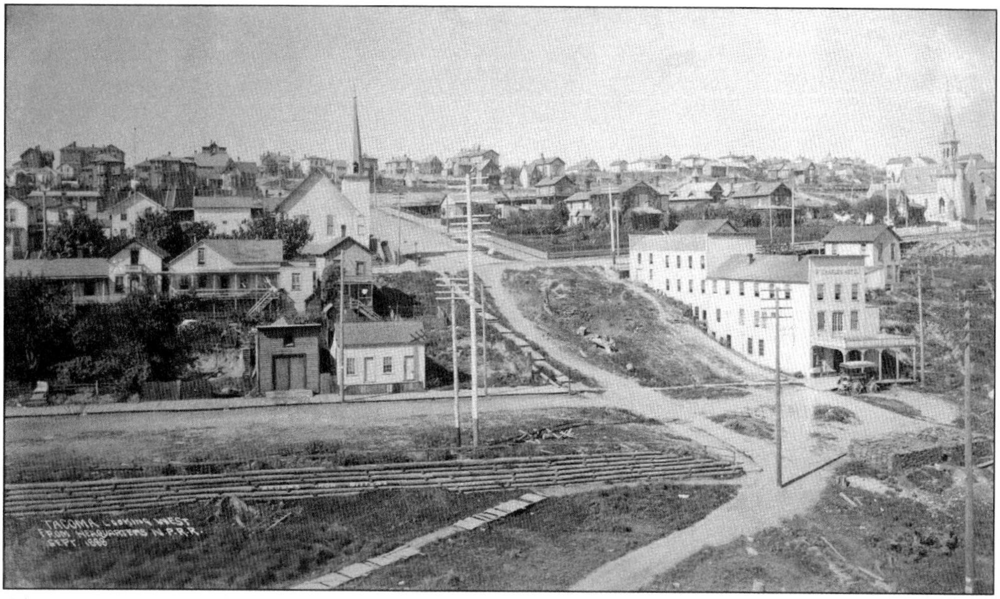

Above, sometime in the 1880s, T. H. Rutter looked westward from the Northern Pacific Railroad headquarters' roof to document the church spires and residences that show downtown Tacoma as a place where most people walked wherever they needed to go unless they could afford a horse and buggy. The undeveloped land would ultimately become the sites for the Tacoma City Hall, the Elks Temple, and the Spanish Stairs that are still a part of the urban landscape. Atop the hill and to the right, the Union Club constructed its meeting rooms in 1888 (below) at 539 Broadway. The organization members considered the building as a place where Tacoma's elite could wine and dine in appropriate fashion.

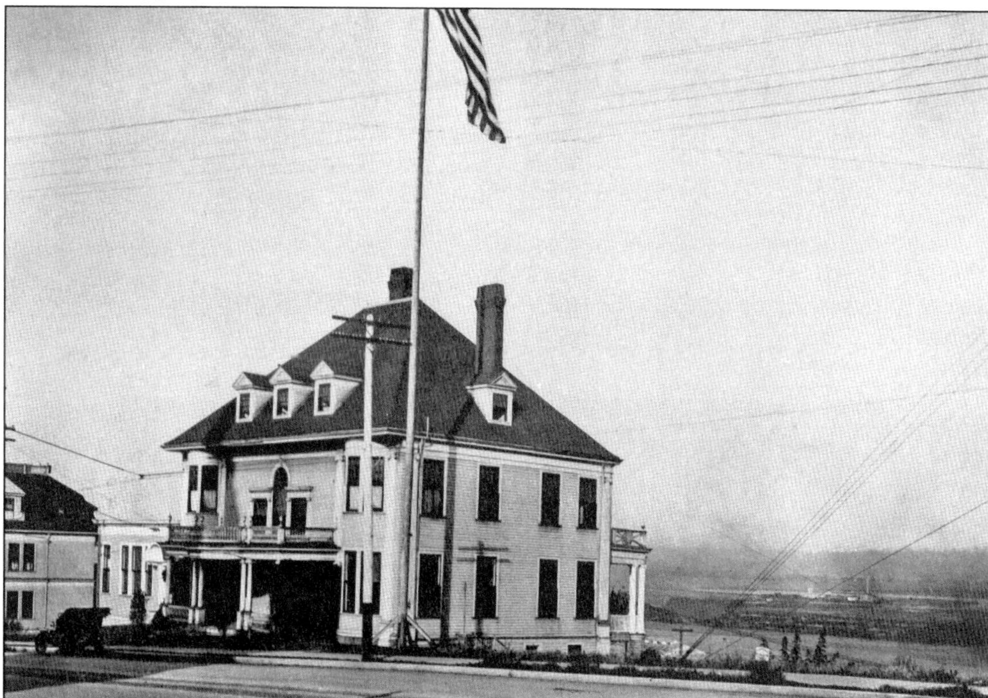

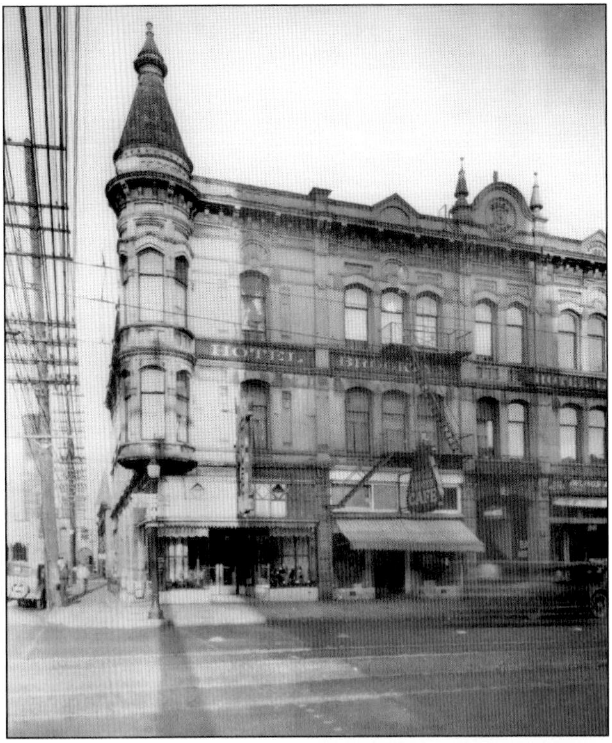

The architectural firm of Farrell and Darmer designed the Union Block in 1888. Located at 1301 Pacific Avenue, it served local business firms into the 1930s. The Hotel Grandolfo opened its doors in 1889, but by the time this photograph was taken, the name had changed to the Hotel Brooklyn. The Tacoma Railway and Motor Company carbarn can be seen in the distance. (Courtesy of Tacoma Public Library.)

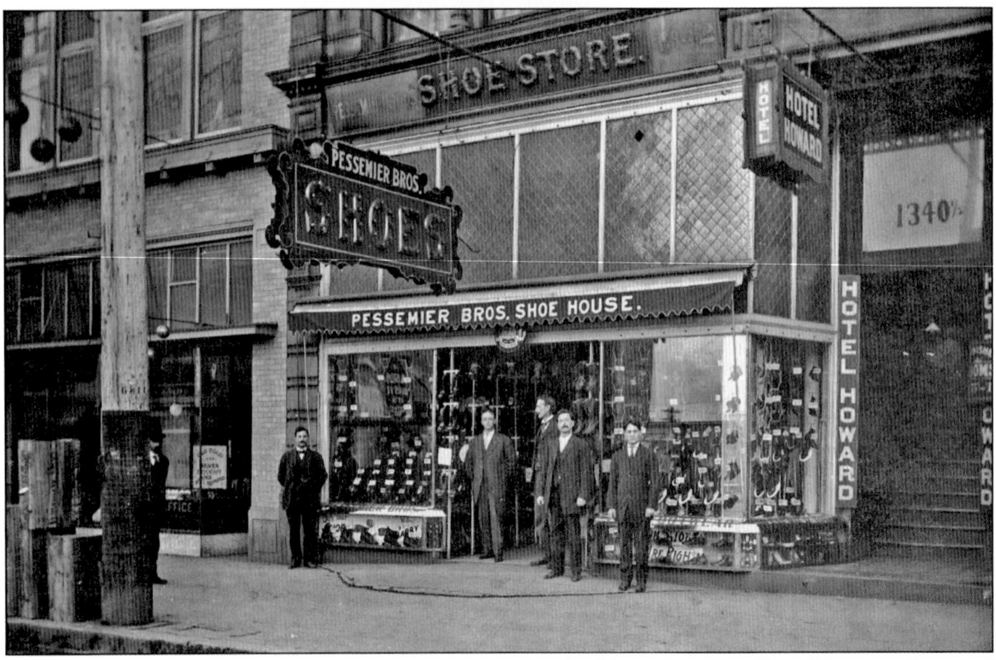

The Citizens Bank at 1340 Pacific Avenue was another building that Farrell and Darmer designed in 1888. Its various uses, besides the bank, included the Coast Vaudeville Theater, hotels under various names, and the Pessimer Brothers' Shoe Store. In 1961, the *Tacoma Daily Ledger* would report that William Pessimer had been in business for 50 years at the same location. The men in this undated photograph are not identified.

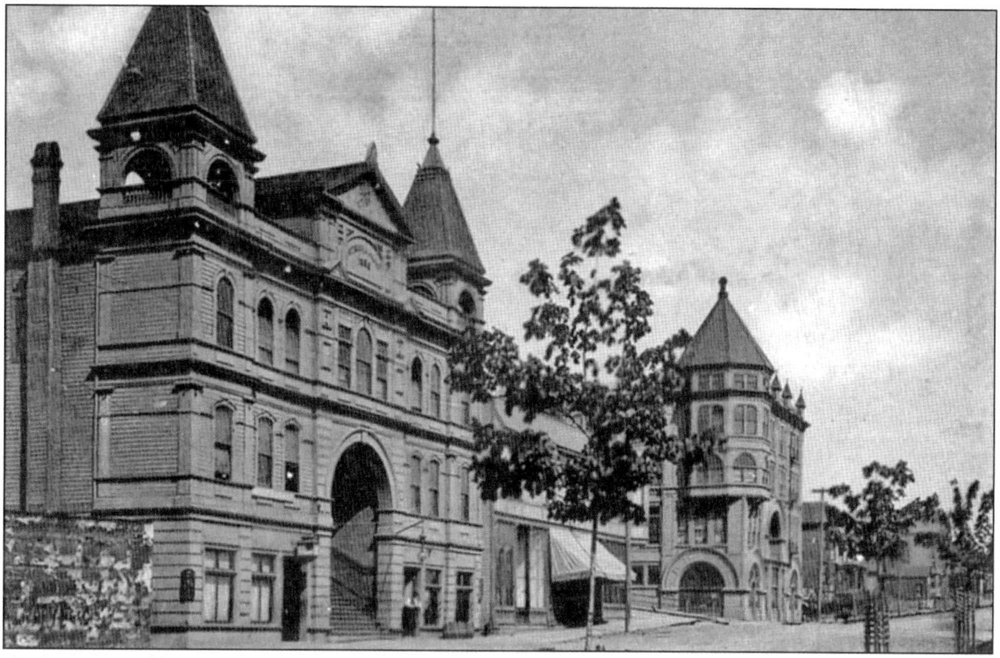

Architect Carl Darmer was a German immigrant, so it is fitting that he designed Germania Hall in 1889 (above). Located at 1308 South Fawcett Avenue, the building was a social and fraternal home for the large German population in Tacoma. It also served as a meeting place for the local militia. In 1912, Democratic Party members met here to nominate Woodrow Wilson as its candidate for president. The Astor House is seen in the distance in this undated view. Constructed in 1889 and located at 1152 South Fawcett Avenue, the building underwent several name changes over the years, ending its life as the Sampson. Photographer Chapin Bowen took this image around 1927. (Above courtesy of Thomas R. Stenger; below courtesy of Tacoma Public Library.)

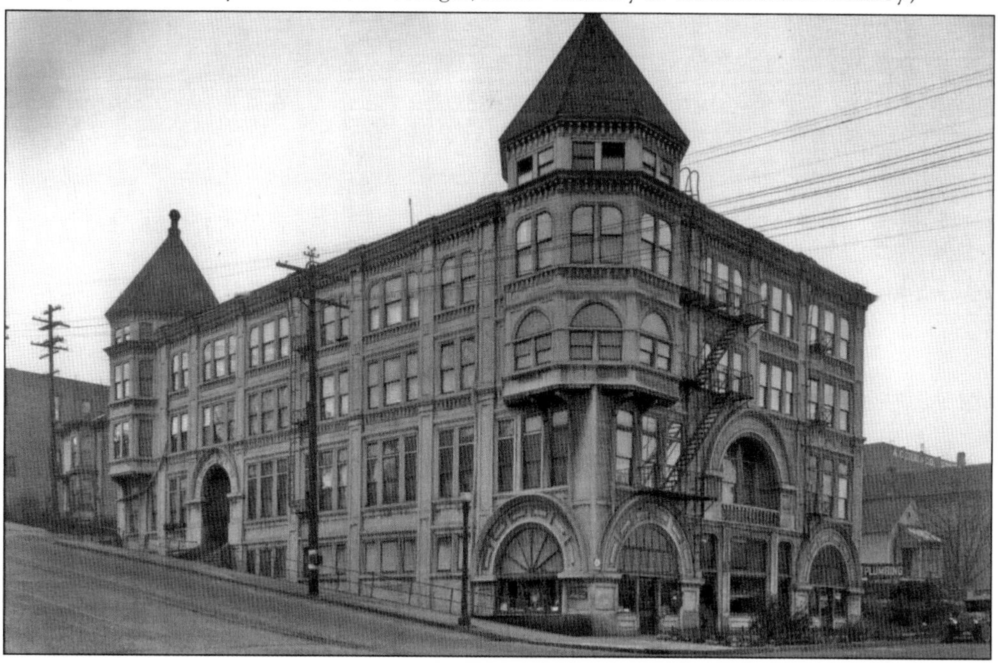

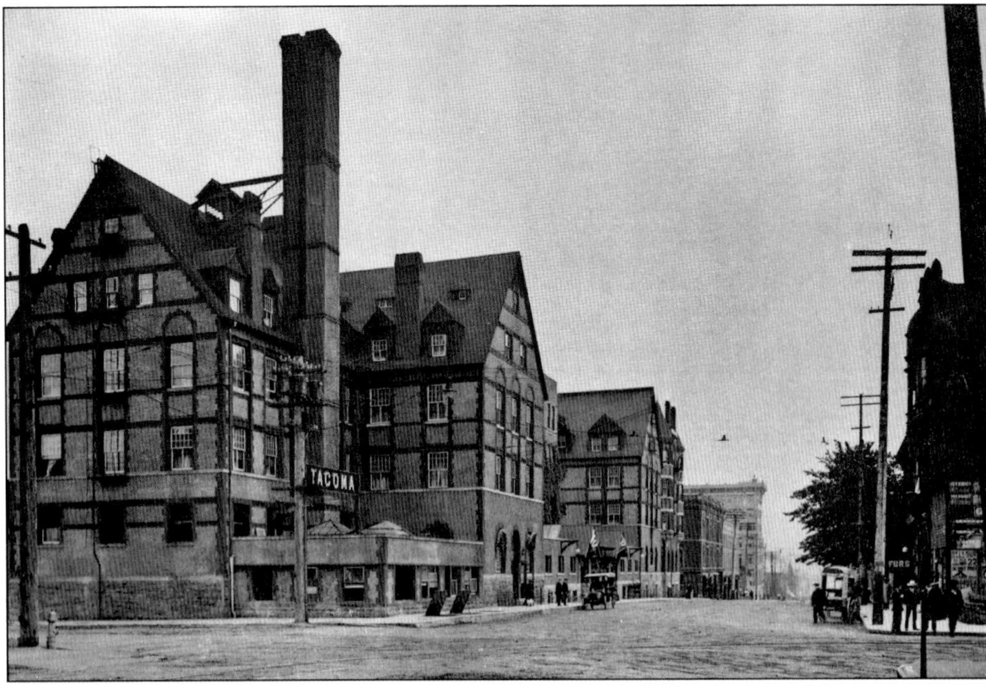

From its small beginnings in 1887, the Tacoma Hotel expanded over the years. This was the place to stay, meet, and be seen by Tacoma's elite. Ambassadors, U.S. presidents, and popular military officers were constant guests. By the time this undated photograph was taken, the hotel dominated South A Street. The Mason Block and Perkins Building can be seen in the distance.

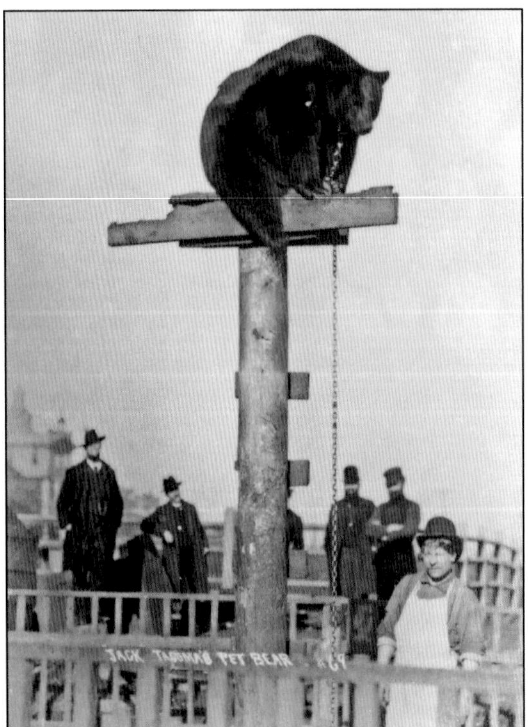

"Jack the Bear" was a regular fixture in the Tacoma Hotel, especially in the saloon where barkeepers kept him supplied with beer. He was gentle, tame, and loved by all. Unfortunately, a rookie policeman did not know this when Jack decided to wander down the streets of Tacoma one night in 1889. The poor creature was shot and killed. Tacoma's mourning included poetic odes to Jack's memory.

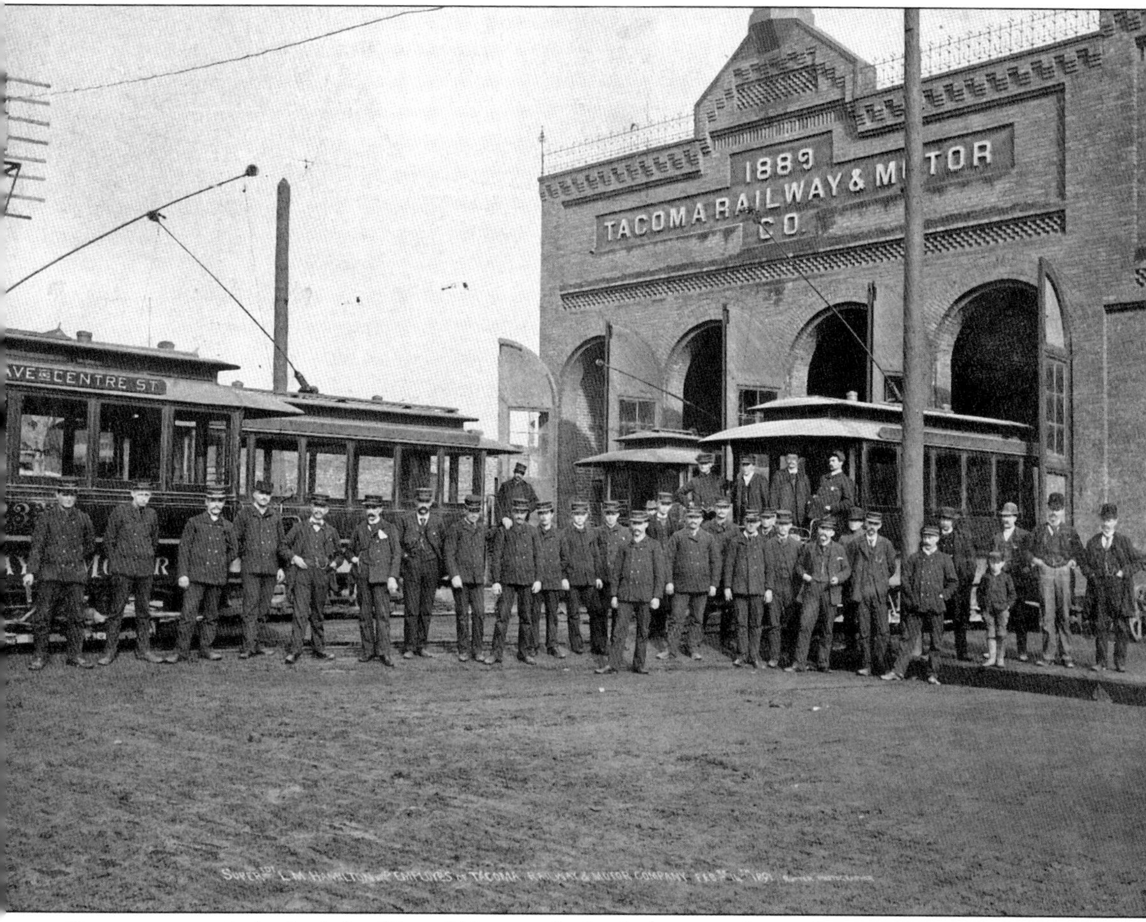

Streetcars revolutionized the City of Destiny. Indeed, this new form of transportation created central business districts in every city in the nation. With streetcar lines extending outward from the downtown area, families could move to residential areas located away from the bustle of commercial activity. And as households moved, new business blocks arose in their stead. Unlike today, however, the development of a local transportation system was not an orderly process. Various companies requested, and received, franchises from the city council to develop the various "suburban" lines. The Tacoma Railway and Motor Company constructed this power facility at 1301 South A Street in 1889 and soon grew to become the major transportation developer in the city. So that people could navigate the hills westward of downtown, the firm also established a cable car system that traversed South Eleventh and Thirteenth Streets. In this 1891 view, Thomas Rutter photographed unidentified streetcar conductors posing in front of the company's facility.

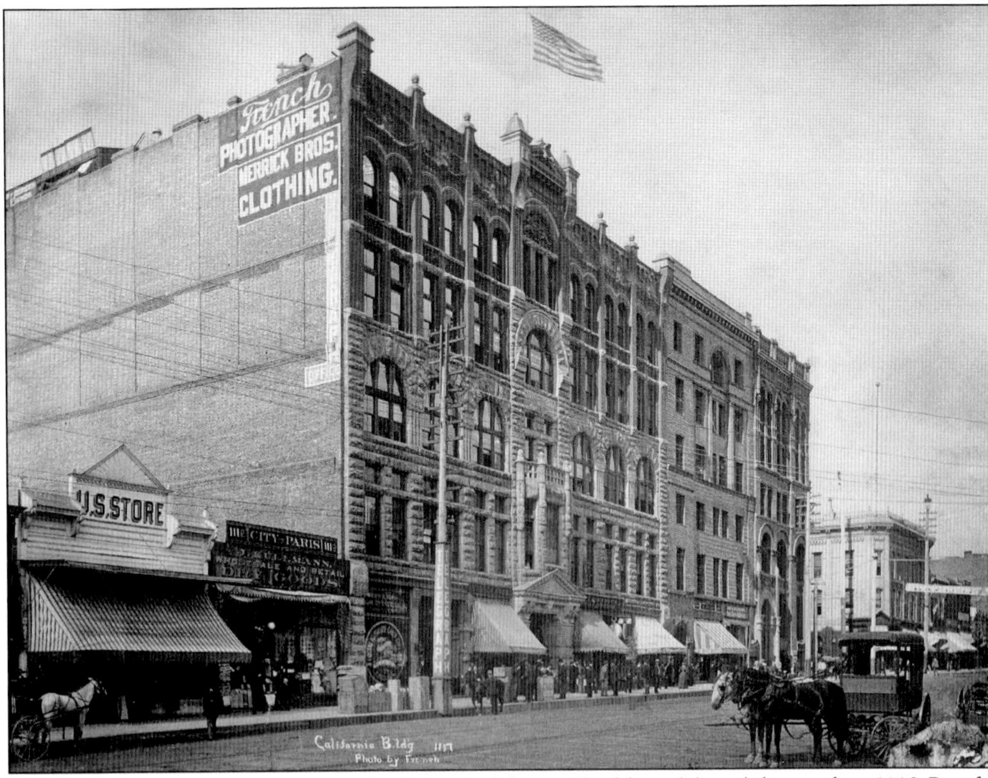

In 1892, Arthur French photographed the California Building (above) located at 1110 Pacific Avenue. As with many buildings constructed in 1889, many uses were found here, including pharmacies and clothing stores. Also this year, at 1501 Pacific Avenue, John W. Sprague—part of the Northern Pacific Railroad elite—commissioned the architectural firm of Pickles and Sutton to design a multiple-use building (seen below). By 1935, when Chapin Bowen took this photograph, the Tacoma Drug Company occupied the building. (Above courtesy of Tacoma Public Library.)

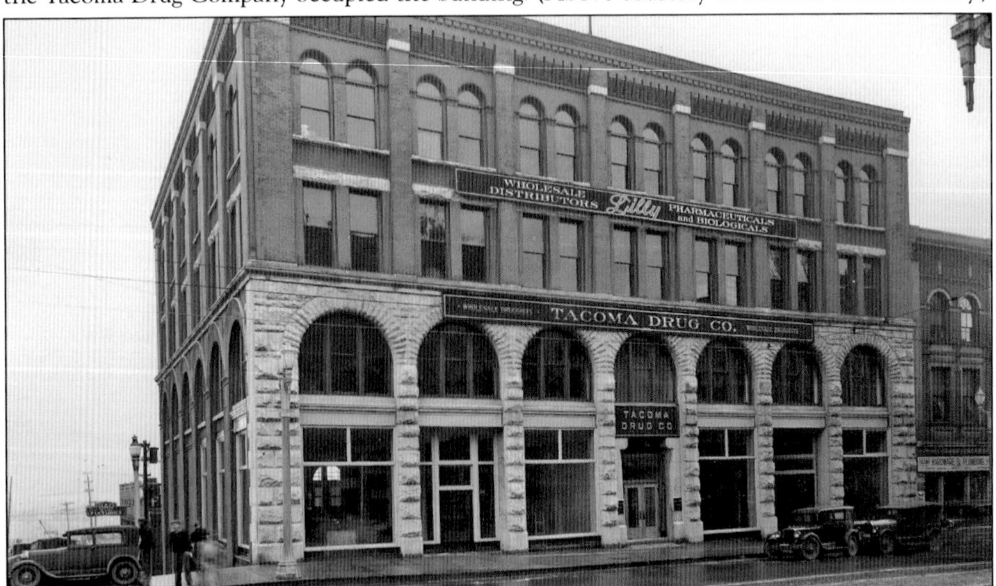

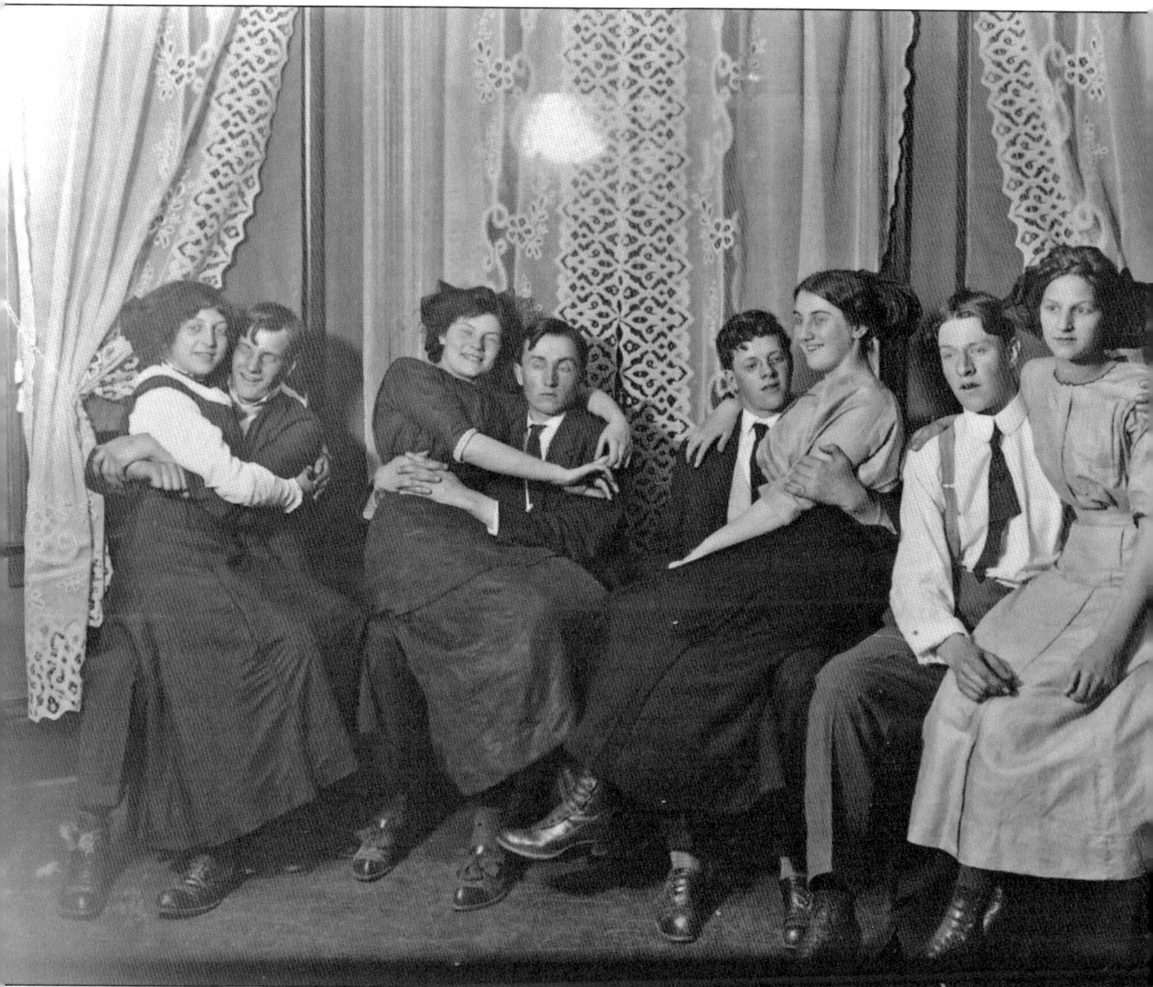

As noted previously, matters of law and order—or vice—concerned early Tacomans. Questions of outlawing such activities as prostitution, gambling, and saloons (or to legalize their existence) periodically dominated city council discussions. Its solution was a combination of both tolerance and control. Formally, the council established zones where owners of saloons could obtain licenses to conduct their businesses. Informally, city fathers established a system whereby prostitutes could establish their houses in certain areas of downtown Tacoma. One such area was "Opera Alley," located on Court C between South Ninth and Eleventh Streets. Gambling during the early years was completely uncontrolled. The result was high-scale corruption throughout Tacoma's history, at least on the part of city officials and policemen willing to accept bribes. The photographer, along with the date of this image, is unidentified. It is a portrait of a group of "Tacoma Girls" posed with their clients. (Courtesy of the Douglas County, Oregon, Museum.)

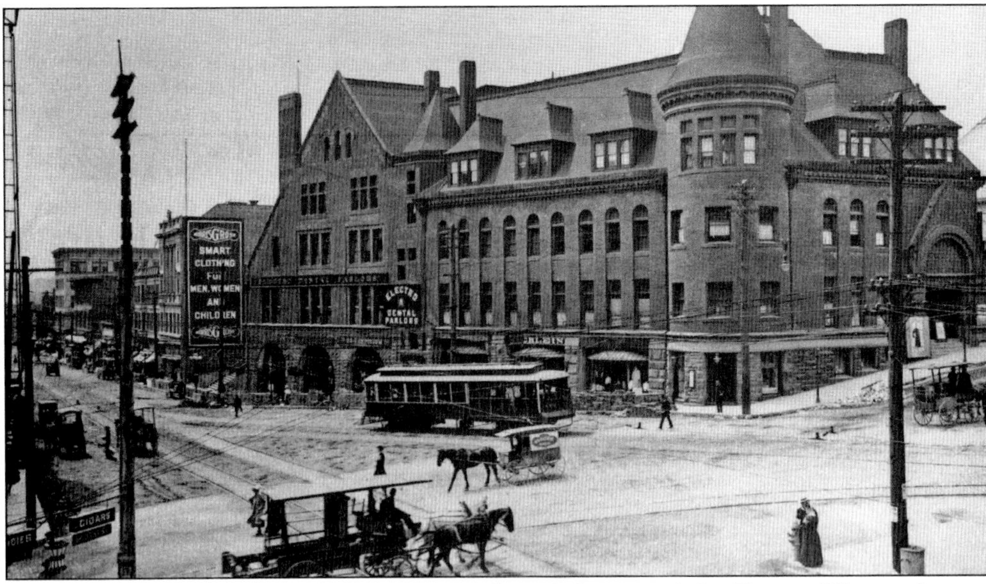

Early Tacoma promoters saw the Tacoma Hotel on A Street and the Tacoma Theater, located at 902 Broadway and completed in 1889, as the two major gems in the city's crown. While there were many vaudeville—and later motion picture—theaters downtown, the Tacoma Theater was promoted as a place where world-renowned opera singers would perform among sets that featured live animals on stage.

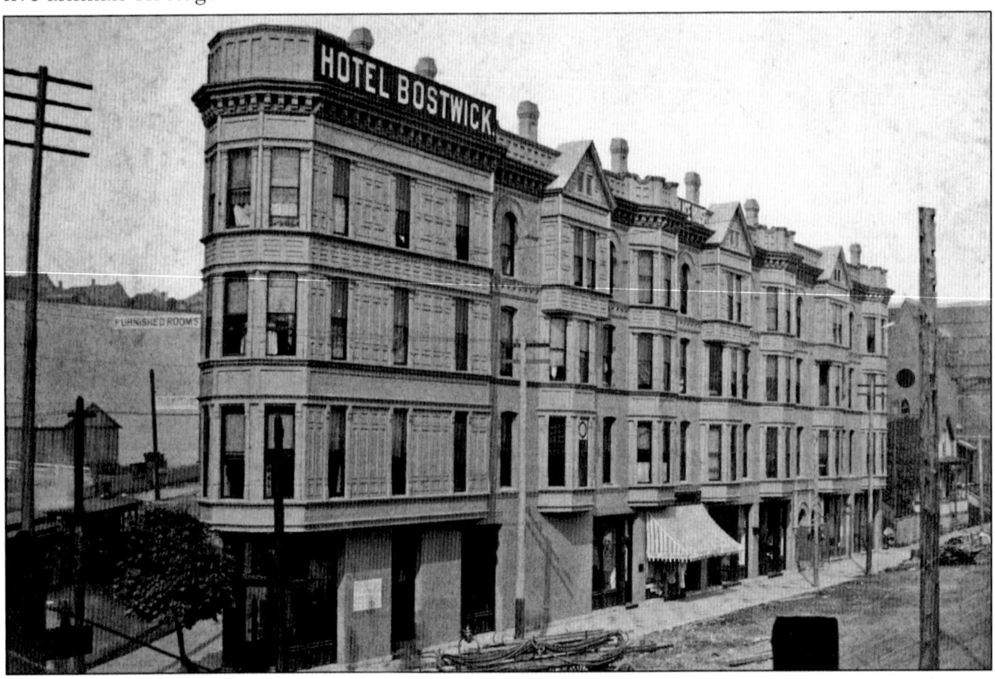

In 1889, Tacoma architect O. P. Dennis designed a flatiron building for Dr. H. C. Bostwick, one of the city's first physicians. The site at 755 St. Helens Street was originally his residence. Those who stayed in his hotel would have had a perfect view of the Tacoma Theater located just across the street. In 1892, the first Chinese merchant allowed in the city after the 1885 expulsion used one of the first-floor commercial spaces.

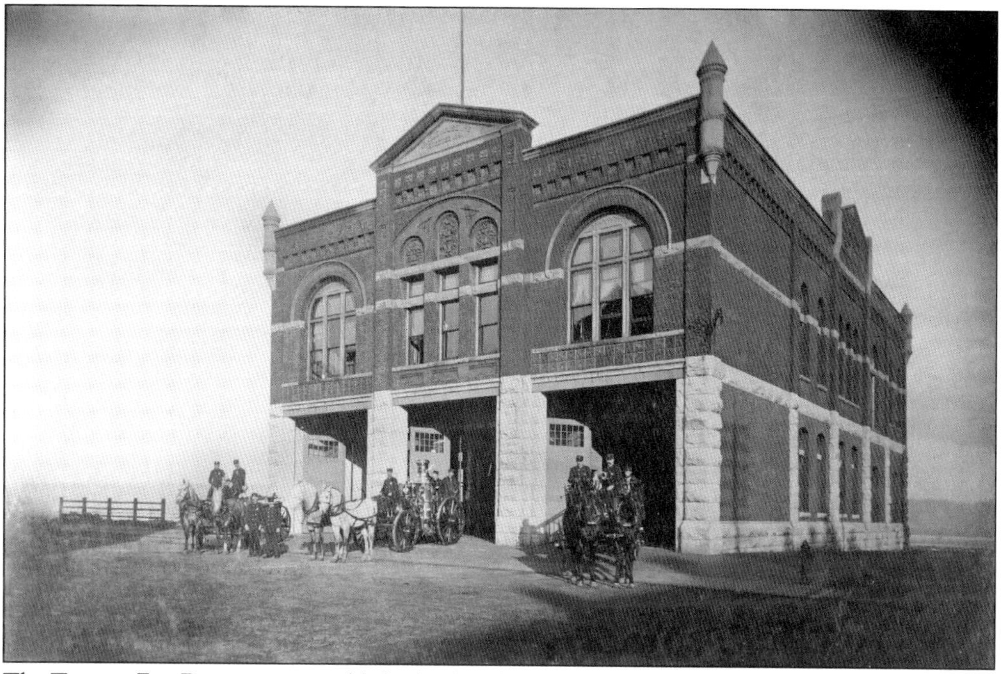

The Tacoma Fire Department established its headquarters at 823 South A Street after constructing Engine House No. 6 in 1890. From horse-drawn, steam-powered firefighting equipment to modern-day fire trucks, this station served downtown Tacoma for over half a century. The architectural firm of Hatherton and McIntosh designed the building shown here in an undated photograph.

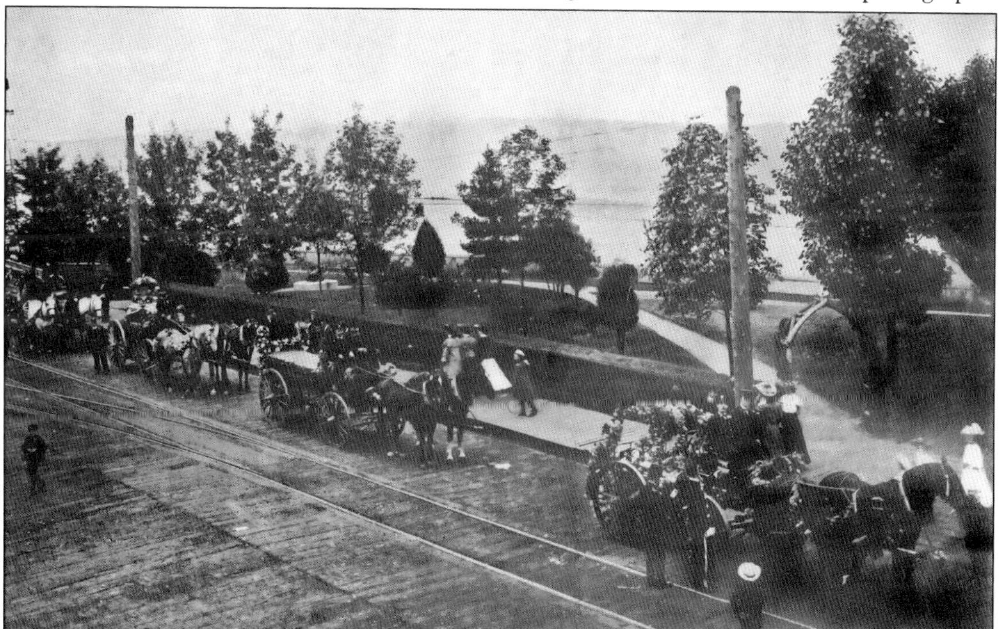

It is unknown who came up with the idea of constructing what is called "Firemen's Park" north of Engine House No. 6. Most likely, the triangular piece of land was too small for a building. But by the early 1890s, when an unidentified photographer captured this view, local citizens were thinking more about parks. This one became the first in downtown Tacoma.

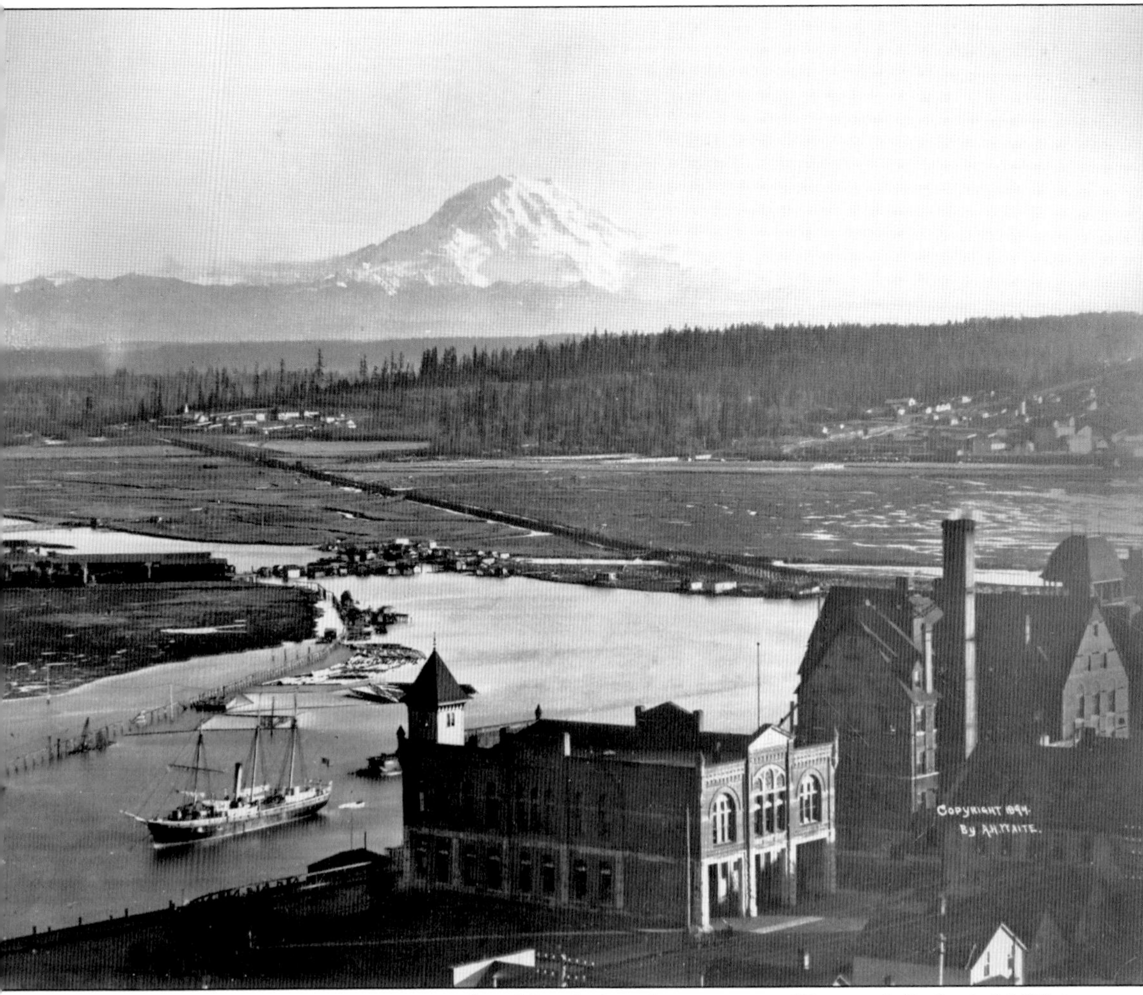

After Engine House No. 6 was completed, but before the creation of Firemen's Park, A. H. Waite made his way to the roof of the Northern Pacific Railroad headquarters building and looked toward Mount Rainier. The image he took documented what downtown Tacomans saw every day during the early years of the 1890s. Up until this time, urban development was limited to the bluff overlooking Commencement Bay and the Puyallup River delta. The Puyallup Indian Reservation, seen in the distance, served as a development boundary until Congress, through the Dawes Severalty Act of 1887, provided the way to divest the Native Americans from their lands. A worldwide economic depression that the nation began to experience in 1893 delayed Tacoma's plans for acquiring Indian land so as to construct a new port. Even so, by the early years of the 20th century, dredging was completed to form the City (now Thea Foss) Waterway, and movement eastward into the Puyallup River delta had begun.

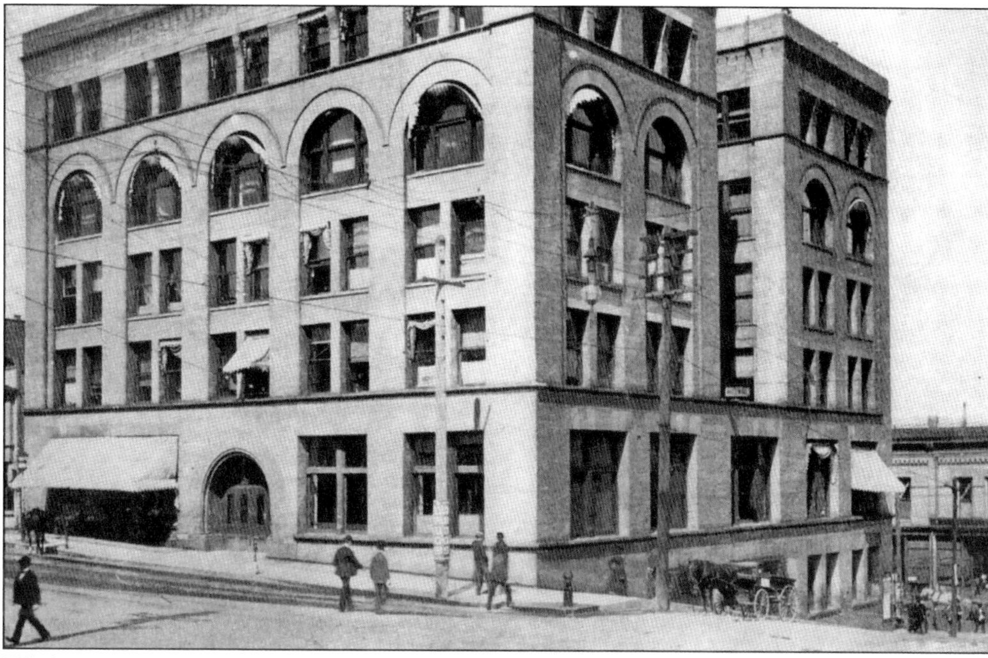

While some Tacomans were looking eastward toward port development, others looked to the west up the tiered hillside forming downtown. In 1890, at 949 Broadway, the Fidelity Trust Company oversaw the construction of a bank building. There were natural springs located underneath the building that provided it with water. The First Presbyterian Church was constructed on this site in 1882 and was moved to make way for the commercial building.

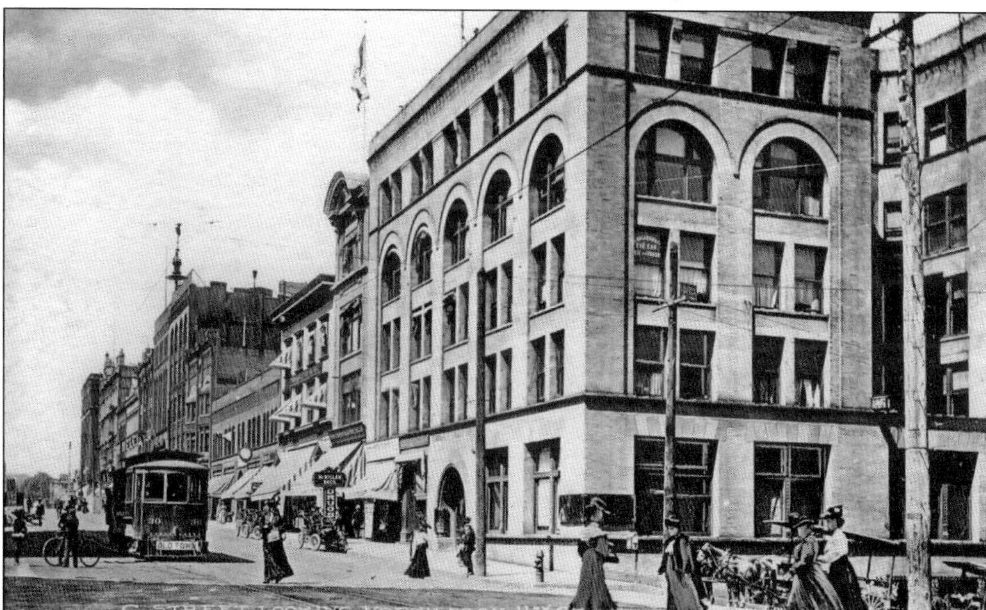

In 1890, the Tacoma Chamber of Commerce commissioned an unidentified photographer to document urban development north along Broadway from South Eleventh Street. Among the buildings seen in this view, besides the Fidelity Trust building, are W. D. Robinson's Dye Works and the Hewitt-Galloway and Snell Blocks. (Courtesy of Thomas R. Stenger.)

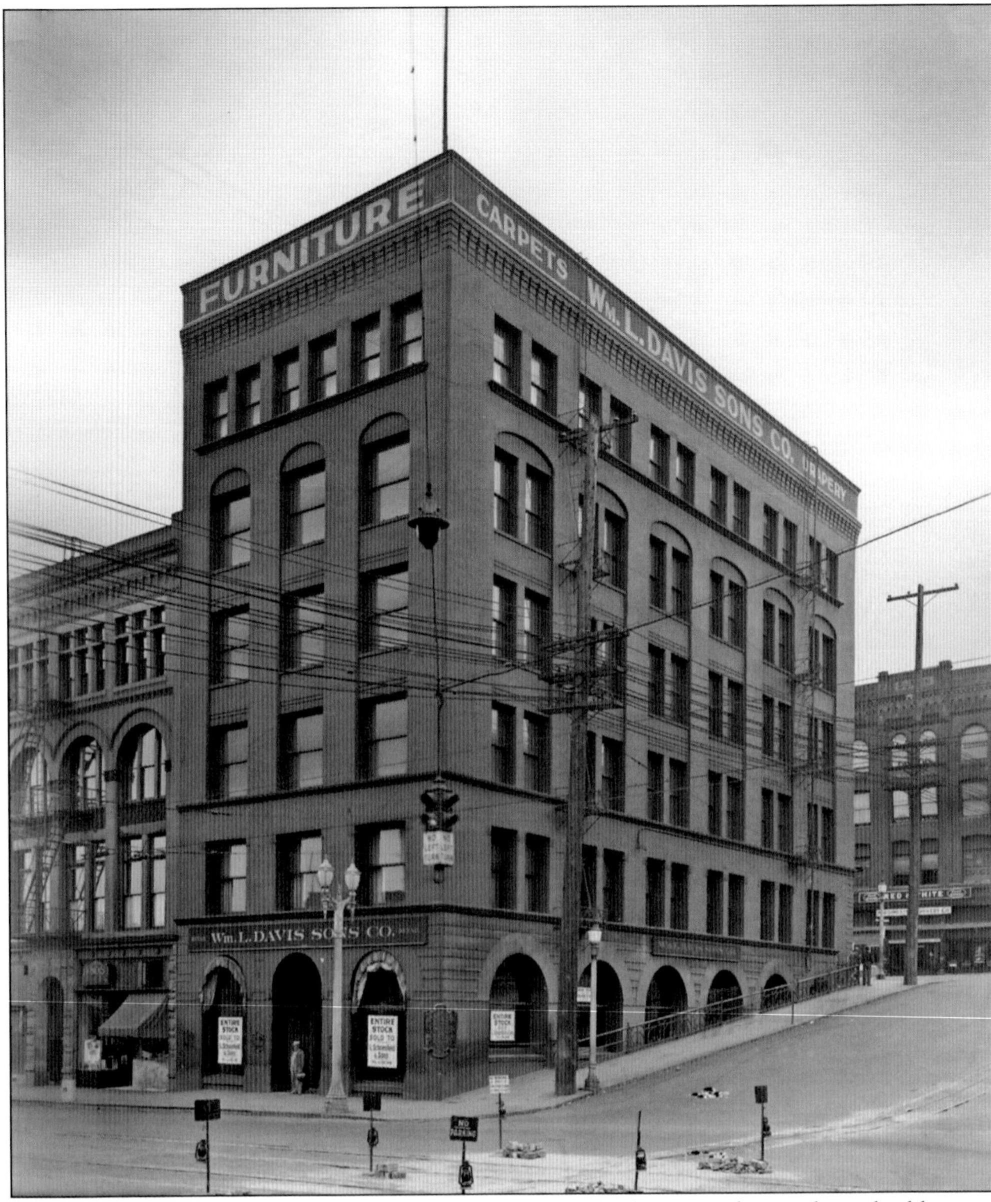

The Chicago architectural firm of Daniel Burnham and John Root designed two buildings in Tacoma: the Fidelity building shown previously and the Luzon building, located at 1302 Pacific Avenue and seen here in an undated photograph. The duo was nationally known for commercial designs that paved the way for future skyscrapers (Burnham designed New York's Flatiron Building). They also were responsible for coordinating the design of the 1893 World's Columbian Exposition. Historians herald this Chicago event as the beginnings of the City Beautiful movement in the nation. The Pacific National Bank commissioned the six-story Luzon building in 1890. George Vanderbilt purchased it two years later. While the upper floors were not developed into commercial spaces, over time, variously named banks occupied the first floor. The building still stands as a monument to the work of one of the nation's premiere architectural firms.

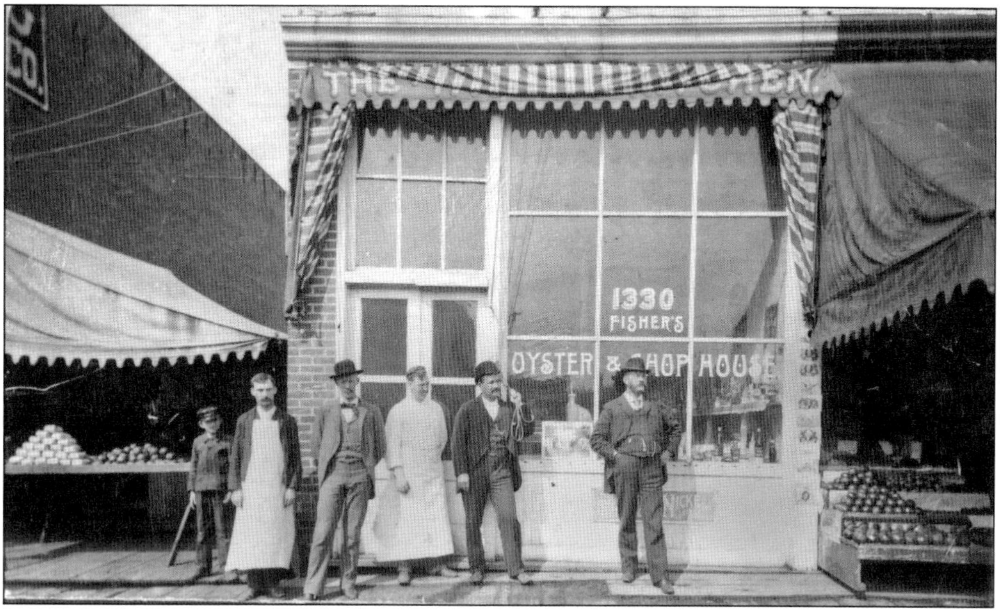

Fisher's Oyster and Chop House was one of many small restaurants locals would find in downtown Tacoma during its early history. In this undated photograph, owner Al Fisher, wearing a derby hat, posed in front of his 1330 Pacific Avenue shop. M. A. Dillon is located third from his left. The names of the remainder of the group are not known.

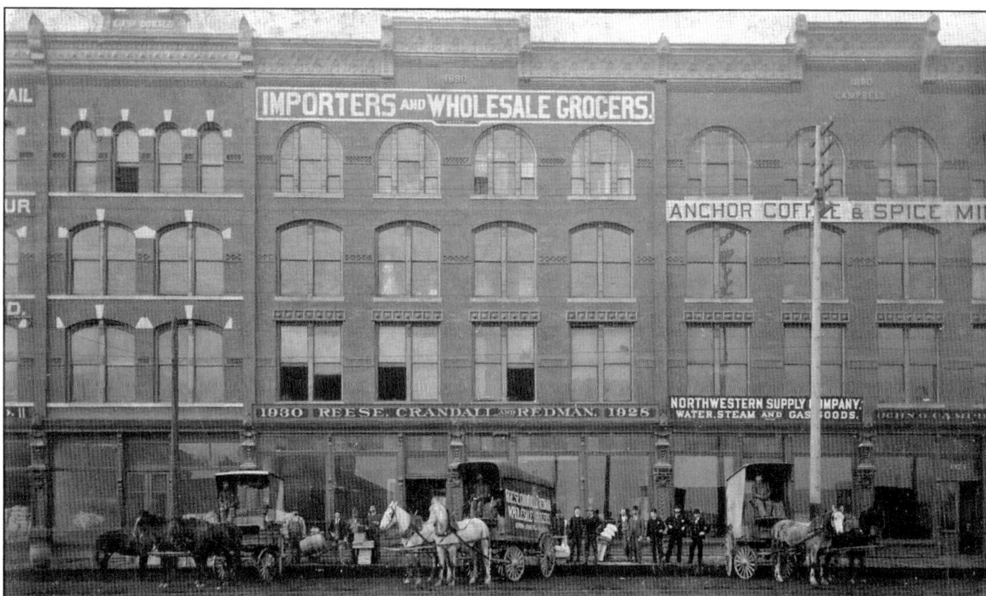

As businessmen constructed their commercial buildings within the core of downtown in the 1890s, Pacific Avenue farther south was becoming a place for wholesalers specializing in grocery products. The firm of Reese, Crandall, and Redman was located at 1928 Pacific Avenue. By 2004, this building along with its neighbors had become part of the University of Washington Tacoma campus. (Courtesy of Thomas R. Stenger.)

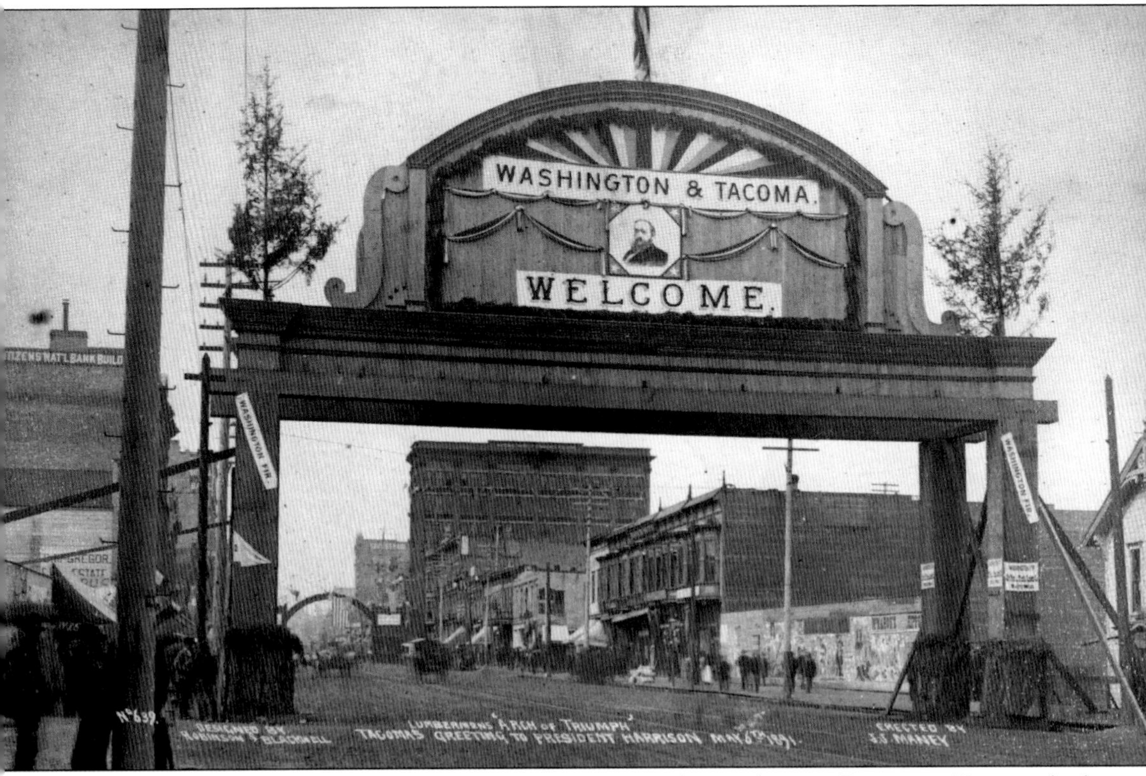

On November 11, 1889, Washington became a state. Earlier in the year, Benjamin Harrison had been inaugurated as president. Two years later, he became one of the first federal executives to tour the West, arriving in Tacoma on May 6, 1891. Why he came is unknown, but it is possible he was campaigning for reelection against Grover Cleveland. Tacomans greeted him and his wife, Caroline, as only an up-and-coming city could. Buildings were draped with flags and bunting while decorative arches lined Pacific Avenue. One, constructed at South Tenth Street and Pacific Avenue—and seen in the distance in this Thomas H. Rutter view—was made with sacks of grain and flour announcing, "Washington Can Feed All Mankind." Farther south along the street near South Fifteenth and Pacific Avenue, another ornate arch welcomed the president. This event was not the last time that Tacomans welcomed national dignitaries: Pres. Theodore Roosevelt would come in 1903. Even so, the Harrison visit did symbolize that the Pacific Northwest was now politically linked to the rest of the nation. (Courtesy of Thomas R. Stenger.)

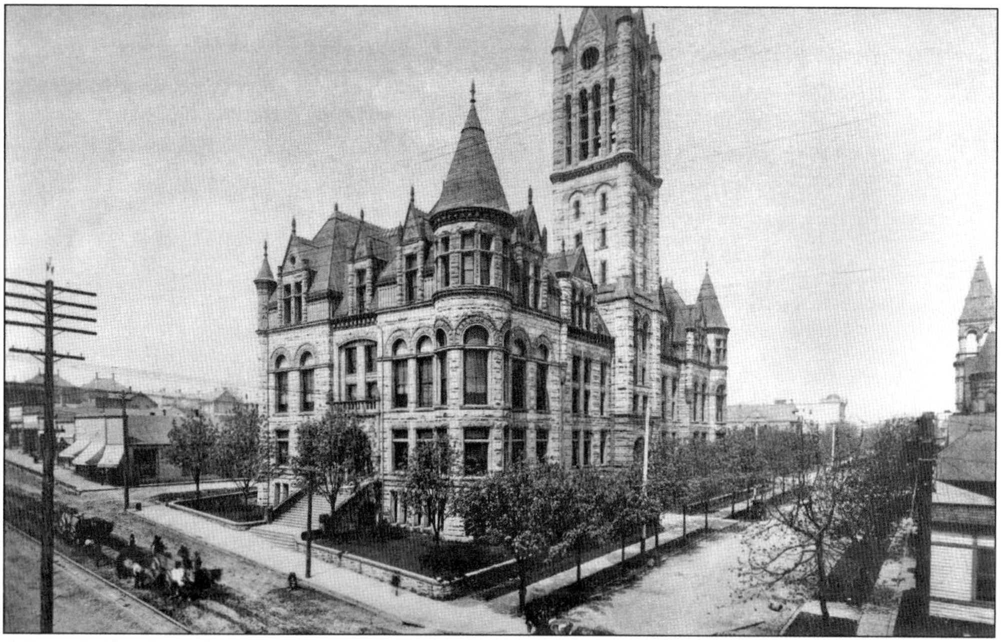

After 1885, when the Pierce County seat was moved from Steilacoom to Tacoma, offices were located in a two-story framed building on Broadway. Running out of room, county commissioners commissioned the architectural firm of Proctor and Dennis to design a new facility located at 1012 South G Street. Dedicated in 1892, Pierce County officials worked in this building for over half a century.

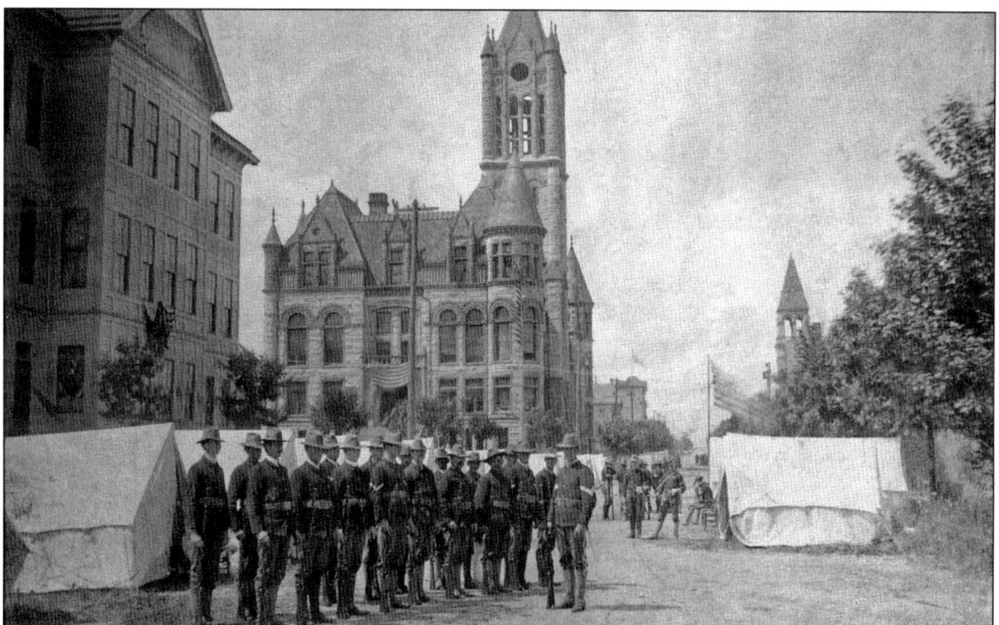

In this undated view, a photographer used the Pierce County Courthouse as a backdrop for a muster of Tacoma's militia, the forerunner of today's National Guard. The names of the men gathered here are unidentified, but they apparently are preparing for an inspection. It is possible that some of these men would deploy to the Philippine Islands following the 1898 Spanish-American War.

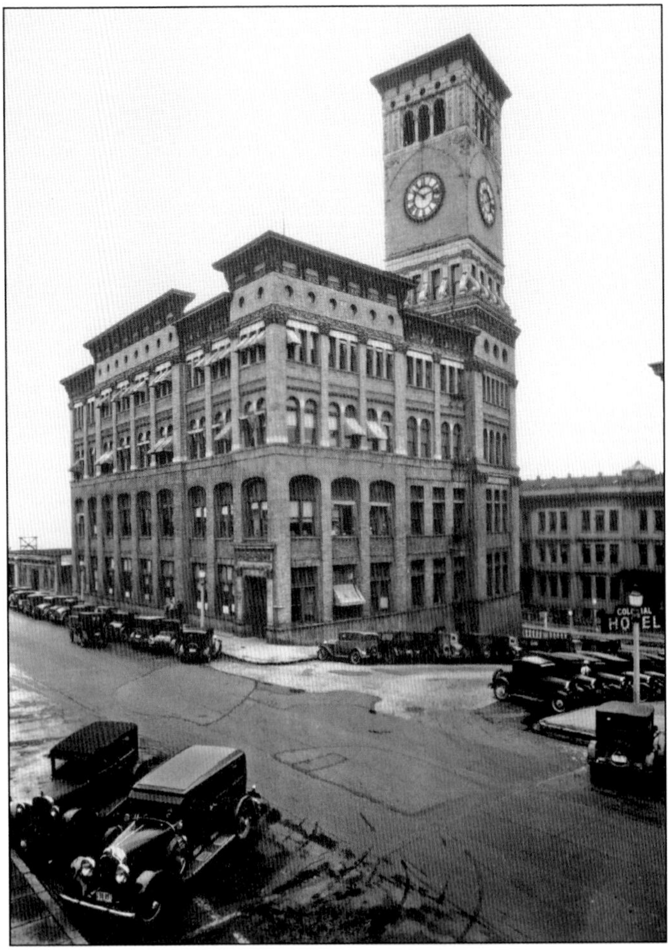

Initially there were two city governments: Tacoma City (Old Tacoma) and New Tacoma. The two combined in 1885. City business was first conducted in various buildings around town, including the chamber of commerce building on Pacific Avenue. By 1892, however, both the City of Tacoma and the chamber of commerce had acquired lots for new buildings: the chamber at 625 Commerce Street and the city at 773 Broadway. The two entities swapped lots and building designs, leaving Tacoma's citizens with the city hall shown at left in this undated view. Below in 1923, an unidentified photographer captured the chamber of commerce building shortly before a new hotel took its place. The San Francisco architectural firm of Hatherton and McIntosh designed both buildings. (Below courtesy of Tacoma Public Library.)

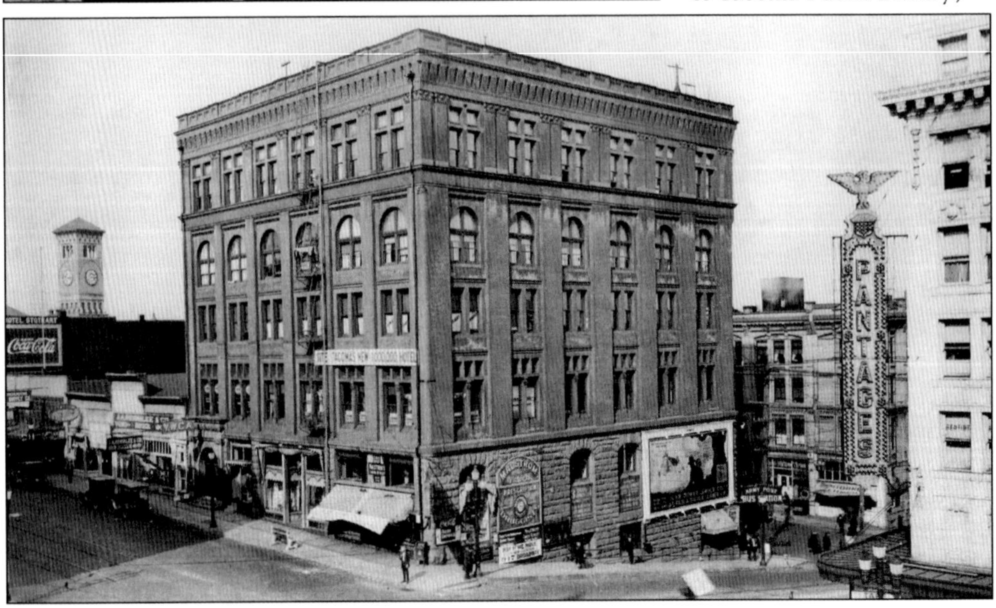

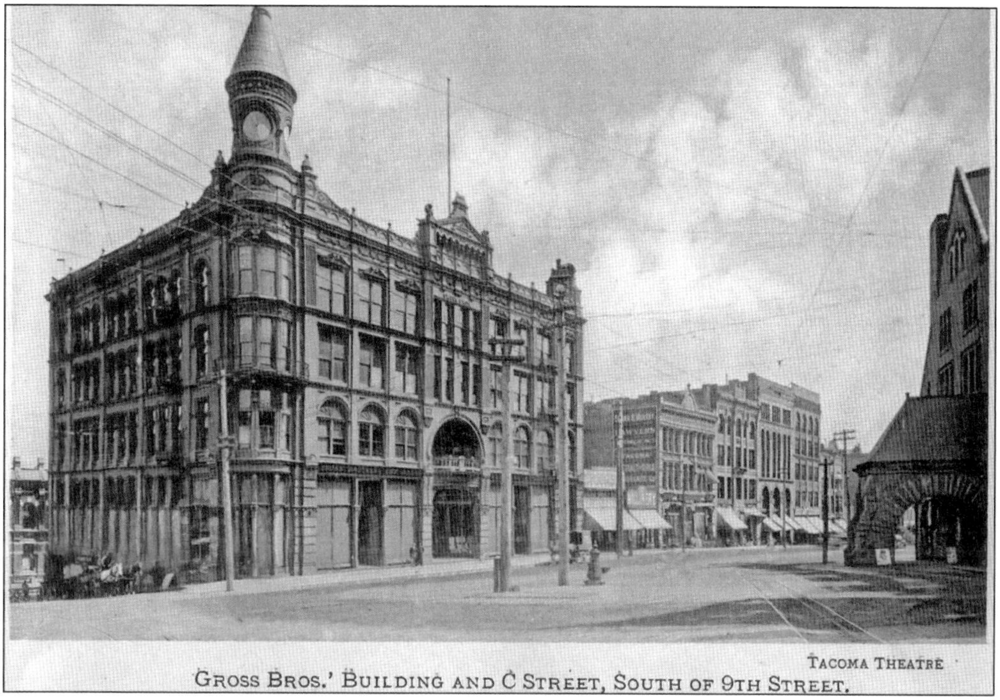

The emergence of large department stores was one byproduct of the streetcar, with the Gross Brothers establishment one of the first of many in downtown Tacoma. The cornerstone for their business located at 901 Broadway was laid in 1889, and the store remained in business until 1916. (Courtesy of Thomas R. Stenger.)

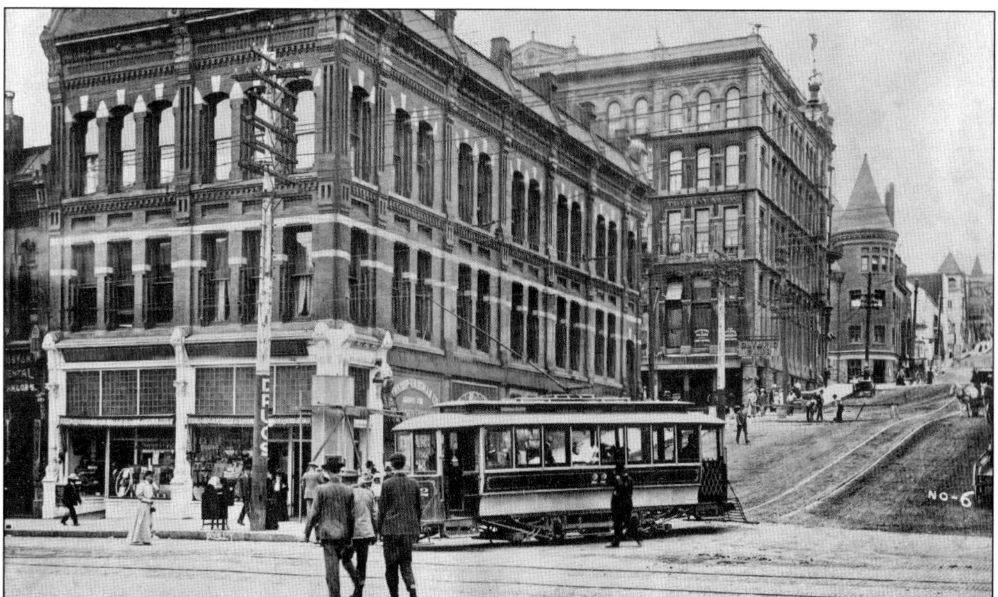

Tacomans in the 1890s ready to ride this streetcar could look west along South Ninth Street and see progress. The trolley is ready to stop in front of the Wright building facing Pacific Avenue. Behind it is the Gross Brothers Department Store. The turret of the Tacoma Theater can be seen in the distance. (Courtesy of Thomas R. Stenger.)

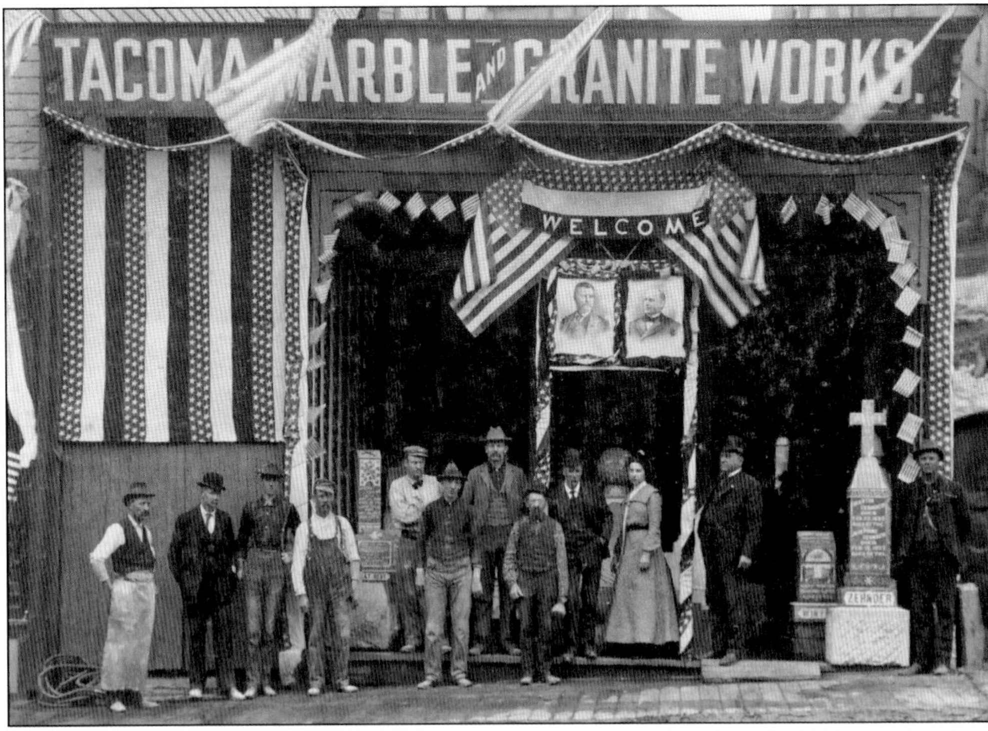

Not all downtown businesses were grandiose. In 1900, a group of unidentified folk posed in front of Thomas Sizer's Tacoma Marble and Granite Works on South Ninth Street. These carvers of tombstones appear to be celebrating the reelection of William McKinley as president of the United States in 1901. His running mate, Theodore Roosevelt, would become president the following year and pay a visit to Tacoma in 1903.

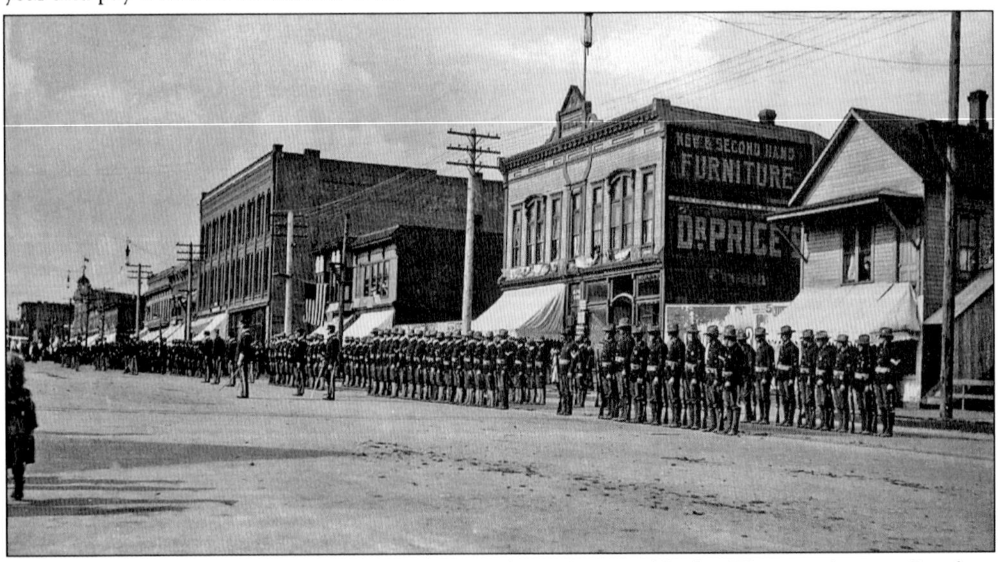

On July 5, 1900, Paul Lehman used the buildings along the 1100 block of Tacoma Avenue South as a backdrop when photographing members of the Washington Guard, Company H, 1st Regiment. The review was part of the city's Fourth of July that year, one that Tacomans remember because of a streetcar accident that killed 37 people. (Courtesy of Tacoma Public Library.)

Three

1900–1920

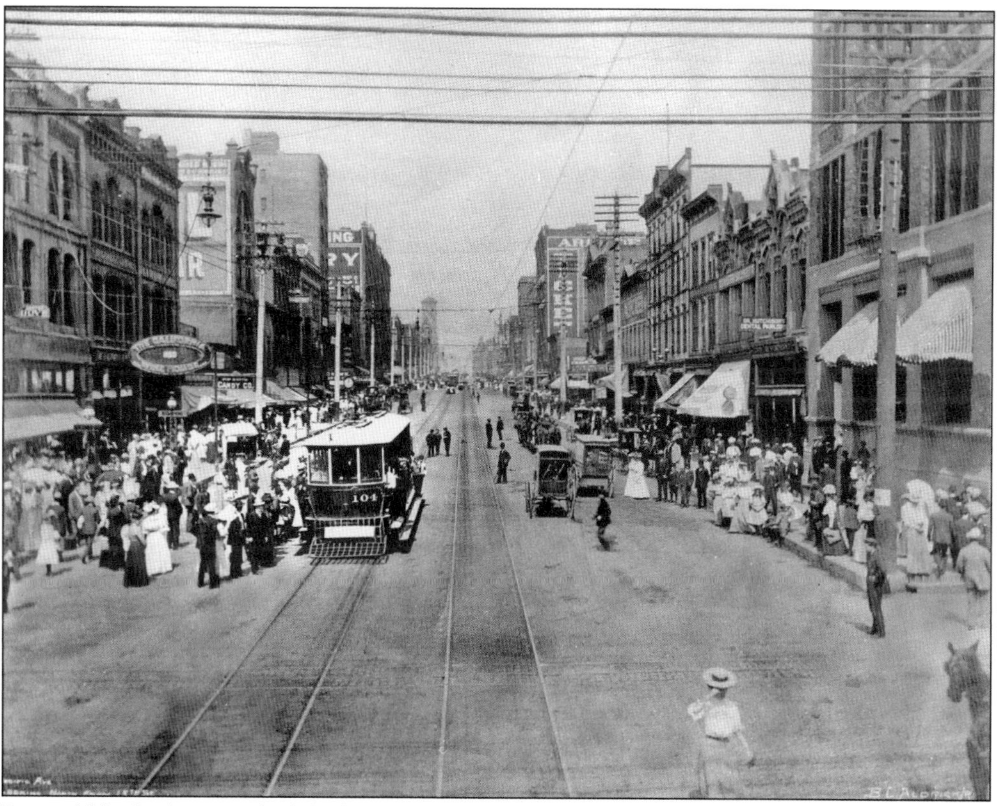

Byron Aldrich photographed the bustle along Pacific Avenue north from South Thirteenth Street sometime after 1902. In the view, men, women, and children are concentrated on the arrival and departure of streetcars along the thoroughfare while horse-drawn vehicles traverse its curbside edges. Little did Tacomans know at the time that soon the automobile would be added to the urban landscape.

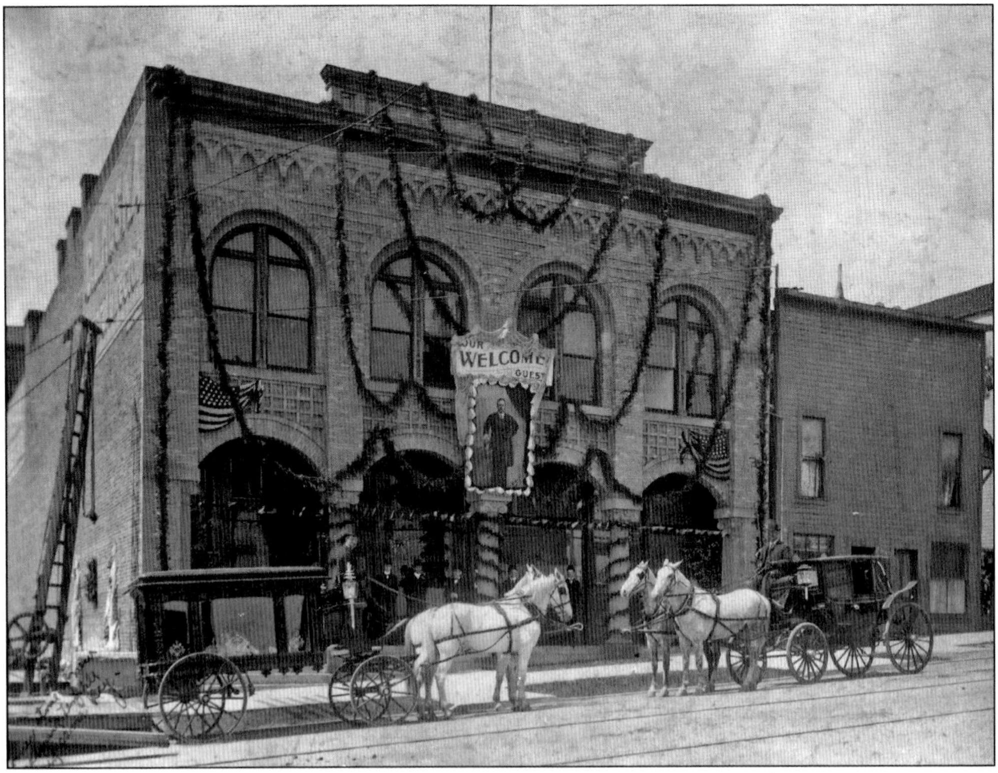

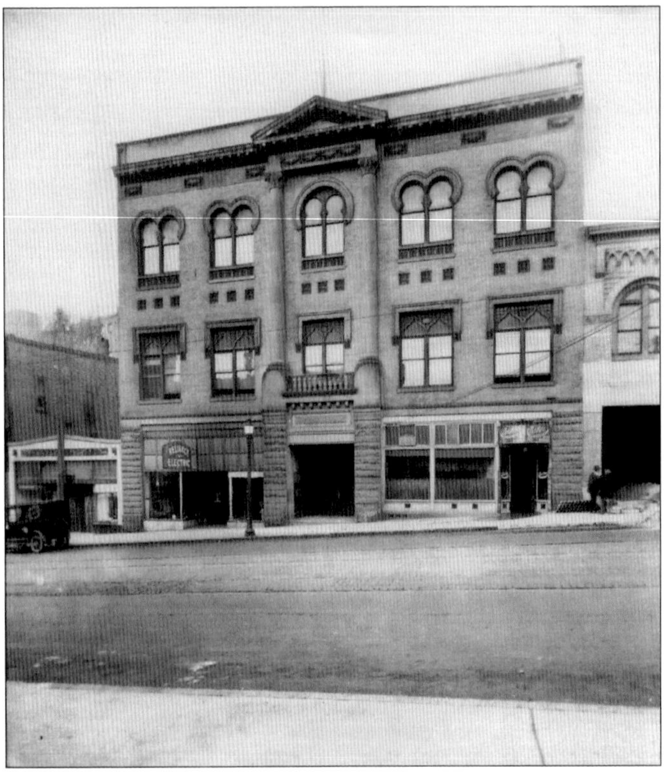

Conrad Hoska's mortuary was one of Tacoma's earliest. While some mourners opted for a streetcar funeral to Tacoma or Oakwood Cemeteries, Hoska provided horse-drawn hearses posed above in front of his business located at 730 St. Helens Avenue. The building is decorated to honor the 1903 arrival of Pres. Theodore Roosevelt, whose visit to Tacoma included laying a cornerstone for the Masonic Temple, seen at left at 734 St. Helens Avenue. After 1929, when this building and Hoska's mortuary were demolished to make way for the Medical Arts Building, the cornerstone—in 1956—was moved to the New Tacoma Cemetery. (Below courtesy of Tacoma Public Library.)

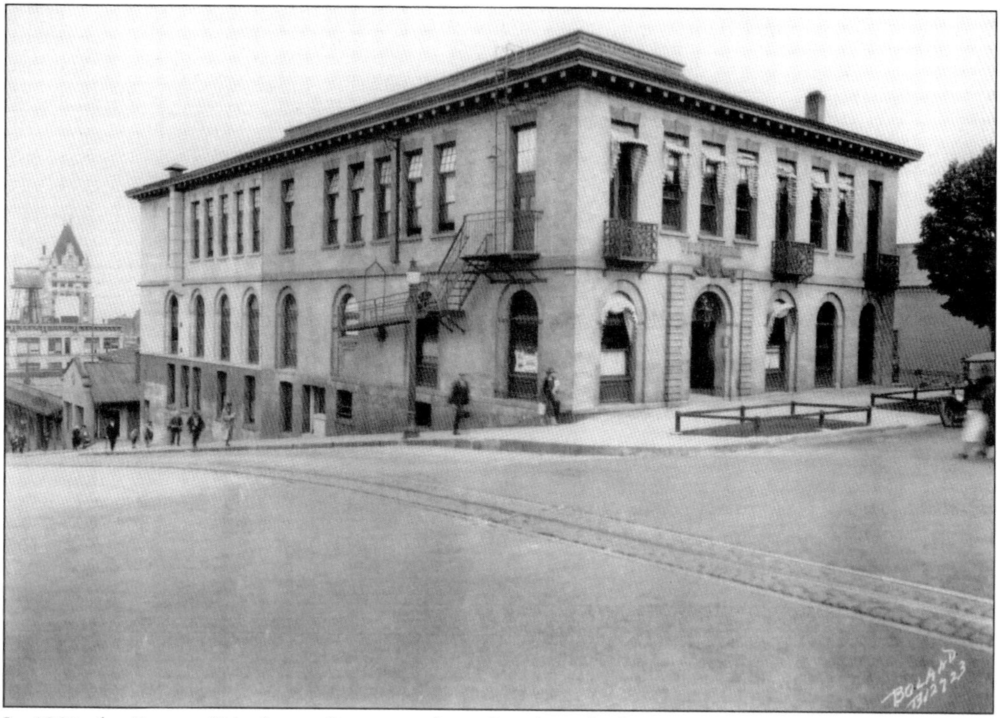

In 1901, the Sunset Telephone Company, later Pacific Telephone and Telegraph, announced the construction of its headquarters at 1101 Fawcett Avenue. This was to be the home for the "hello" girls, reported the *Tacoma Daily Ledger* that year. Marvin Boland photographed the building in 1927 shortly after its new rear addition was completed. (Courtesy of Tacoma Public Library.)

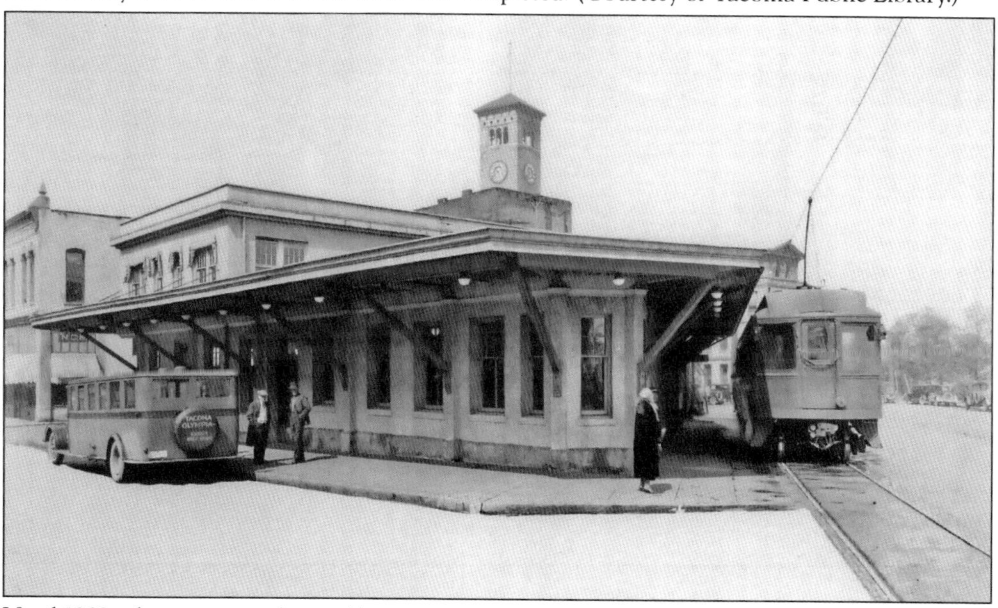

Until 1902, when an interurban rail line was constructed to link Tacoma and Seattle, travelers would have to ride a ferry. Both passengers and freight could now depart from the Puget Sound Electric Railway depot at 712 A Street. In 1937, an unidentified photographer showed the depot at a time when motor buses were beginning to replace the trolleys. (Courtesy of Tacoma Public Library.)

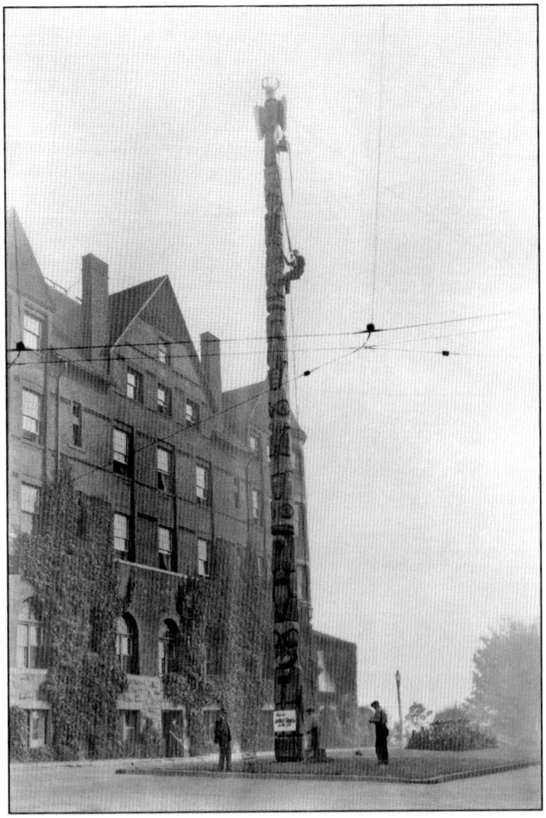

Tacoma businessman William Sheard and banker Chester Thorne commissioned a totem pole to be placed at South Tenth and A Streets near the Tacoma Hotel. The reason is unknown, although probably the two men thought it would do honor to local Native Americans, even though such structures were not a part of the Puyallup Indian culture. Alaskan natives on Vashon Island carved a cedar pole provided by the St. Paul and Tacoma Lumber Company; it was then shipped to the site in 1903. A halo of lights encircled the top of the totem, and the view at left, taken by an unidentified photographer, might be showing the replacement of lightbulbs. In 1918, after America's entry into World War I, Victory House was constructed behind the pole and became the focus of bond drives. (Above courtesy of Tacoma Public Library; below courtesy of Thomas R. Stenger.)

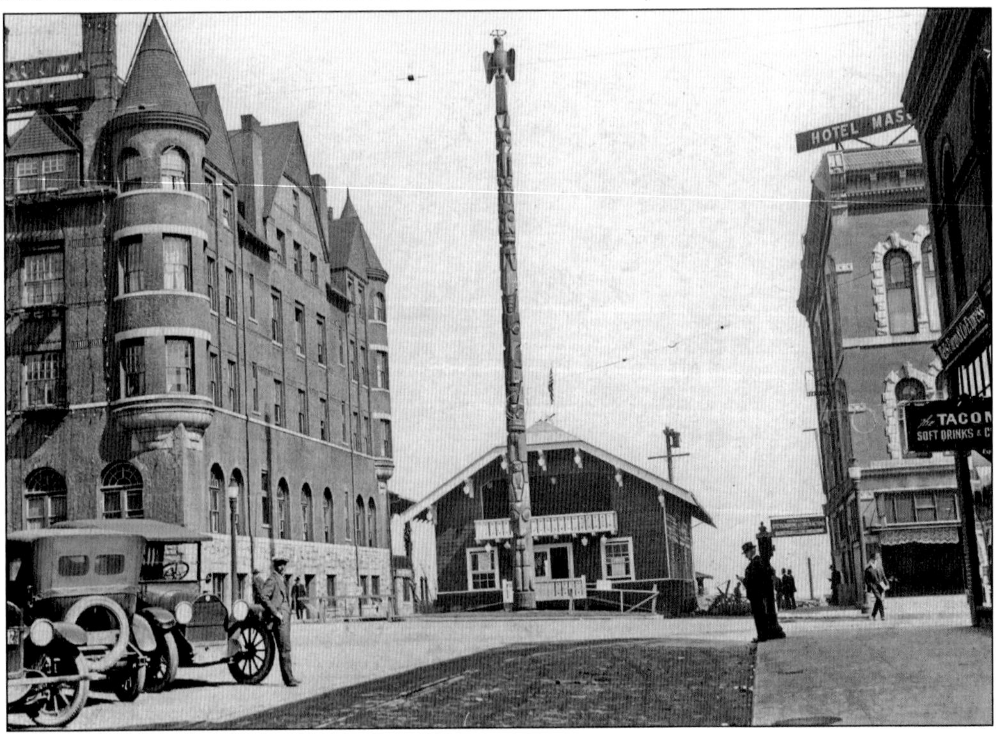

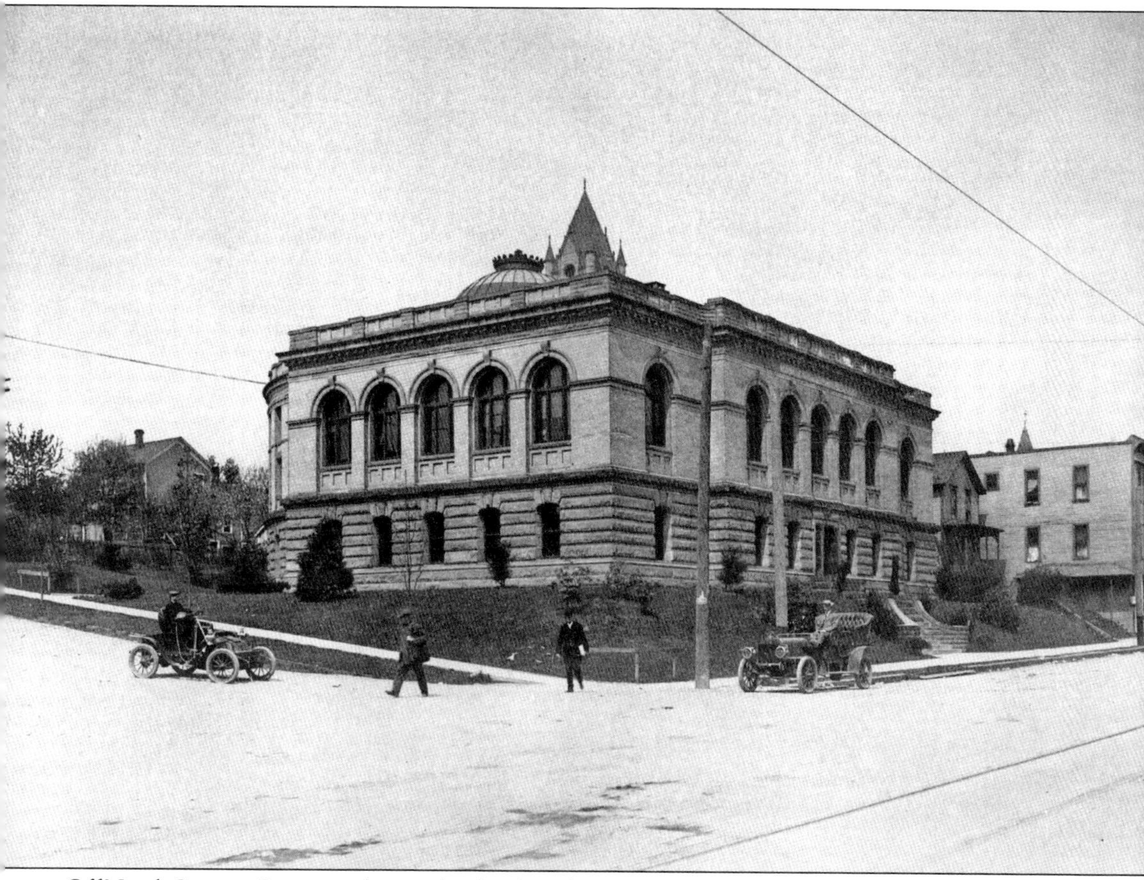

Off North Stevens Street, in the area he developed, a marker honors Allen C. Mason as the founder of Tacoma's first public library. Not much is known about the Mason Library except to note that in 1900 the City of Tacoma loaned his 6,000-volume library to Whitworth College—then occupying the Mason estate—provided it was opened to the public two days a week. One year later, the city announced that Andrew Carnegie was to provide funds for a new downtown library. By the end of the year, the council had decided on a site located at 1120 (now 1102) Tacoma Avenue South. The New York architectural firm of Jardine, Kent, and Jardine designed the building complete with a resplendent glass dome. The Tacoma Public Library opened to the public on June 5, 1903. Today part of the original Carnegie building houses the Northwest Collections Division.

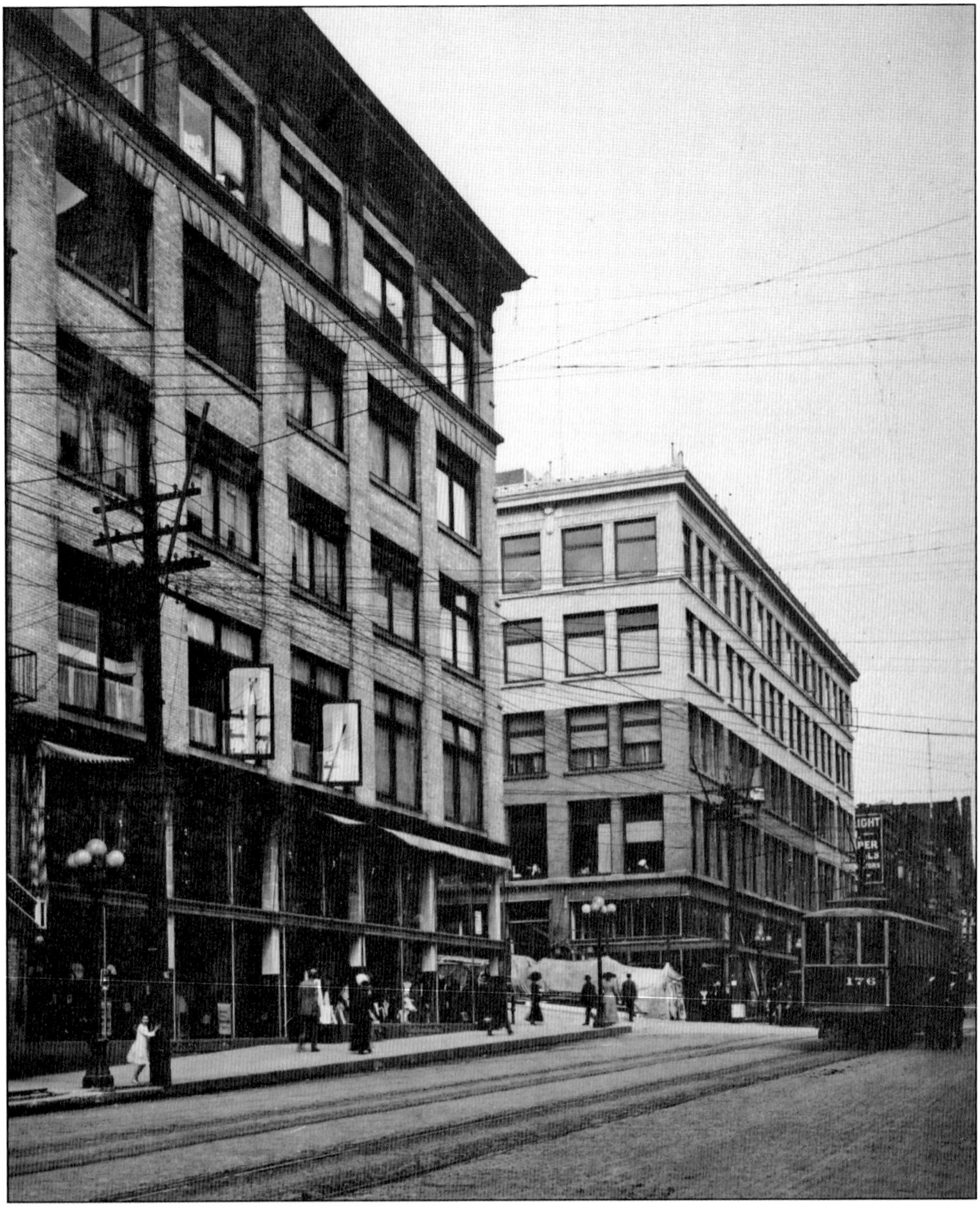

Shoppers today take the department store for granted. At the beginning of the 20th century, however, they were still quite novel. At that time, people expected to go to a variety of shops for furniture, other household needs, clothing, books, pharmacy products, baked goods, groceries, pianos—a major source of entertainment—and sheet music. As previously noted, the Gross Brothers store on Broadway, established in 1889, was the first to create an earlier version of one-stop shopping. Peoples Store, designed by architect Carl Darmer, opened in 1895 at 1101 Pacific Avenue. The emergence of these "palaces of commerce" did not initially cause the foreclosure of the small business but simply provided another shoppers' option. They were, in other words, another reason for families to ride a streetcar from their respective neighborhoods and go downtown. Sometime after 1911, an unidentified photographer captured two of the newest department stores on Broadway that were attracting the attention of Tacomans.

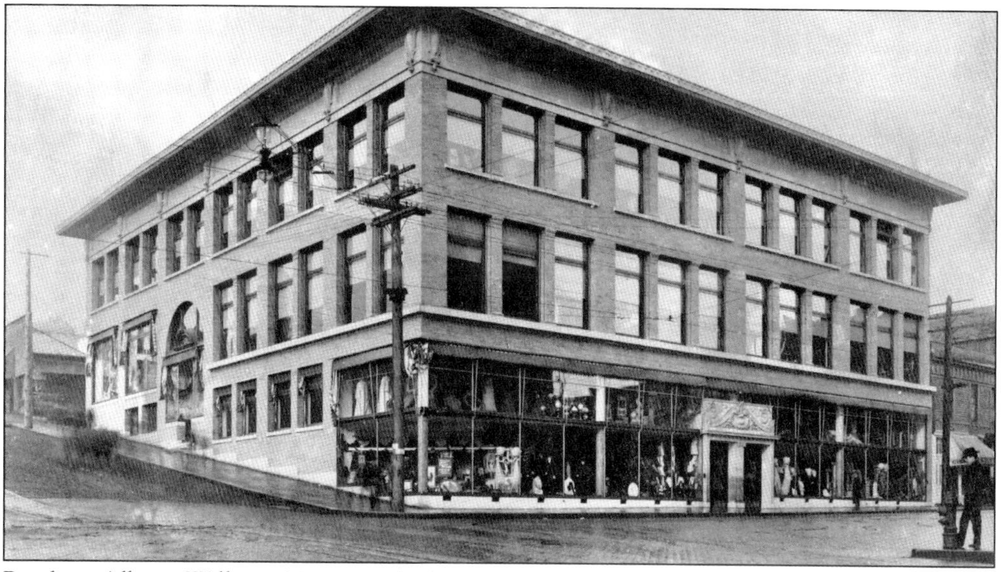

Brothers Albert, William, Henry, and Charles Rhodes established a coffee shop in downtown Tacoma in 1892. Within a decade, they decided to construct a department store at 950 Broadway and commissioned architects Ambrose Russell and Frederick Heath to design the building. "All roads lead to Rhodes" became the advertising slogan after its opening in 1903. An unidentified cameraman photographed the building before two more stories were added.

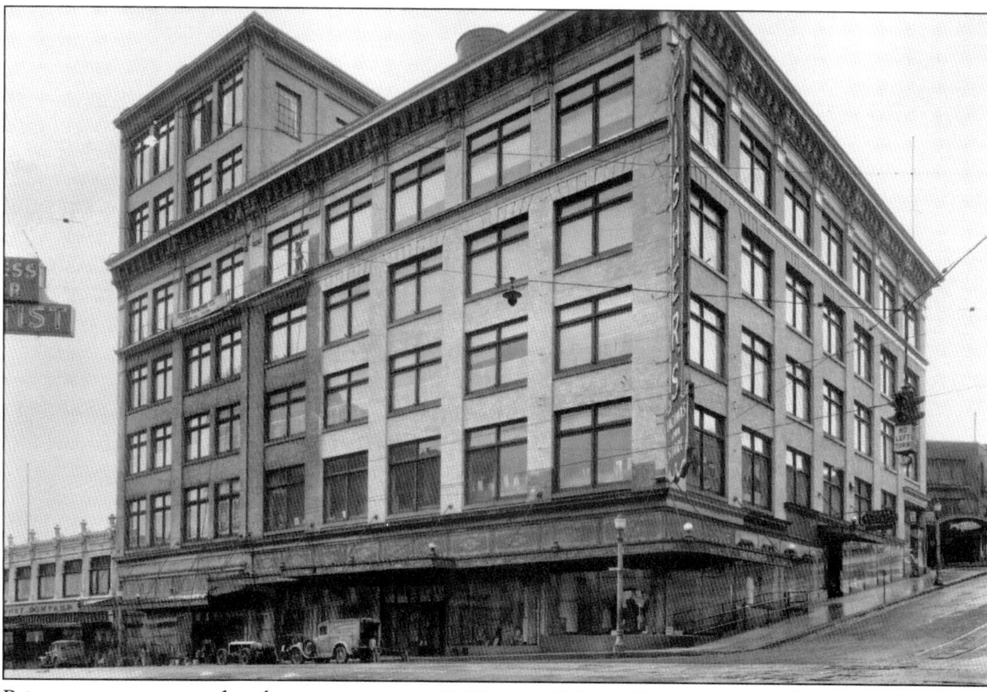

Prior to constructing his department store, F. Garrett Fisher sold shoes. In 1905, he commissioned architect Frederick Heath to design a building across South Eleventh Street from Rhodes at 1104 Broadway. Early Tacomans knew the store as Fishers (or Stone-Fishers) and remember it for "Fisher's Famous Silk Sales." In 1952, it became the city's Bon Marche Department Store that remained at this site until moving to the Tacoma Mall in the mid-1960s.

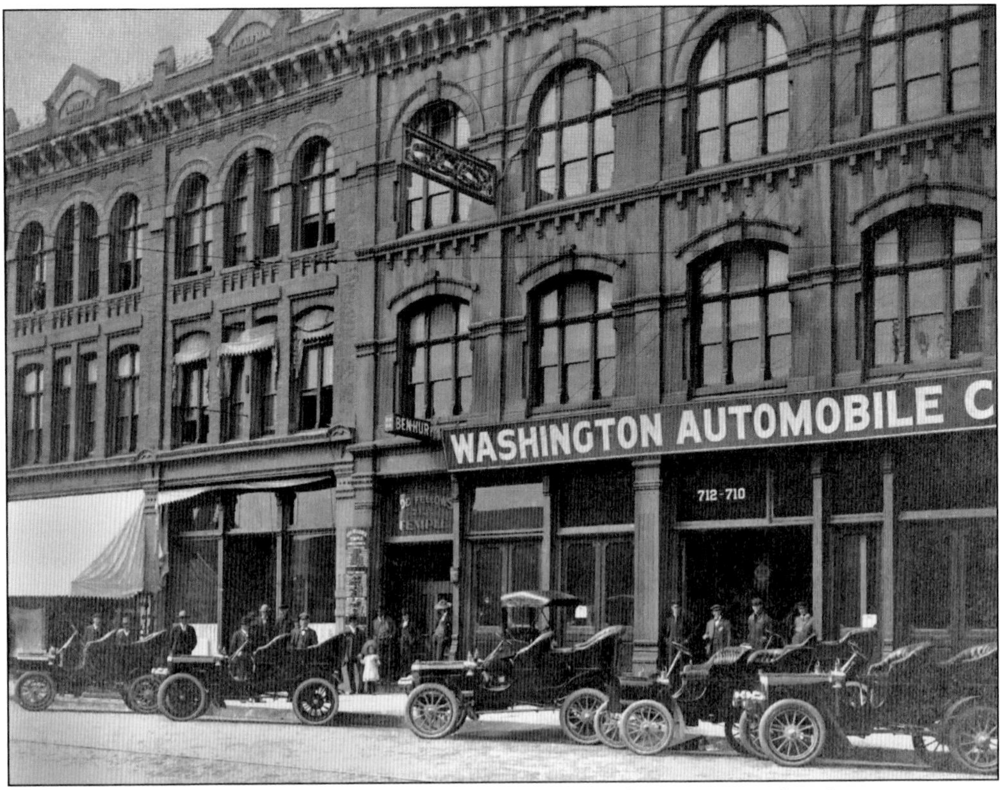

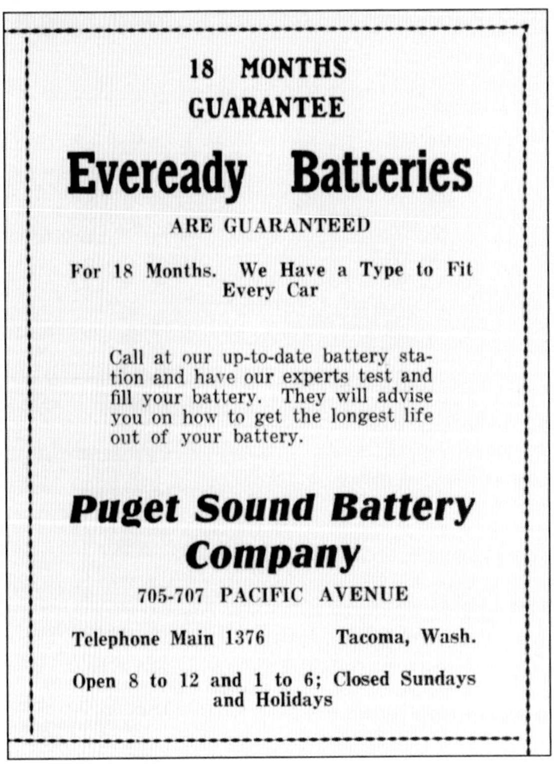

At the same time that downtown Tacoma was being shaped by streetcars, and horse drayage was becoming a thing of the past, the automobile appeared on the scene. Unknown to Tacomans at the time, and like the trolley before it, this mode of transportation was to reshape the city again. During the first decade of the 20th century, only the wealthy could afford the "horseless carriage," with the *Tacoma Daily Ledger* reporting weekly on which members of the elite bought what make and model of car. In 1905, the Washington Automobile Company (above), located at 710 Pacific Avenue, became the first local dealership. By the 1920s, listings in Tacoma's city directory were classified to include everything from dealerships to used cars, car parts, taxies, and moving vans. The advertisement at left was printed in a 1919 brochure.

Thanks to new technologies, such as the elevator and steel-frame construction, Tacoma developers were building upward, creating the city's first skyscrapers. In 1906, the Fidelity Trust Company announced that Daniel Burnham would design a six-story addition for the original 1890 building at 949 Broadway. Completed in 1909, the roof had a rooftop weather tower.

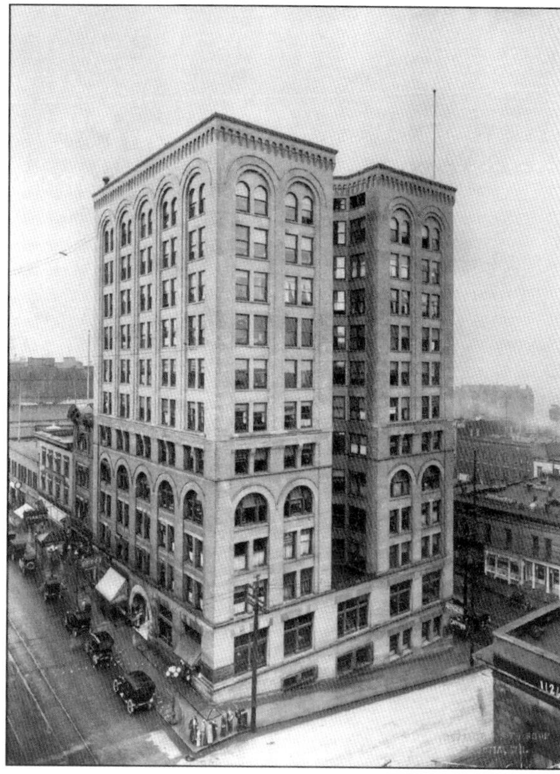

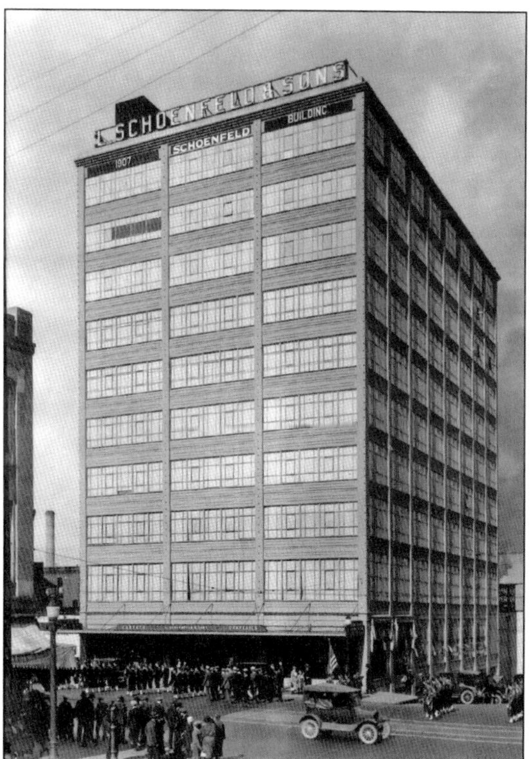

At 1423 Pacific Avenue, Peter Sandberg built what promoters called the "oldest reinforced concrete skyscraper on the West Coast." Tacoma's Frederick Heath served as the local architect for the project. In 1922, the firm of L. Schoenfeld and Sons purchased the building and two years later opened what a *Tacoma Daily Ledger* reporter called "one of the Coast's large furniture plants."

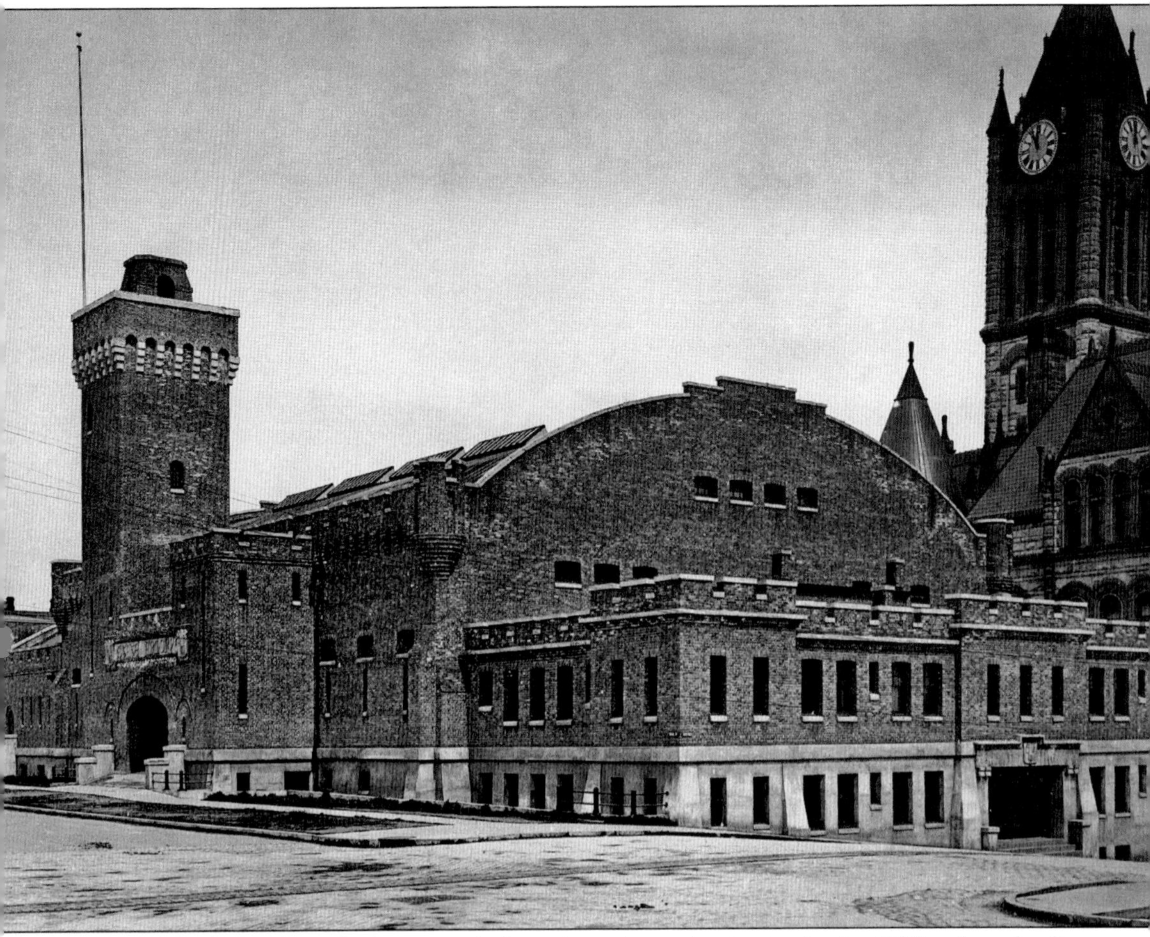

Tacomans have always had a strong link to the military, beginning in the 1880s when the first militia companies were formed. By the beginning of the 20th century, units of the Washington National Guard were mustering at a site near American Lake south of the city. Also at this time, the Washington State Legislature provided funds for the construction of local armories where members of the guard could receive training in the arts of warfare on a regular basis. In 1907, Russell and Babcock designed this medieval-like fortress, located at 715 South Eleventh Street, for the Washington National Guard. Following its dedication, it became more than a training facility for local units of cavalry and infantry. Pres. William Howard Taft met an overflow crowd there in 1911. The building became the site for everything from rose shows to boxing matches and dances at a time when Tacoma had few places to accommodate large groups of people. Its location just west of the Pierce County Courthouse created a spectacular view from Tacoma's downtown.

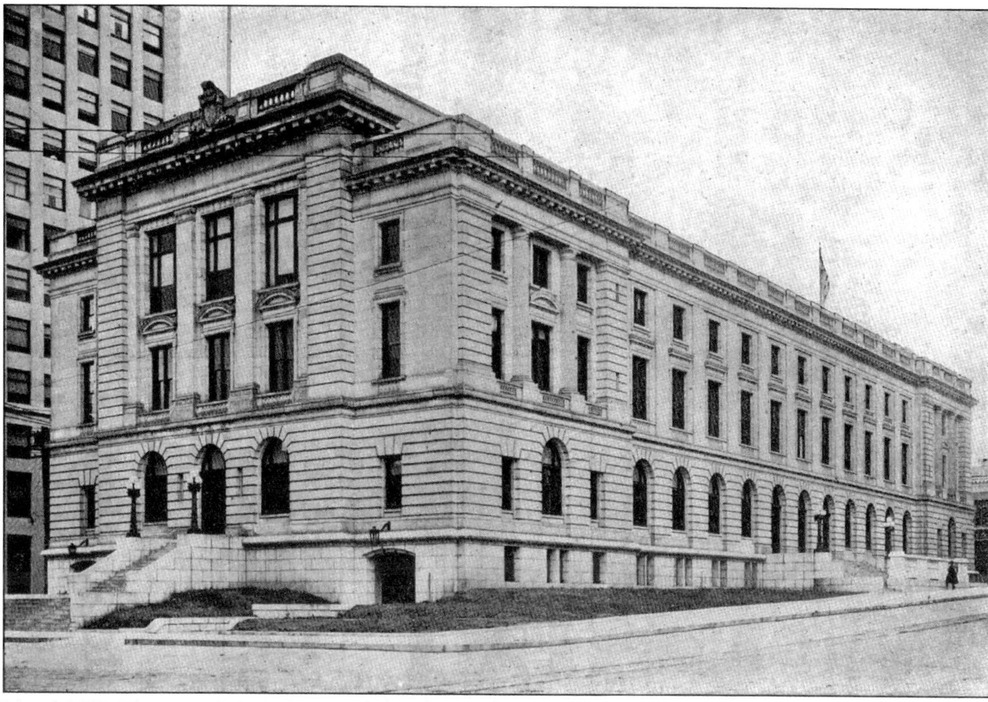

Until 1910, Tacoma did not have a federal courthouse. In that year, this building at 1102 A Street was dedicated both as a post office and as the courtrooms for federal judges. In 1974, over a half century after an unidentified photographer took this 1919 view, federal judge George Boldt would make his decision establishing equity for Native American fishermen.

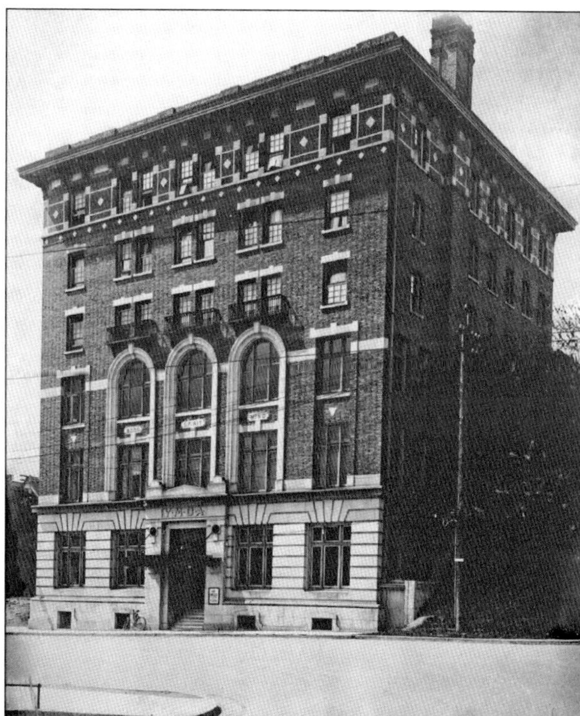

Tacoma's Young Men's Christian Association (YMCA) was founded in 1883 to meet the needs of workers encountering the unhealthful conditions of urban industrial society. The dedication of the organization's first quarters, located at 714 Broadway, occurred in January 1910. Besides sleeping quarters, the facility at various times had a gymnasium, lounge, and restaurant, along with educational programs to aid the worker.

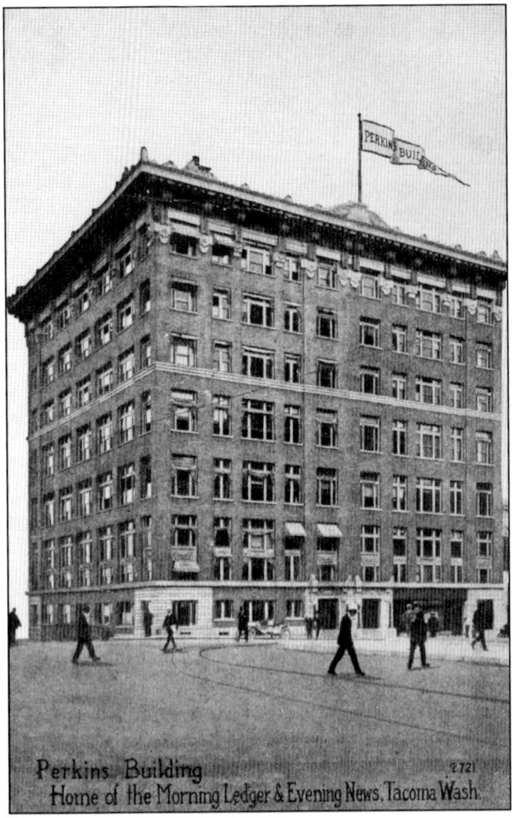

Before radio and television revolutionized the communication industry, local newspapers were the primary source of information and entertainment. And by the early years of the 20th century, the newspaper they read identified a Tacoman's politics. The *Tacoma Daily Ledger* and the *Tacoma Daily News* were Republican, while the paper that ultimately became the *Tacoma News Tribune* was Democrat. Reporting was biased, and editorial mudslinging was standard fare. By 1906, Sidney Albert Perkins dominated the local scene by owning both the *Ledger* and *News* and by constructing a building at 1101 A Street (at left) for his offices and press. Four years later, the Tribune Building was constructed at 711 St. Helens Avenue (below). In this view, folks have gathered outside the newspaper office to check the score of a World Series baseball game some time in the 1920s.

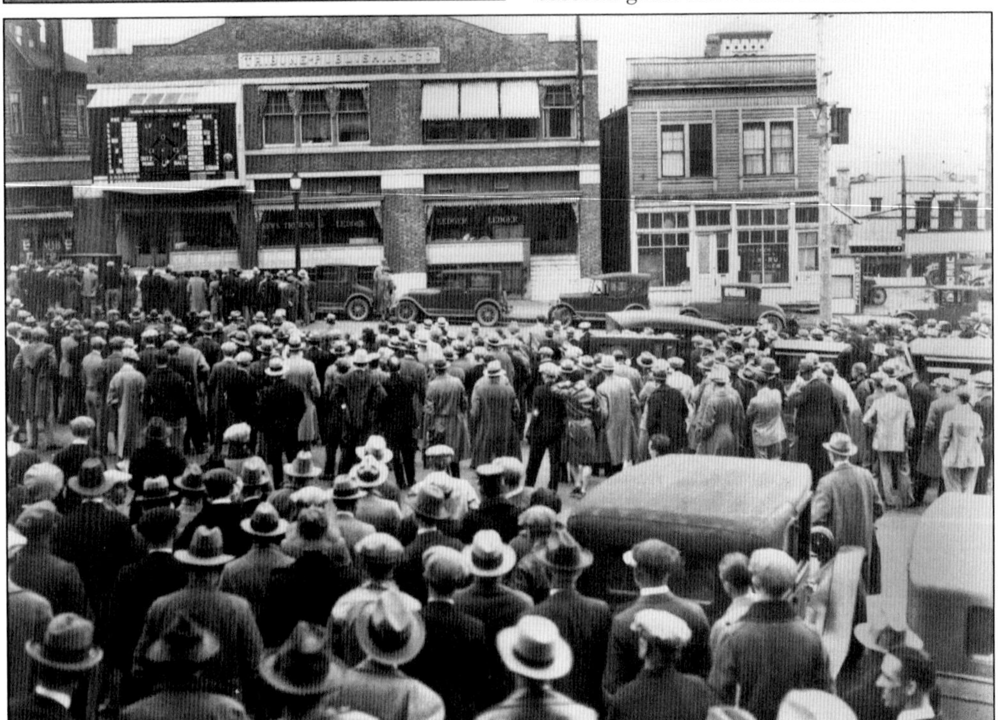

In 1900, Frederick Weyerhaeuser acquired thousands of acres of timberland then owned by the Northern Pacific Railroad Company as a part of its land grant. At first, the timber company's offices were in the railroad headquarters building on Pacific Avenue. By 1910, Weyerhaeuser was ready to begin construction of the Tacoma Building at 1017 A Street. The company moved into it in 1912.

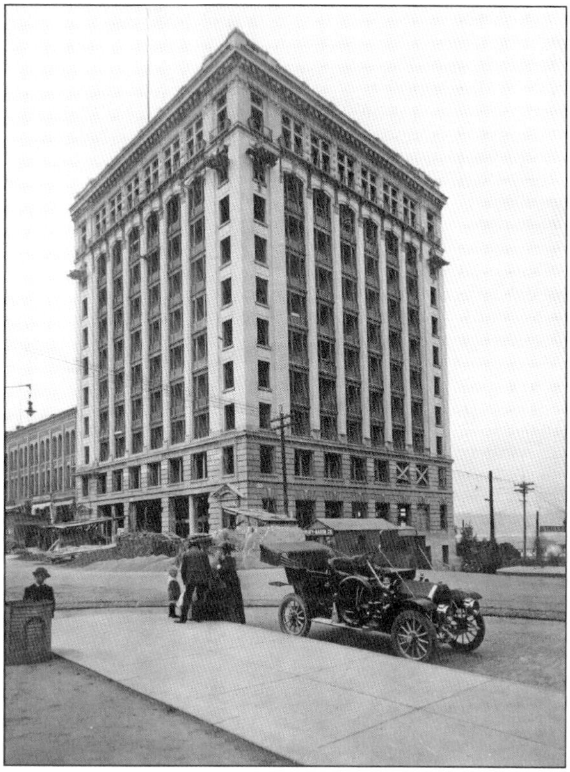

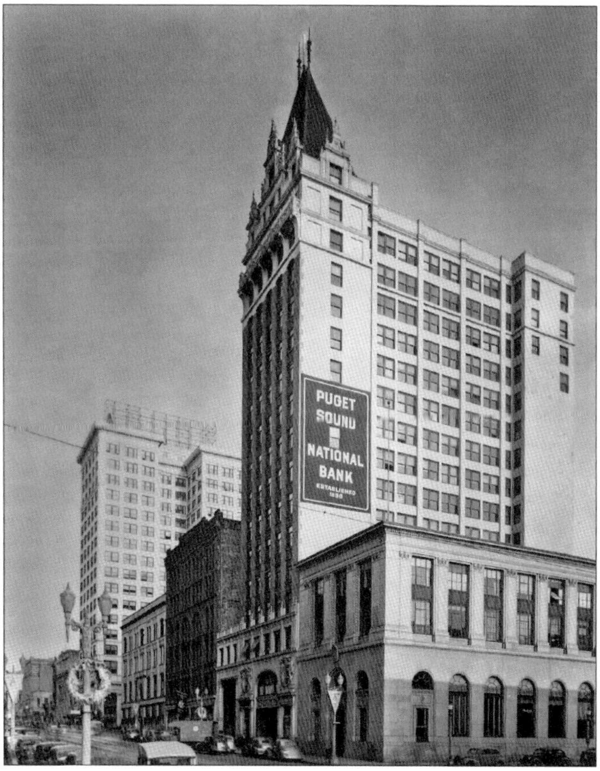

At the same time Weyerhaeuser's skyscraper was rising on A Street, another was underway at 1117 Pacific Avenue. Designed by Frederick Heath, who put his offices in the upper tower, the Puget Sound National Bank occupied the building for years. Until the construction of Seattle's Smith Tower in 1914, the building, seen in this 1939 photograph, was considered the tallest building on the West Coast.

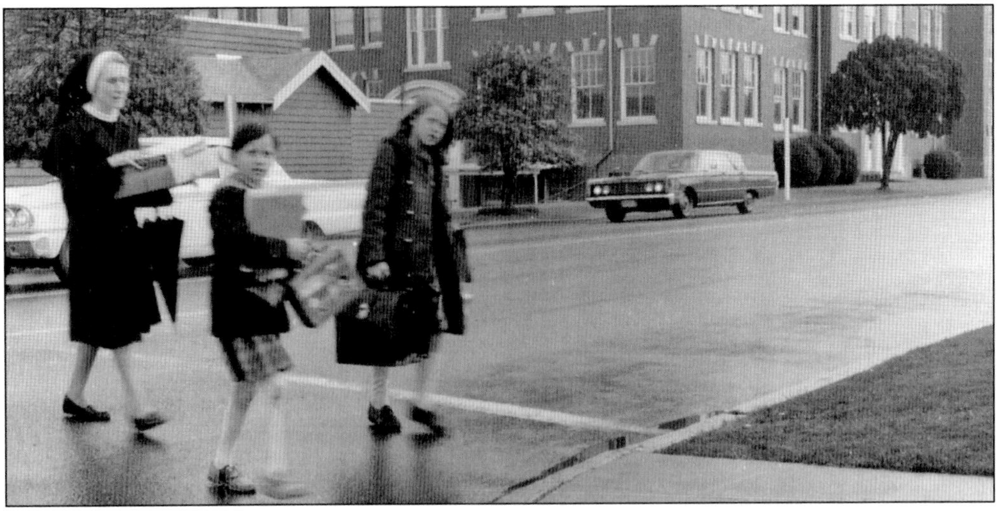

Religious institutions always played a role in the history of downtown Tacoma, with St. Leo Roman Catholic Parish church, school, and convent ultimately dominating the east side of Yakima Avenue South beginning at South Thirteenth Street. The school at 1323 Yakima opened its doors to students in 1912. The Knights of Columbus also held an evening school in the building. (Courtesy of Tacoma Public Library.)

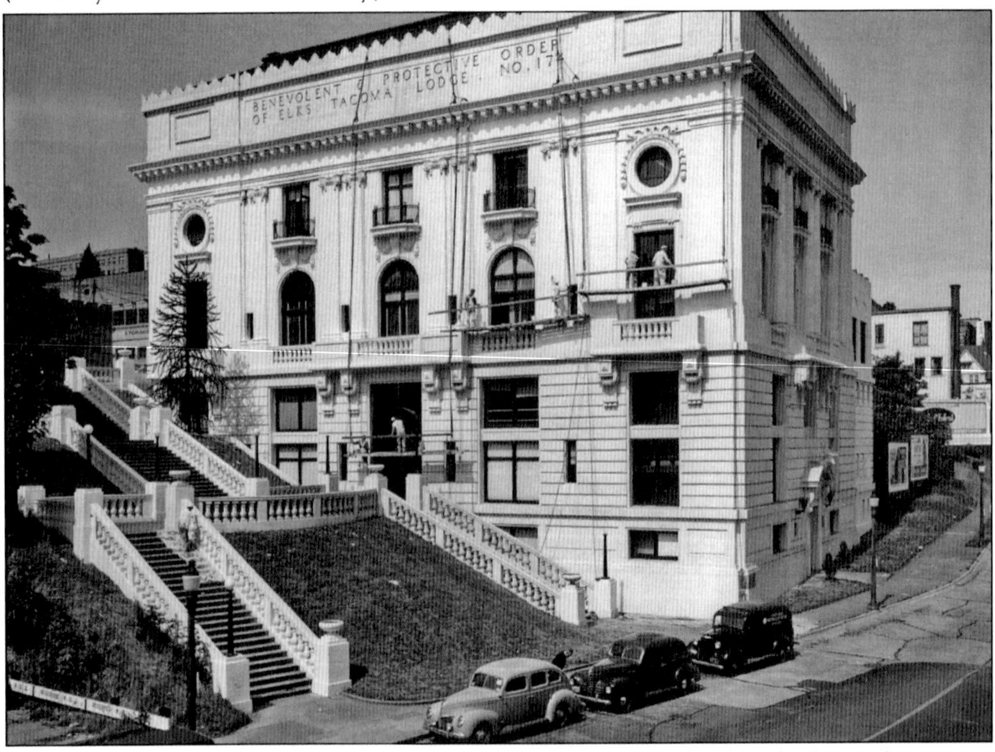

The Elks Lodge, one of Tacoma's many fraternal organizations, also found a home downtown. Planning for its headquarters at 565 Broadway began in 1914, and the dedication was held in 1916. Architect E. Frere Champney designed the "Spanish Stairs" that connect Broadway and Commerce Street as a fire escape for the building, pictured here in 1947. (Photograph by Richards Studio; courtesy of Tacoma Public Library.)

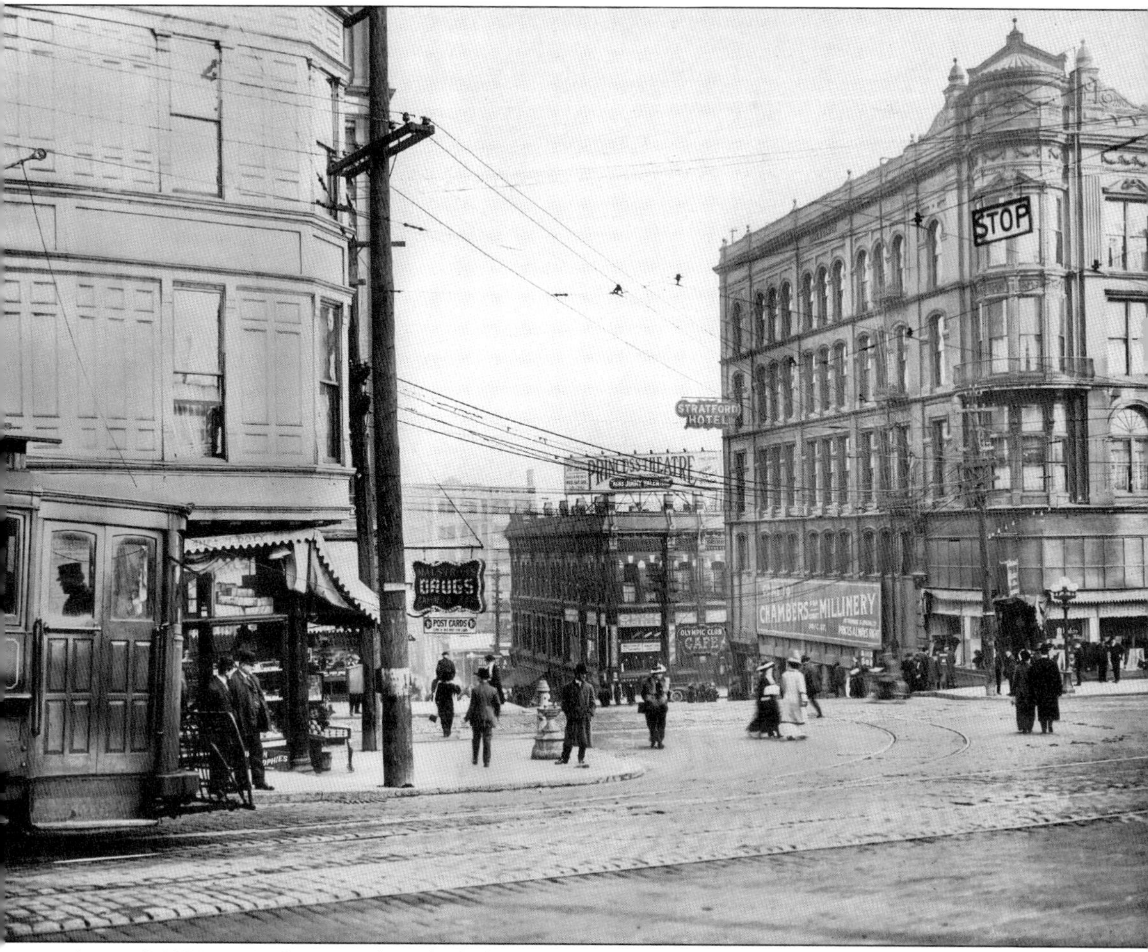

Around 1914 or 1915, an unidentified photographer stood in the middle of St. Helens Avenue and South Ninth Street and looked east. A rooftop billboard advertised a movie in the Princess Theater, then located in the Wright Building, seen in this view between the Gross Brothers store (right) and the Bostwick Block (left). The Tacoma Chamber of Commerce offices are out of view and behind the Bostwick. The Stafford Hotel occupied the floors above what was then known as the Jones building, while various businesses could be found below the Bostwick Hotel. Dr. H. C. Bostwick was to die in 1916, the same year that major changes were underway at this intersection. Within a year, the Jones block would be gone. In a decade, a new hotel would replace the chamber of commerce building. (Courtesy of Thomas R. Stenger.)

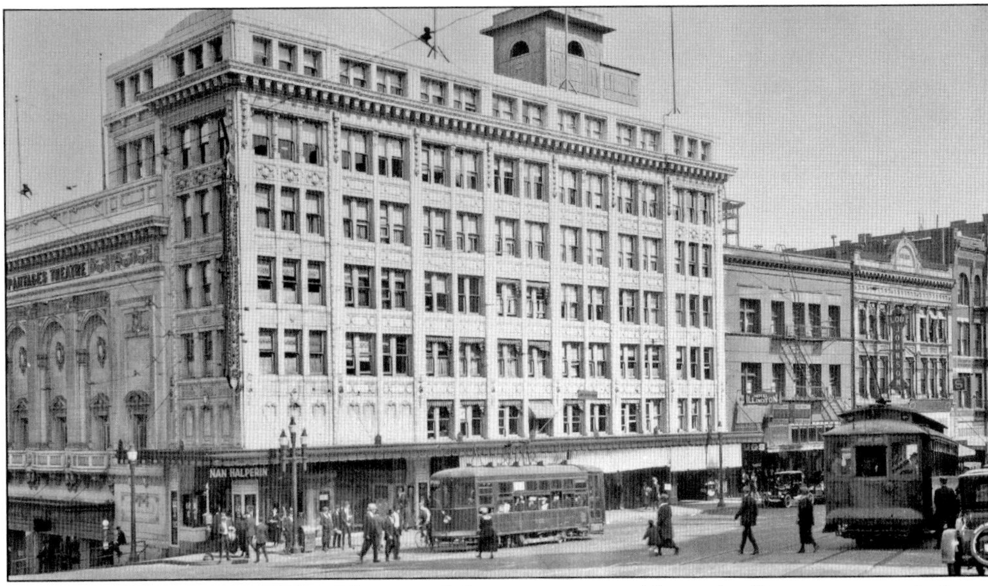

In 1916, building owner William Jones and theater manager Alexander Pantages commissioned architect B. Marcus Priteca to design a vaudeville house at 901 Broadway directly across the street from the Tacoma Theater. Newspaper accounts reported the progress as the old structure was being demolished, steel framing put into place, and terra-cotta applied to the new building. Opening night for the Pantages Theater (above) was in January 1918. Entertainment was not the only amusement, however. In 1920, Franklin D. Roosevelt appeared to castigate the behavior of the Grand Old Party. Four years later, Tacomans attended a memorial service for the late Pres. Woodrow Wilson. Below, sometime in the 1920s, photographer Chapin Bowen captured moviegoers and a regimental band posed in front of the Pantages prior to viewing *Lost Battalion*, a film released in 1919.

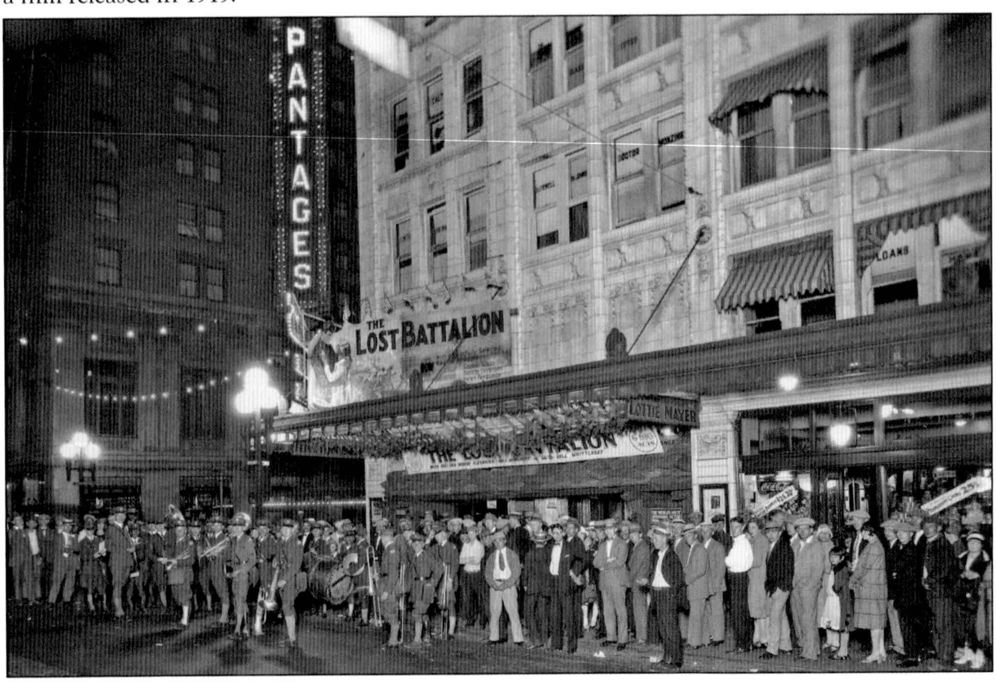

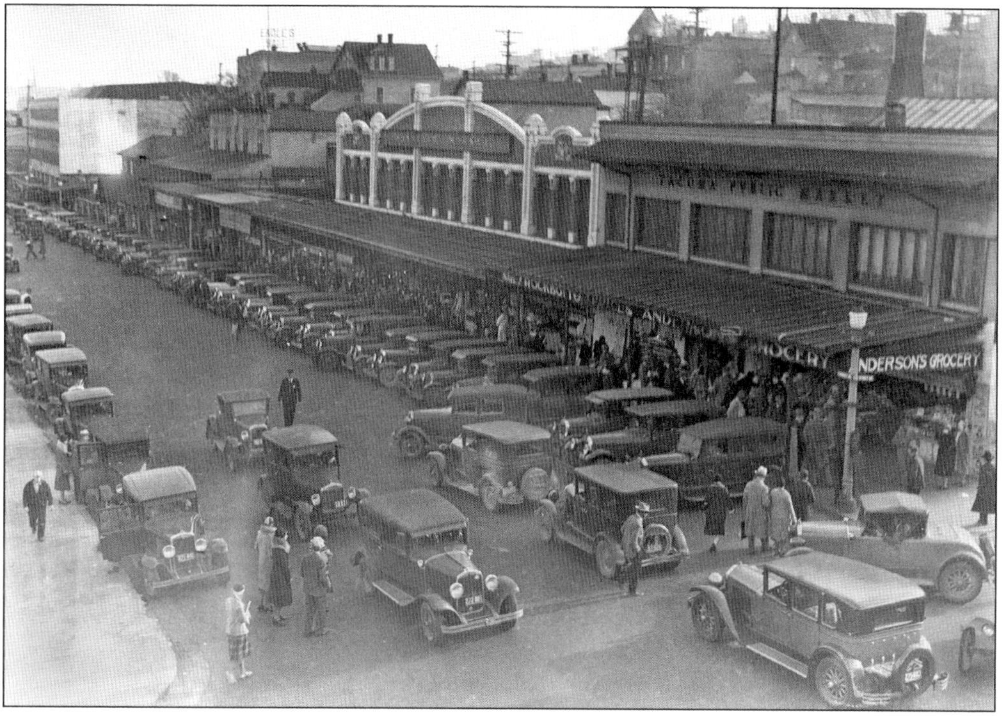

From 1907, when Seattle established the Pike Place Market, Tacomans wanted one of their own. Puyallup Valley farmers also sought a place to sell their fresh produce without having to go through wholesalers. And while the city had attempted several times in the past to establish commercial spaces for such an endeavor, none succeeded. In 1917, however, the Sanitary Public Market (above) opened at 1108 Market Street. Designed by the Tacoma architectural firm of Heath and Gove, it became one of several that gave Market Street its name. Not all vendors were to use the facilities. In the undated view below, a merchant is selling his wares from a sidewalk stand.

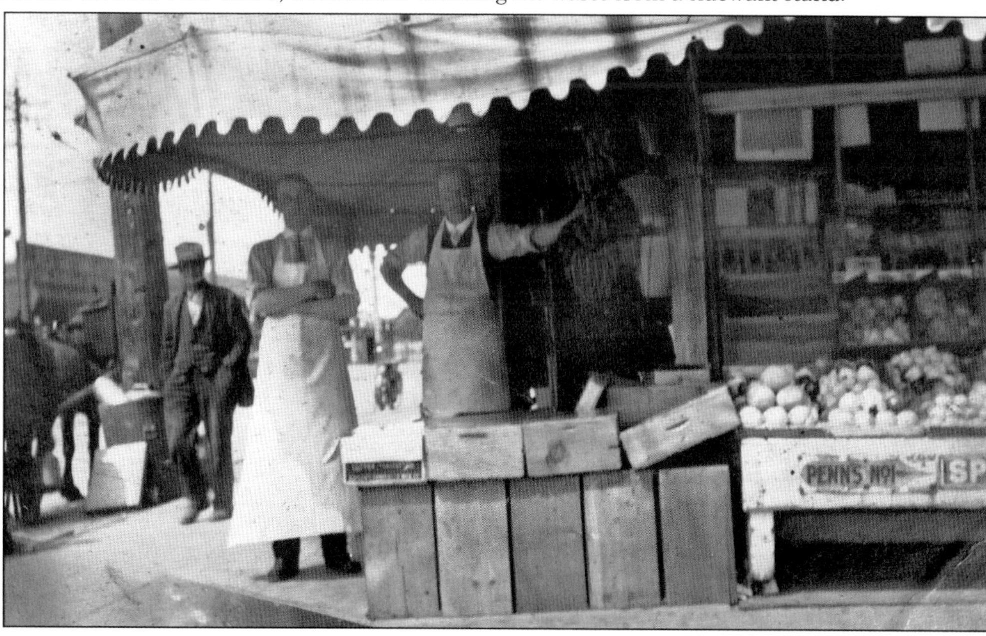

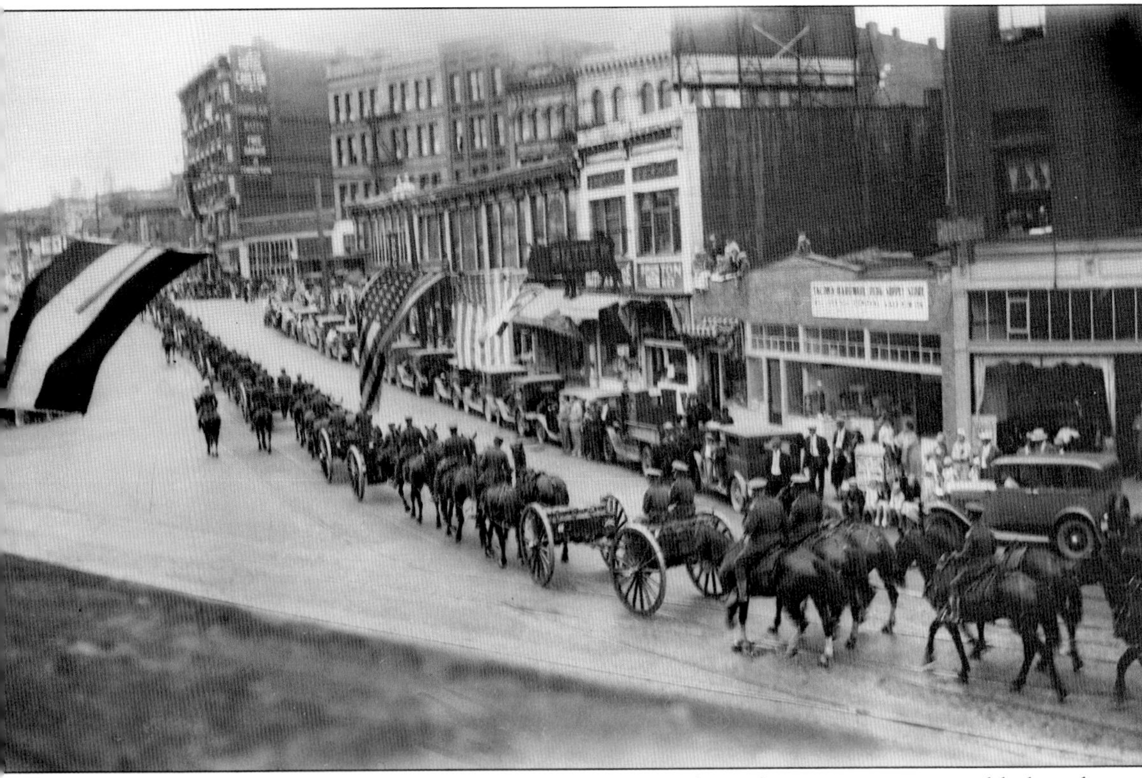

The intersection of Market Street and Jefferson Avenue formed a unique commercial hub tied to its proximity to the earliest Northern Pacific Railroad depot. Here businesses and industry converged, forming almost a separate neighborhood within Tacoma's downtown. The Carlton Hotel—built by Anton Huth, designed by architect Carl Darmer in 1909, and located at 1552 Jefferson Avenue—is a surviving example of the district's urban environment. A trolley station on Jefferson Avenue has not survived, but there are accounts that "streetcar funerals" embarked from this area and the trolleys took the mourners, along with the dear and departed loved one, to local cemeteries in the south end. The photographer and date of this image are unidentified. Apparently a parade is headed north toward Pacific Avenue. The Carlton Hotel can be seen in the background.

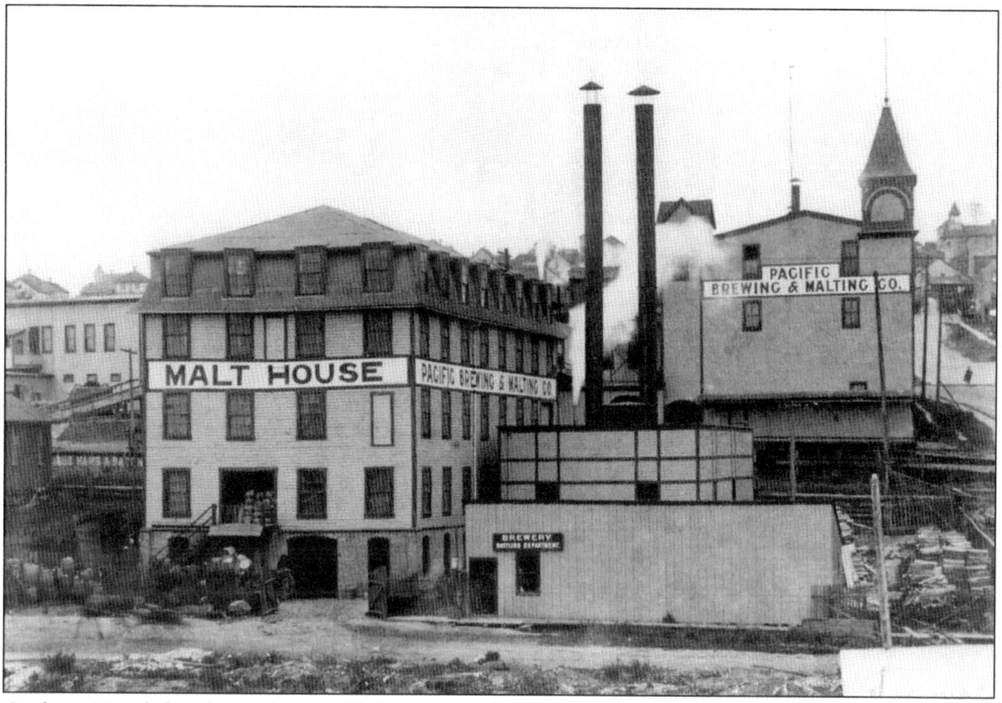

Carlton Hotel developer Anton Huth migrated from Germany to Tacoma in 1888. Prior to his arrival, he had learned how to make beer and in about 1891 commenced to build the Pacific Brewing and Malting Company on Holgate Street in the Jefferson Avenue district of the city. His first complex (above) is shown here in a 1900 photograph. Following this year, Huth, and his architect Carl Darmer, began the process of removing these wood-frame buildings and replacing them with a brick complex (below). By 1916, however, Washington voters opted for Prohibition and beer could no longer be manufactured. The success of his plant, however, enabled Huth to invest in real estate development in Tacoma's downtown. (Above courtesy of Tacoma Public Library.)

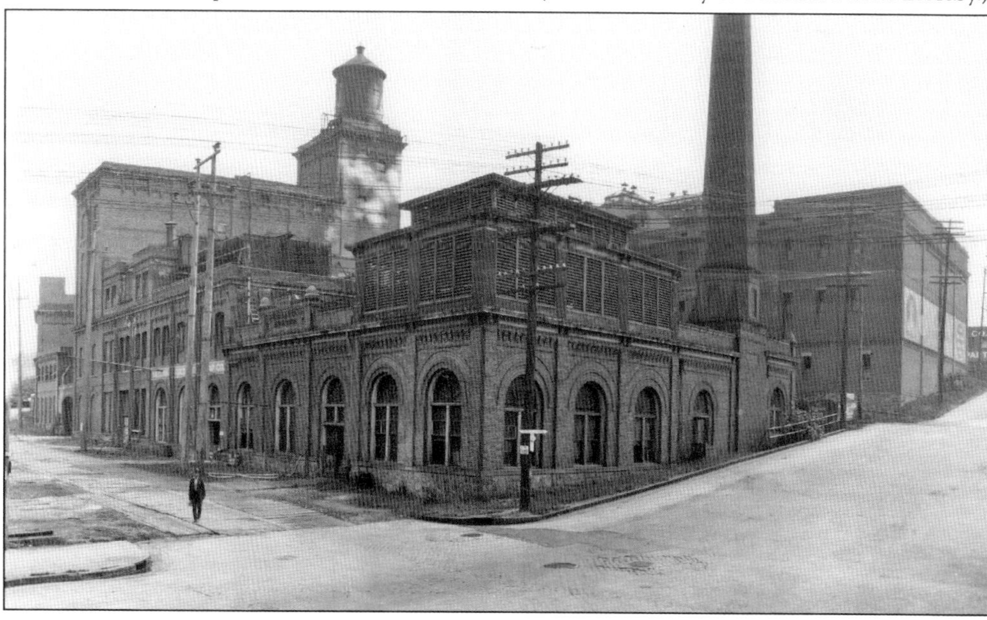

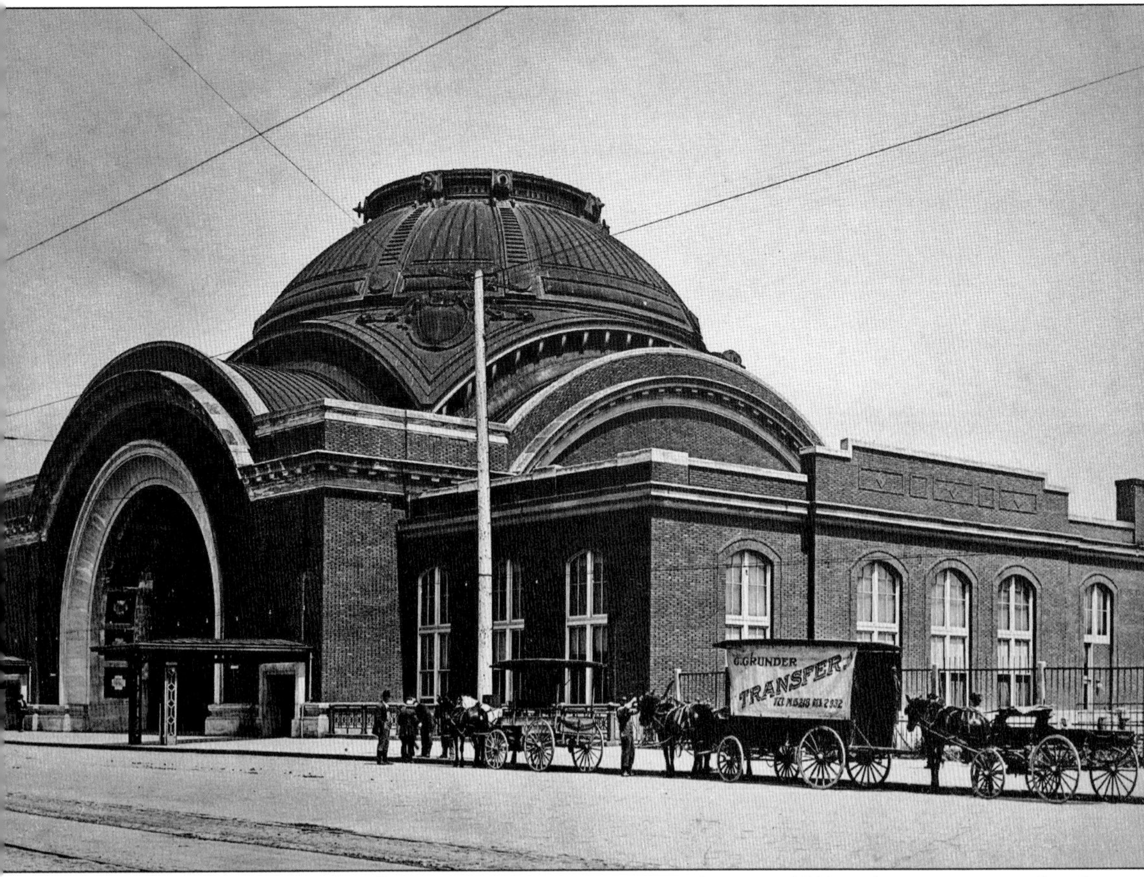

When Tacomans looked at the Union Station upon its completion in 1911, perhaps some considered the possibility that Pres. Theodore Roosevelt's visit to the city in 1903 might have played a role in its construction. The year before, he had authorized the U.S. Department of Justice to file a suit against a conglomerate of railroad interests whose Northern Securities Company would have established monopolistic control over Western transportation. The Supreme Court decision that followed in 1904 mandated the dissolution of the monopoly and thus opened Tacoma's doors to railroad companies other than the Northern Pacific. Among the new competitors was the Union Pacific, which began plans to lay track from its Western termini in Oregon and California. Through a series of negotiations, the Northern and Union Pacific railroad companies agreed to share both track and a single passenger station. The two companies also commissioned the New York architectural firm of Reed and Stem to design the building constructed at 1717 Pacific Avenue.

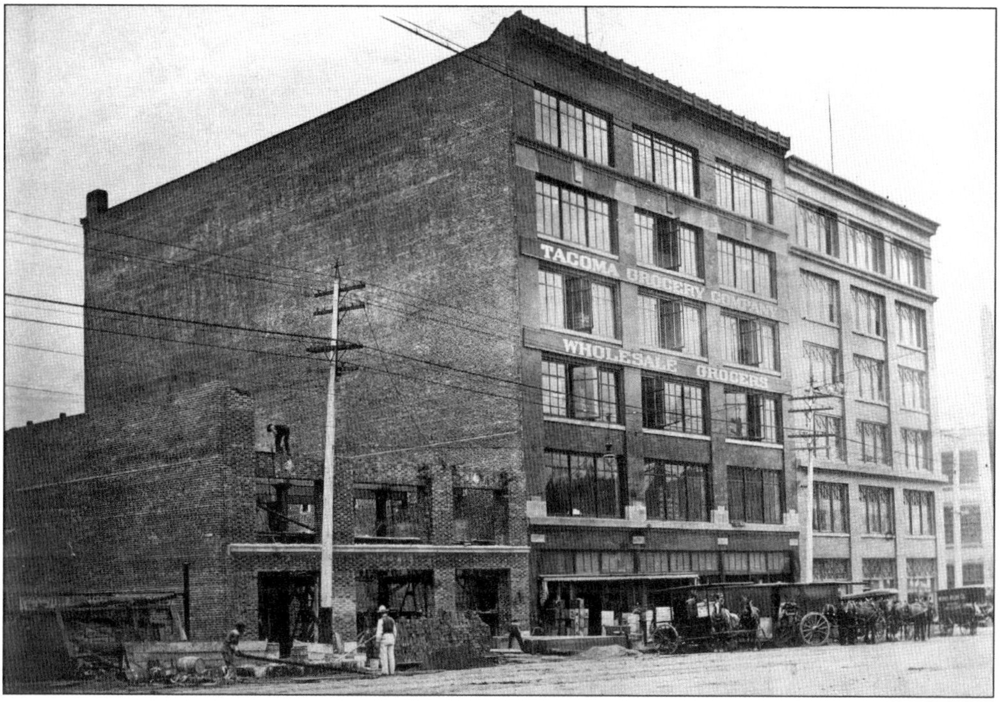

Near the Union Station, wholesale companies continued to build. In this view, taken in 1907, the Hunt and Mottet Company hardware warehouse is under construction at 2114 Pacific Avenue. To the right are the Tacoma Grocery Company (1906) and the Morris-Miller dry goods company (1906).

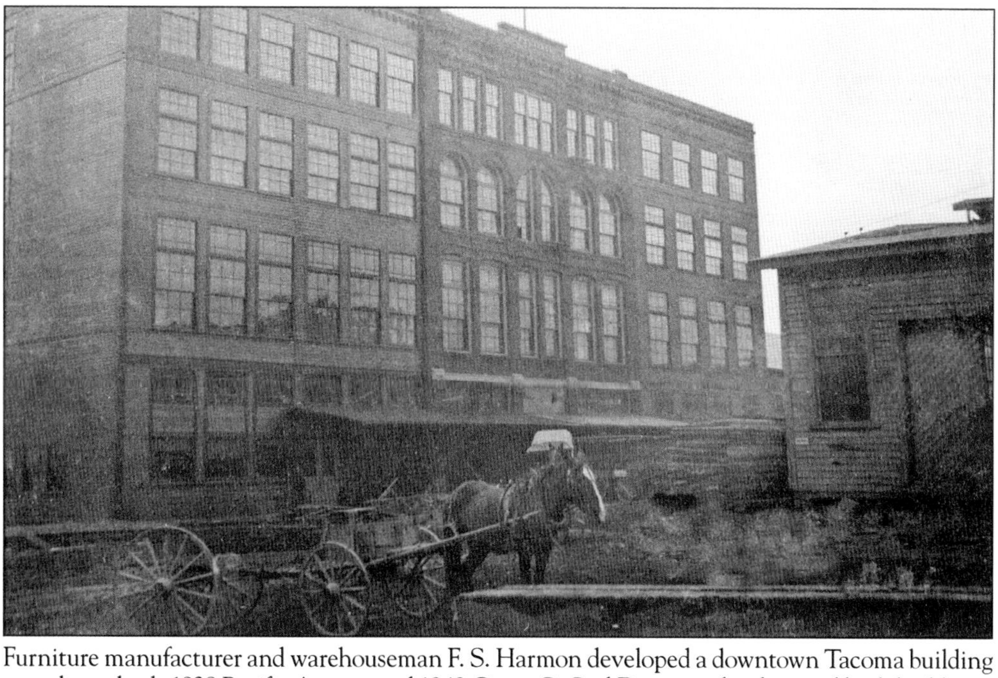
Furniture manufacturer and warehouseman F. S. Harmon developed a downtown Tacoma building complex at both 1938 Pacific Avenue and 1949 Court C. Carl Darmer, who designed both buildings, took this photograph sometime around 1912. The Pacific Avenue site is now home to Harmon Brewing Company, a nearby adjunct to the University of Washington Tacoma campus.

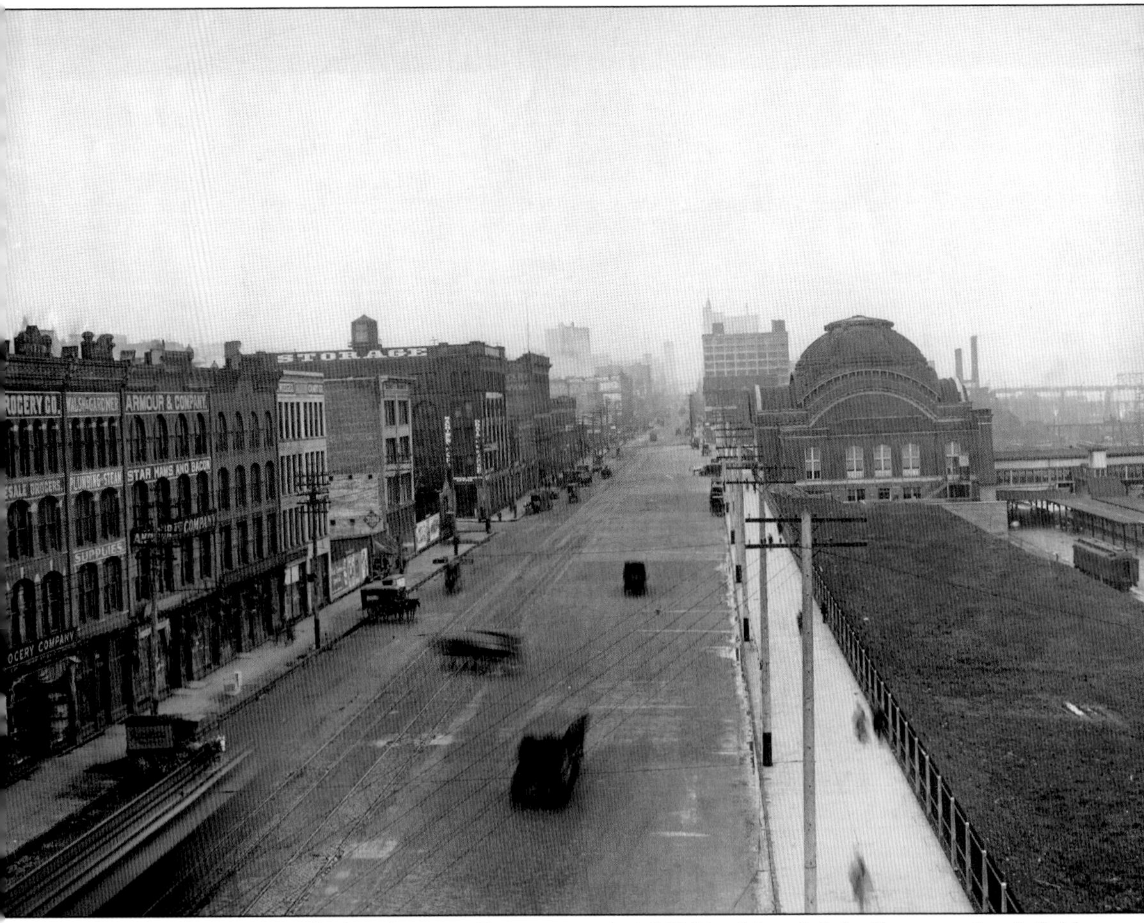

After U.S. Congress declared war on Germany in April 1917, soldiers left for European battlefields from Union Station, shown on the right in this view. After the armistice on November 11, 1918, they returned to the station, some very sick with the influenza pandemic that had encircled the world. Tacomans also succumbed to the disease, many public places and businesses were closed, and the business hardships caused by the disease were amplified by a postwar economic depression. Even so, businesses along the lower reaches of Pacific Avenue were ready for the economic boom that gradually came in the 1920s. Warehouse businesses facing Union Station in this view included drug and grocery companies and dealers in stoves and machinery, coffee and tea, hay and feed, plumbing supplies, candy, furniture, mattresses, and paper goods. On the street, horse drayage was still a part of the urban landscape, along with streetcars and automobiles. By the time of the next war in 1941, only the automobile remained. (Courtesy of Thomas R. Stenger.)

Four

1920–1940

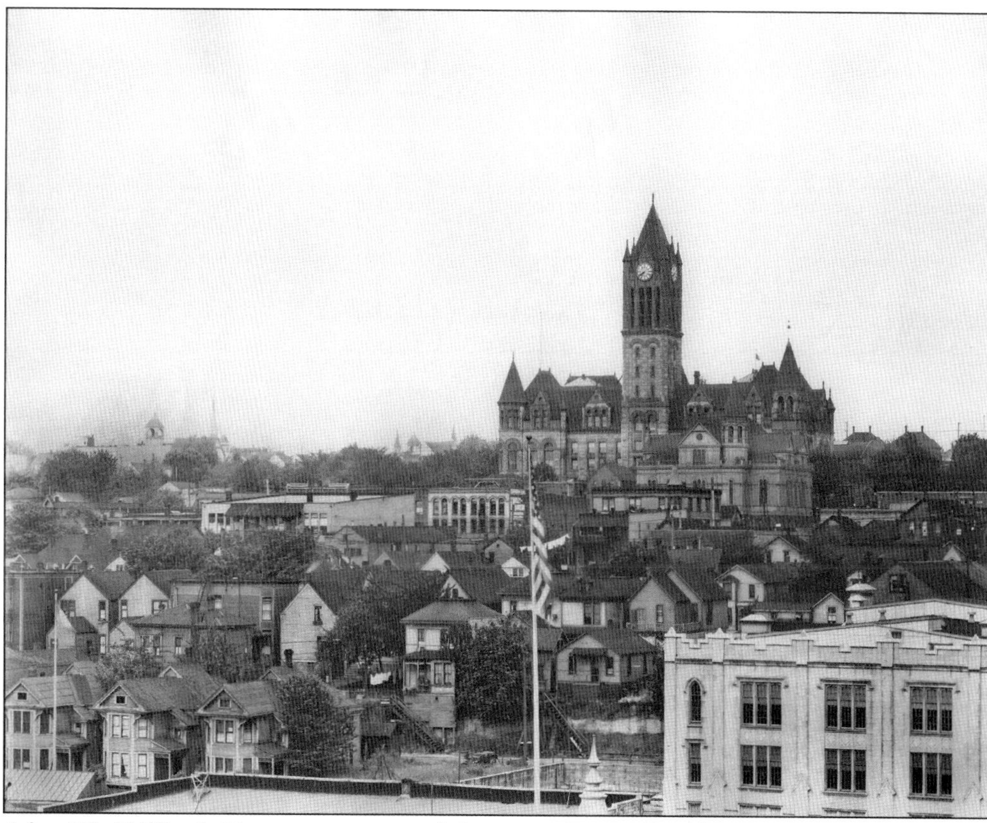

After World War I, Tacomans witnessed the next phase of building construction, one that would see most of the earlier housing, shown here in a 1927 view, demolished and replaced with commercial buildings. The Pierce County Courthouse, however, continued to dominate the skyline. The Baptist church is shown in the lower right in this view.

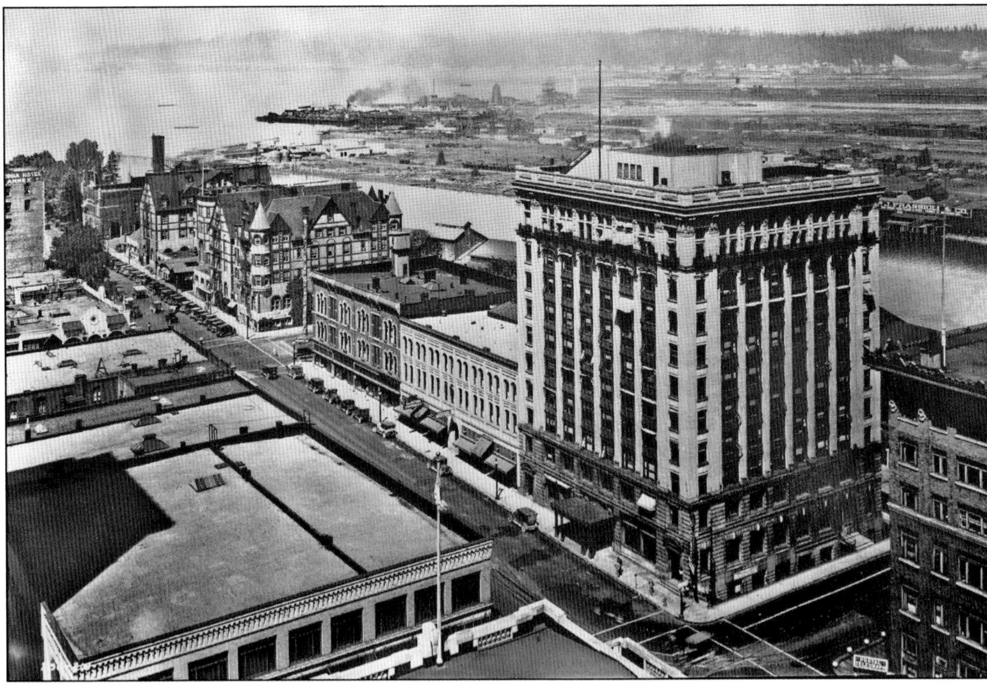

In 1928, a photographer looked northeast and captured A Street from Weyerhaeuser's Tacoma Building to Firemen's Park. The St. Paul and Tacoma Lumber Company, along with the newly constructed Port of Tacoma wharves, are in the distance. By the time the United States entered World War II, both street and port will have undergone significant changes.

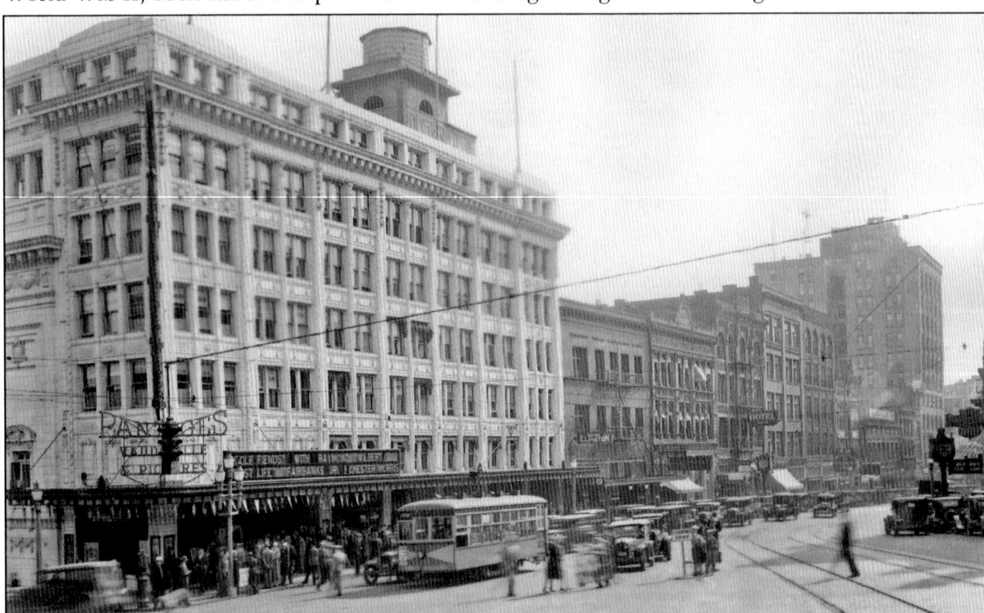

The urban landscape on the east side of Broadway from South Ninth Street would remain the same until later in the 20th century. By 1929, the Pantages was advertising both vaudeville and motion pictures. Small hotels and commercial spaces linked the theater to the Burnham and Root Fidelity Trust building seen on the far right.

"Landmarks fast becoming history," reported the 1919 *Tacoma Daily Ledger* when construction began on the Rust building. William R. Rust, of Tacoma Smelter fame, constructed his high rise at 950 Pacific Avenue. The first tenets were Lundquist-Lilly clothing store, the Ambrose Physiological Clinic, and the W. H. Opie Company, which managed the Rust property.

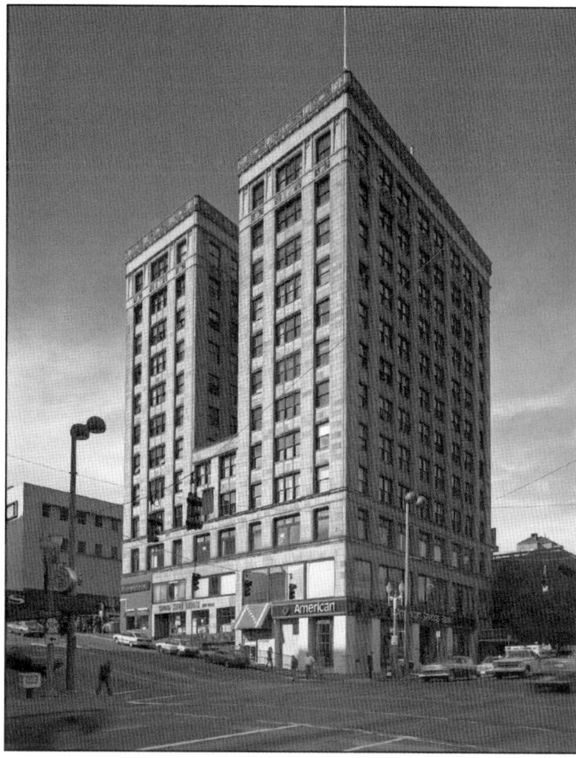

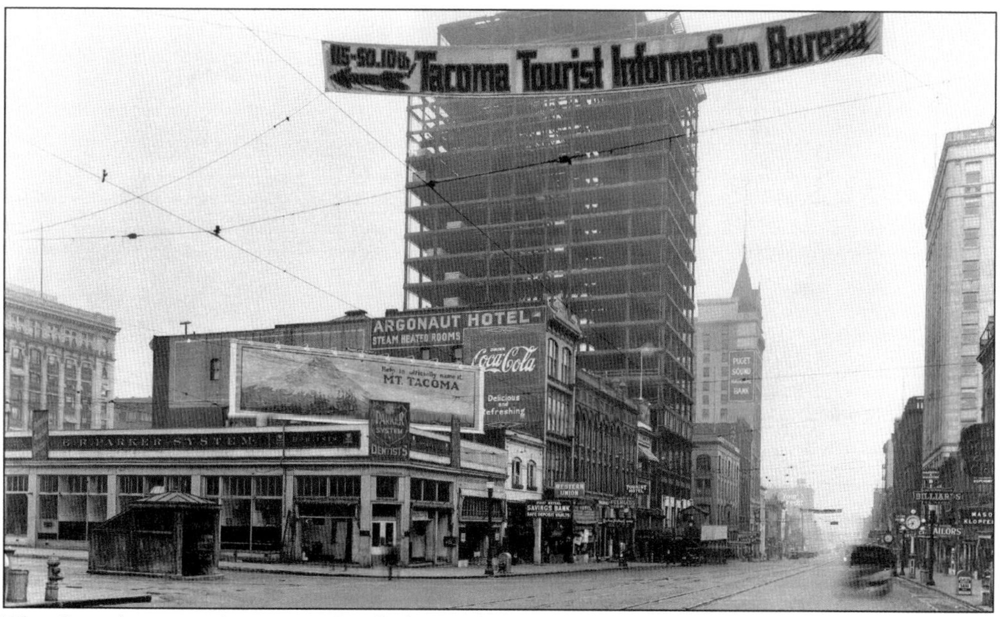

The Scandinavian-American Bank, located across Pacific Avenue from the Rust building, was also under construction in 1919. The bank failed in 1920, however, just as workmen were completing the steel girder framing seen in this view. In 1924, the Washington-California Company acquired the property and completed the structure the following year. The Brotherhood Cooperative National Bank, linked to railroad workers, was one of the first to occupy the renamed Washington Building.

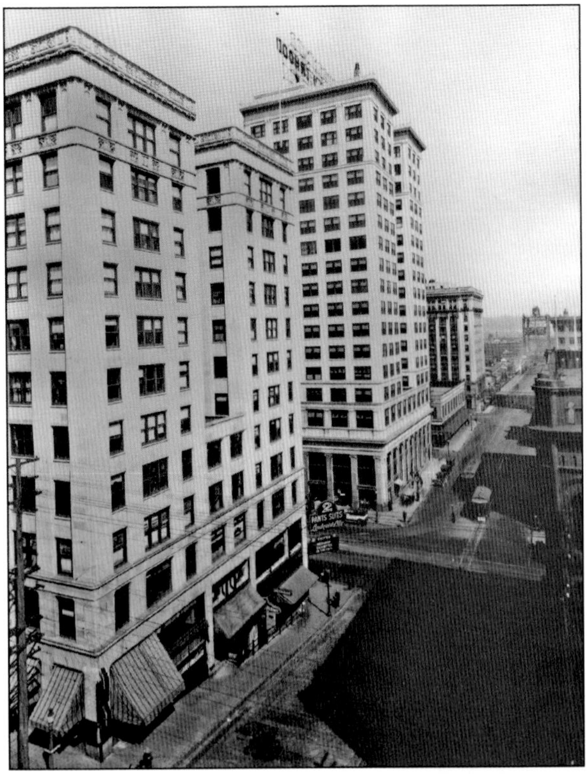

The completion of the Washington Building yielded a striking view of newer buildings when photographed eastward toward the Eleventh Street (Murray Morgan) Bridge in 1927. All three buildings—the Rust (left), the Washington (center), and the Tacoma (right)—in addition to the Murray Morgan Bridge, remain as part of Tacoma's cityscape.

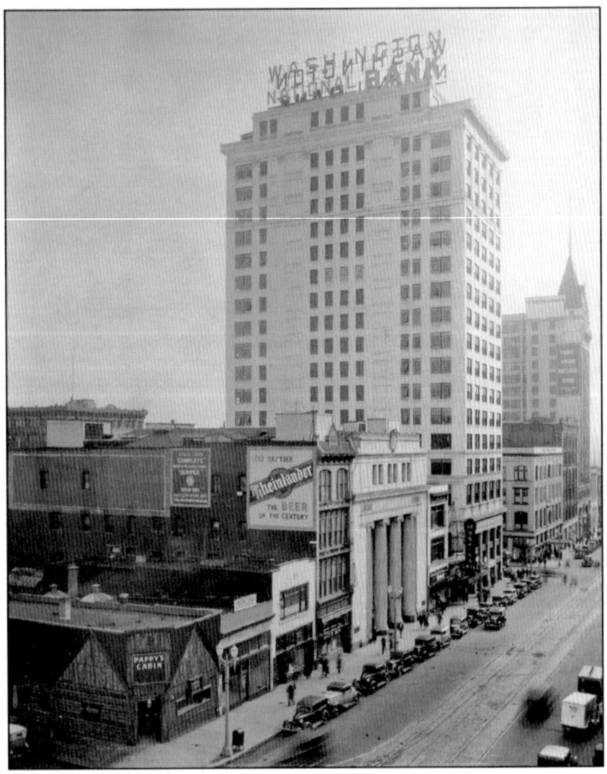

Sometime after 1933, when Pappy's Cabin (seen on the left) opened for business, a photographer provided an image of the east side of Pacific Avenue from South Tenth Street. While the Washington Building dominates the view, the Bank of California is now seen at mid-block. Seattle architect John Graham designed the classical-style structure in 1928.

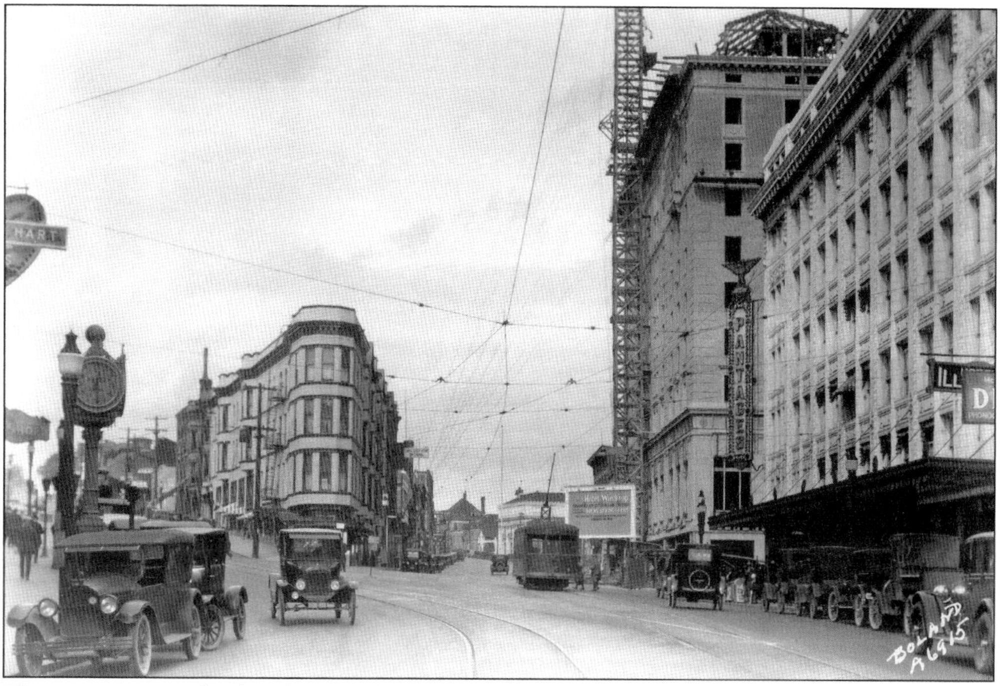

The war years saw the demolition of the Gross Brothers Department Store and the construction of the Pantages Theater. Across from the theater at 773 Broadway in 1923, the chamber of commerce building was demolished and the Winthrop Hotel (above) was constructed. Tacoma architect Roland E. Borhek designed the "new hotel for a bigger Tacoma." The hotel (below) was named to honor Theodore Winthrop, whose book *The Canoe and the Saddle* was an inspiration for naming the city Tacoma. The hotel opened for business in 1925. (Below courtesy of Thomas R. Stenger.)

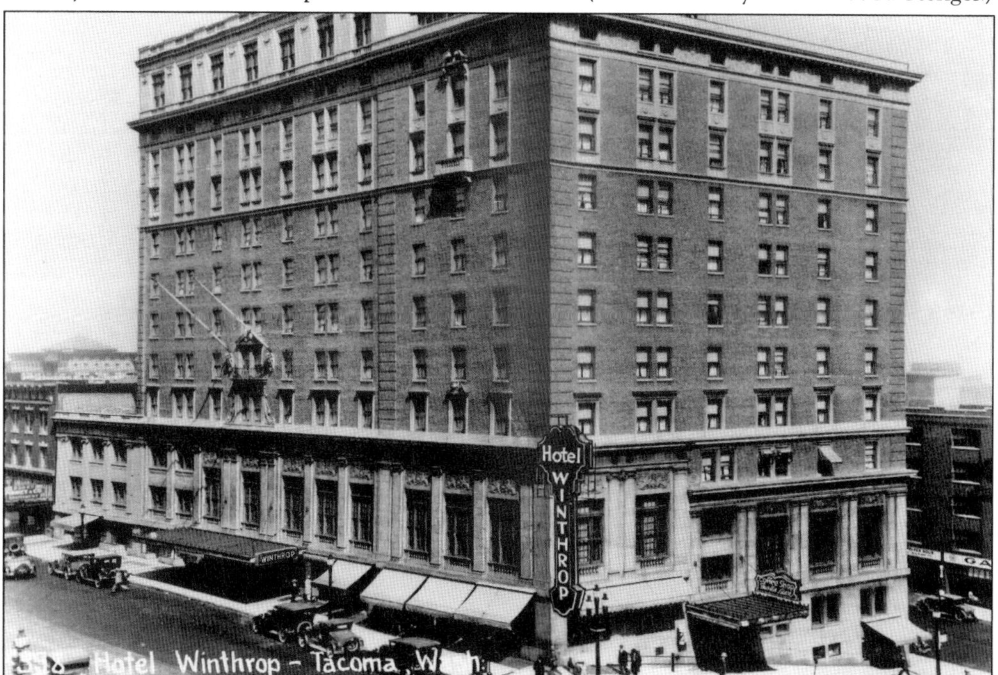

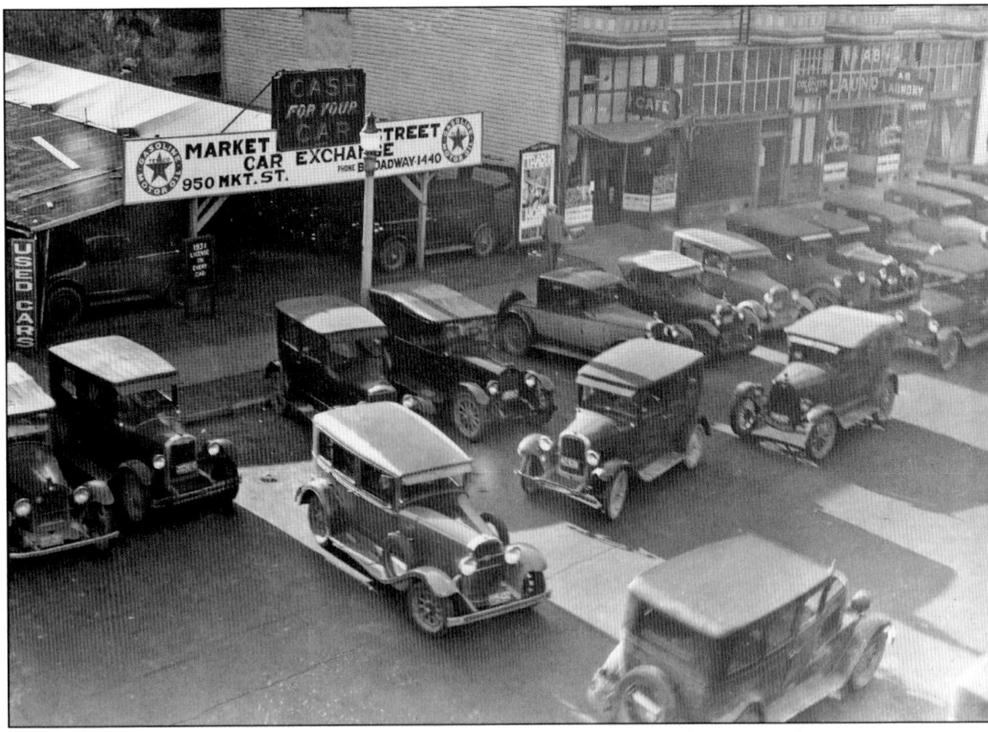

The automobile began to dominate Tacoma in the 1920s and 1930s. There was subsequent congestion and parking problems throughout the downtown, as this 1931 view documents. "Traffic conditions" is the description placed on the image by the unidentified photographer. The Market Street Car Exchange, at 950 Market Street, was a combination used car lot and Texaco gas station.

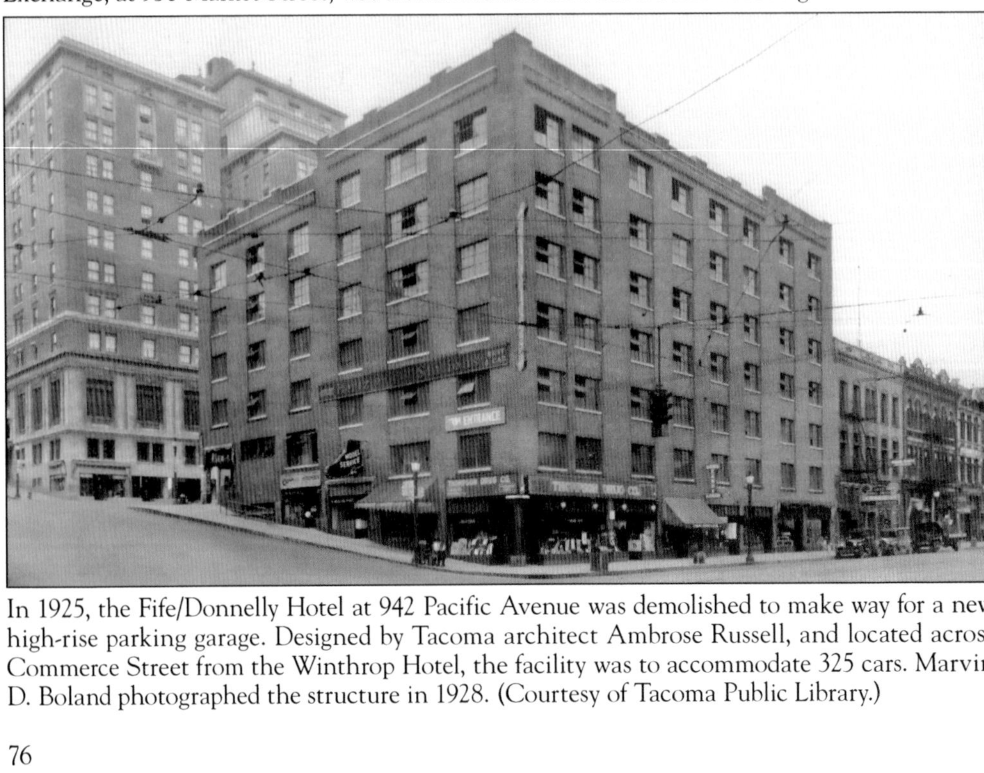

In 1925, the Fife/Donnelly Hotel at 942 Pacific Avenue was demolished to make way for a new high-rise parking garage. Designed by Tacoma architect Ambrose Russell, and located across Commerce Street from the Winthrop Hotel, the facility was to accommodate 325 cars. Marvin D. Boland photographed the structure in 1928. (Courtesy of Tacoma Public Library.)

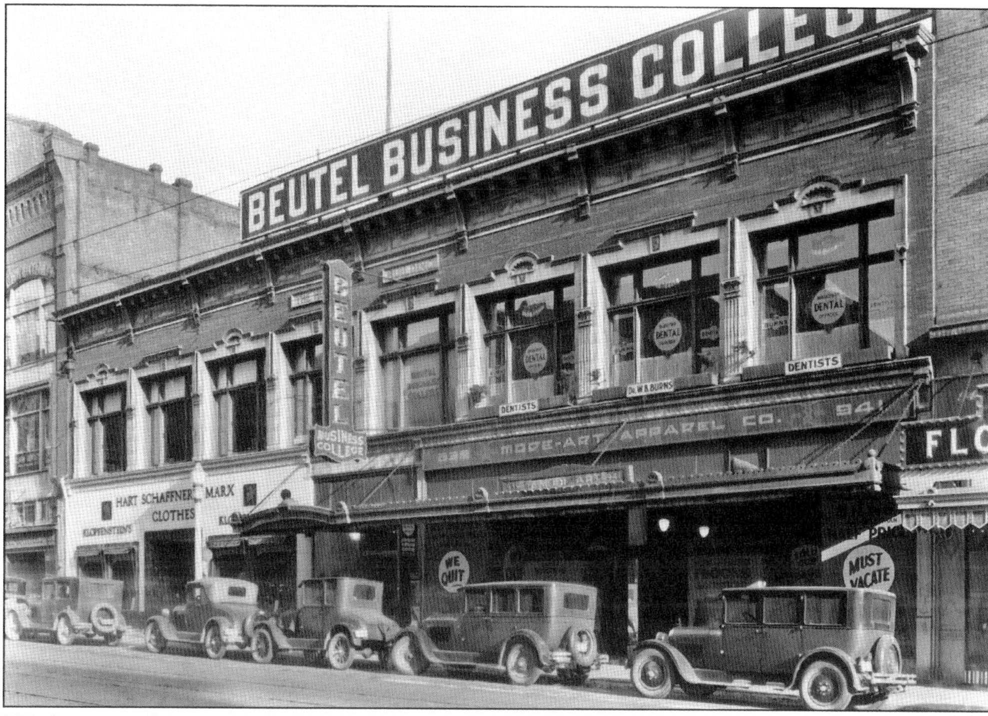

While some of Tacoma's downtown buildings were demolished for the new, others lasted into the 1960s. The Huth building constructed in 1892 at 935 Broadway is one such example. In 1930, at the time of this photograph, Beutel Business College held classes here. So did a men's clothing store. The Mode-Art Apparel Company, however, was going out of business, a victim perhaps of the Depression that followed the 1929 stock market crash.

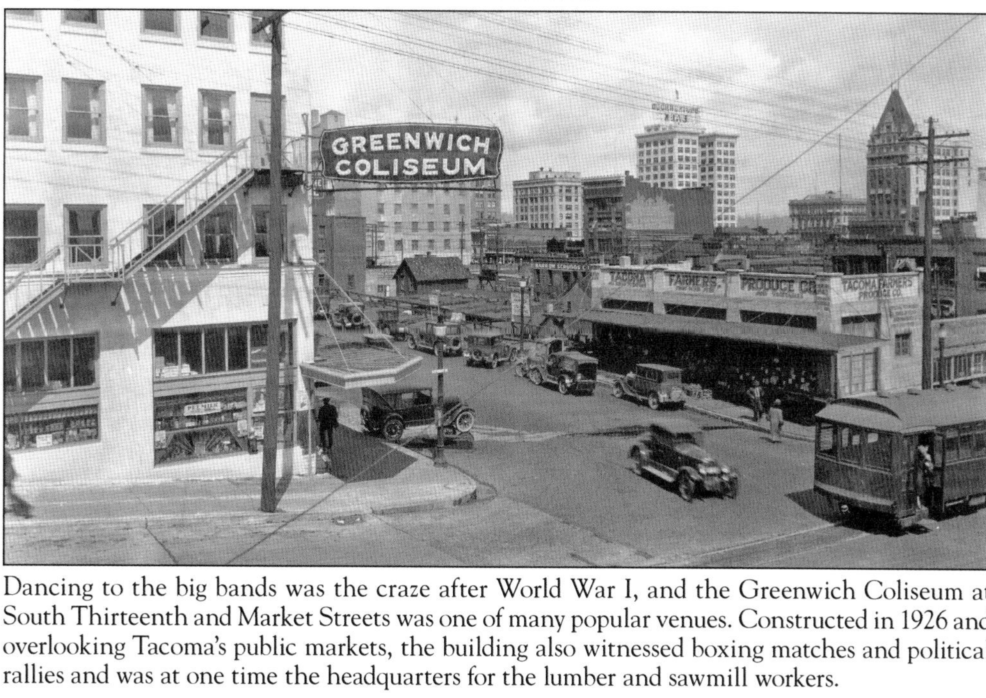

Dancing to the big bands was the craze after World War I, and the Greenwich Coliseum at South Thirteenth and Market Streets was one of many popular venues. Constructed in 1926 and overlooking Tacoma's public markets, the building also witnessed boxing matches and political rallies and was at one time the headquarters for the lumber and sawmill workers.

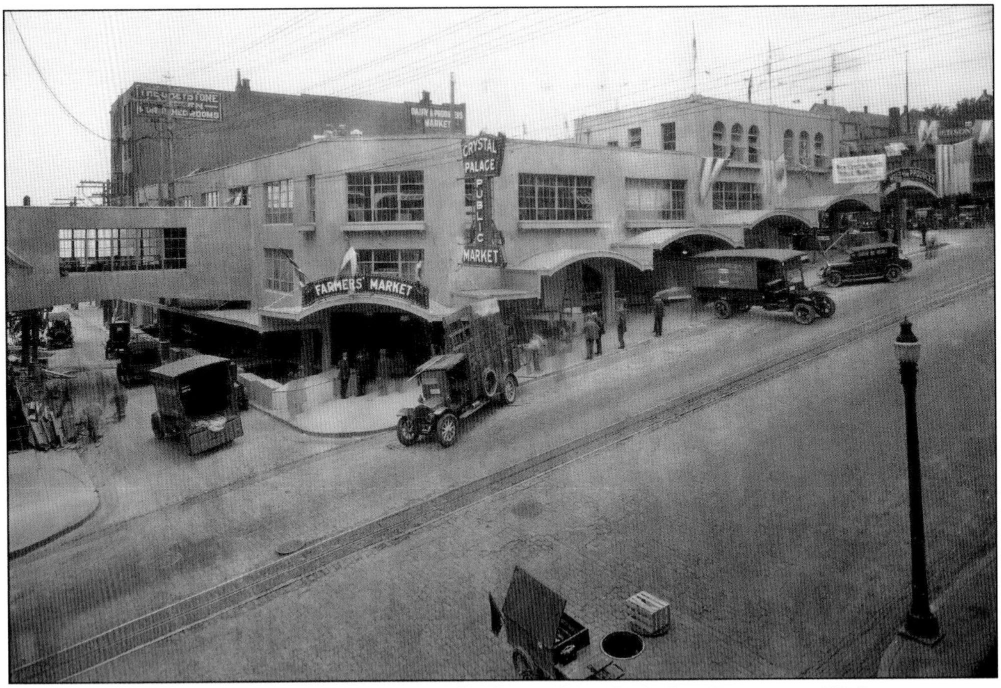

Charles B. Hurley leased the corner of South Eleventh and Market Streets in 1926 to construct a public market. One year later, upon the opening of the Crystal Palace, a *Tacoma News Tribune* reporter referred to it as a mammoth structure (above). Shown below is a 1927 view of the Busy Bee Fruit Company. The total number of vendors is unidentified, but Arthur E. Goodwin was lured from Seattle's Pike Place Market to manage the facility. Also known is that the majority of tenants were Puyallup Valley Japanese farmers, and when they were placed in concentration camps in 1942 at the onset of World War II, the market could not survive.

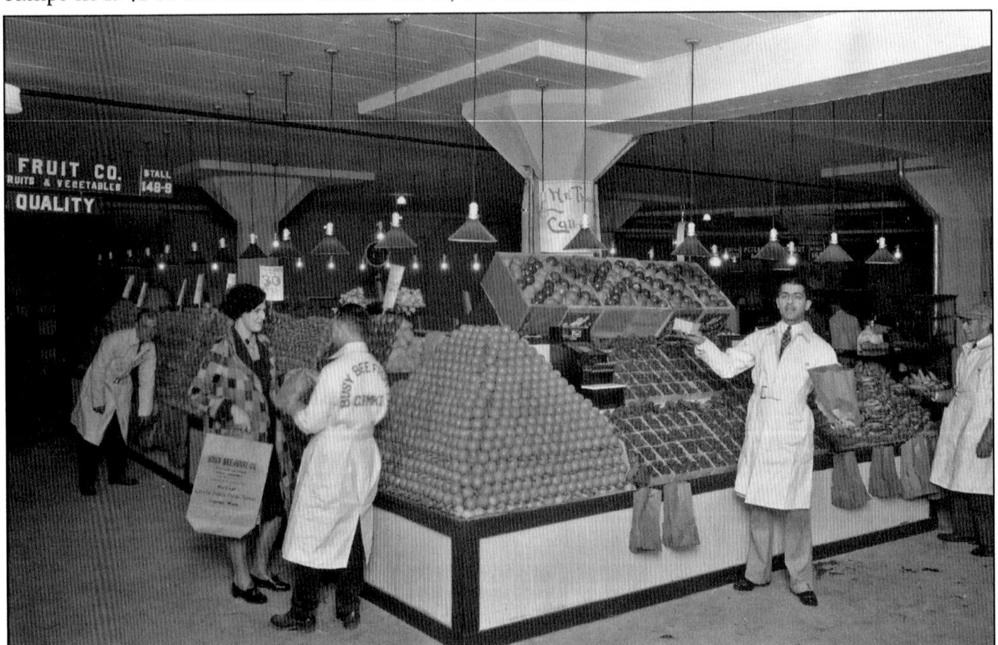

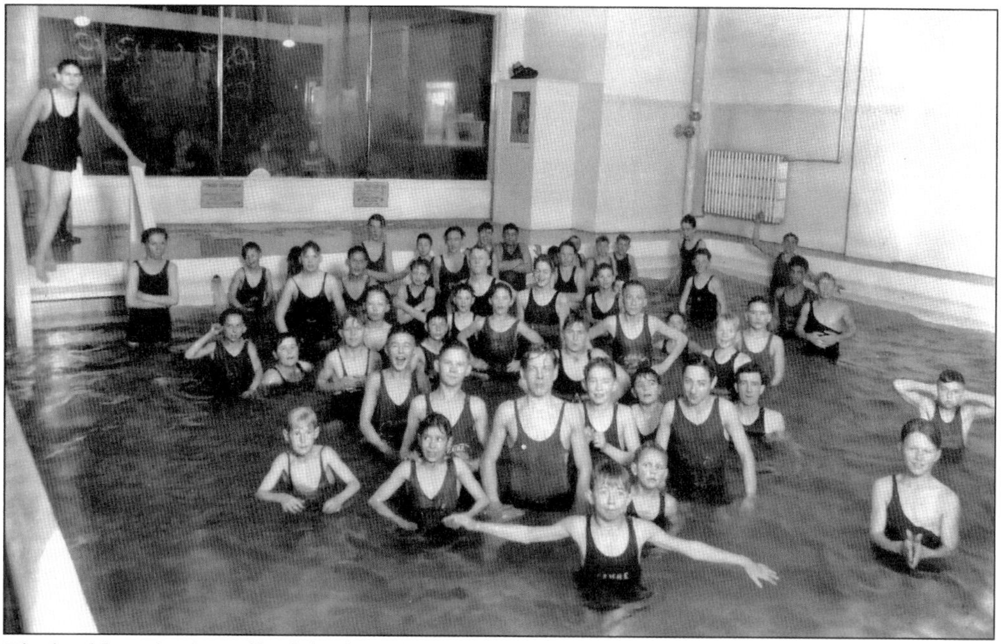

The health and safety of both body and soul was the preoccupation of reformers concerned about families still living close to downtown Tacoma or those individuals who were transient workers or homeless. This concern explains why the central business district and the areas adjacent to it contained such a wide array of Roman Catholic and Protestant churches as well as Jewish synagogues to provide aid and comfort to their parishioners. Tacoma became home to Roman Meal bread in 1912, after its founder, Dr. Robert Jackson, cured his ailing health using an ancient dietary grain formula. In 1927, Dr. R. D. Monaghan dedicated his new Azure Pool at 748 Market Street (above). Marvin D. Boland photographed children in the swimming pool close to this time. The Salvation Army (below in 1940) began its ministry in Tacoma in 1888.

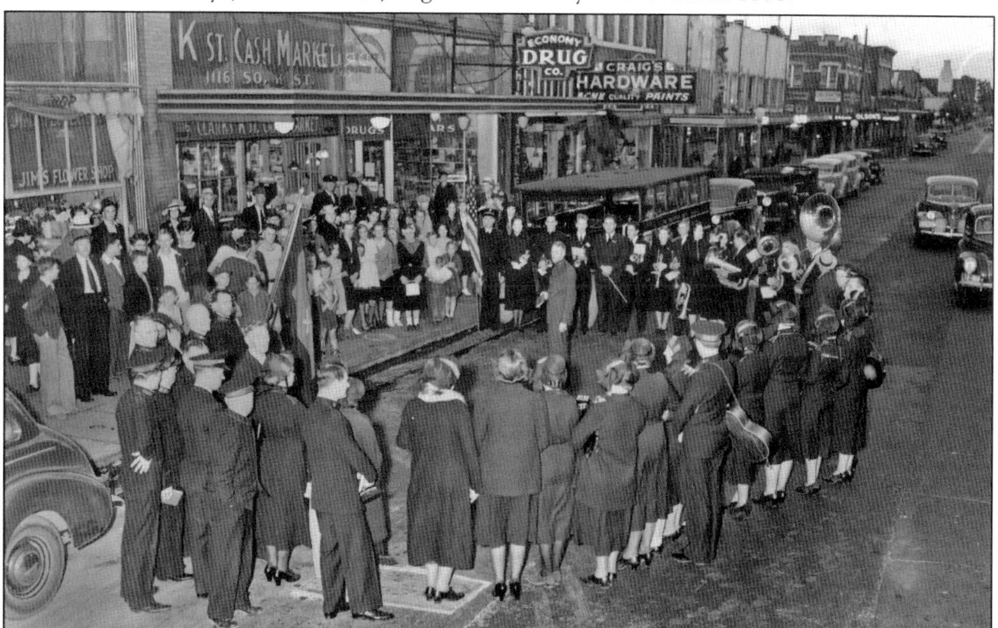

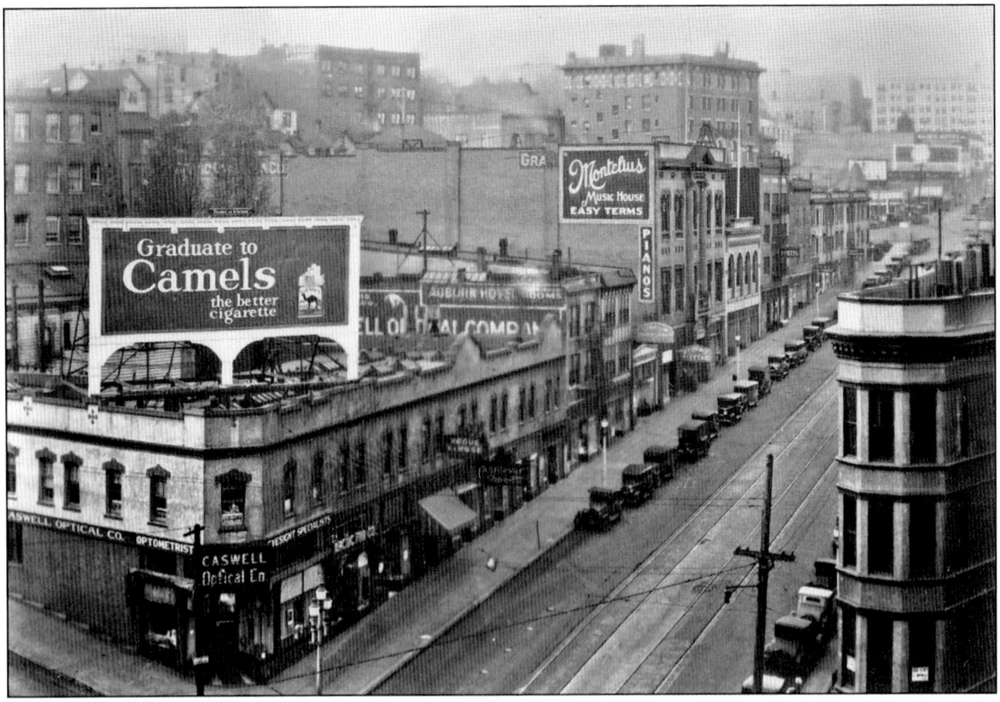

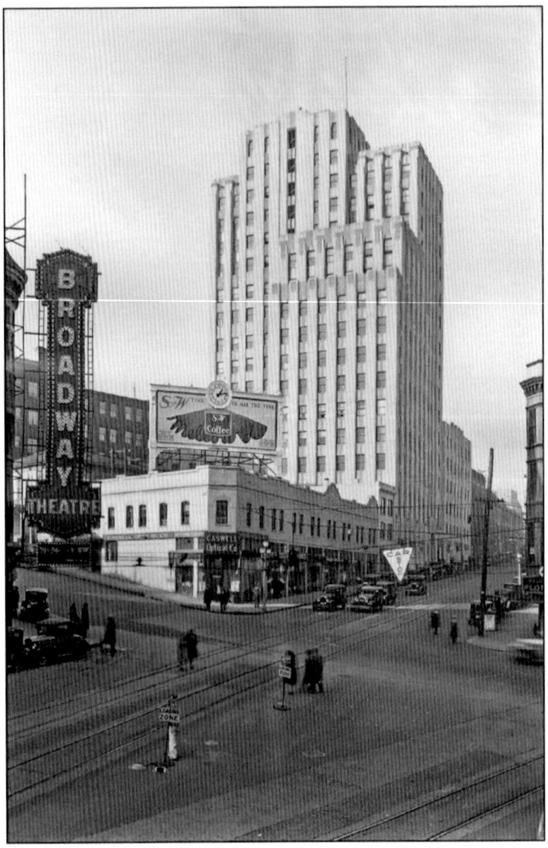

In the late 1920s, St. Helens Avenue looking north from South Ninth Street appeared as it had almost a decade before. The Caswell Optical Company in the foreground was in business by 1914 and still remains there today. Beyond it were, among other businesses, Hoska's funeral parlor and the Masonic Temple. By 1930, the streetscape was to change dramatically through the addition of a new skyscraper.

When the Rhodes Medical Arts Tower was completed in 1931, newspapers heralded it as the "Pacific Coast's first integrated medical complex" and the tallest building in Tacoma. Located at 747 Market Street, the facility included, besides doctors' offices, a pharmacy, the Washington Minor Hospital, and its own parking garage. In 1977, the City of Tacoma purchased, and continues to use, the building for municipal offices.

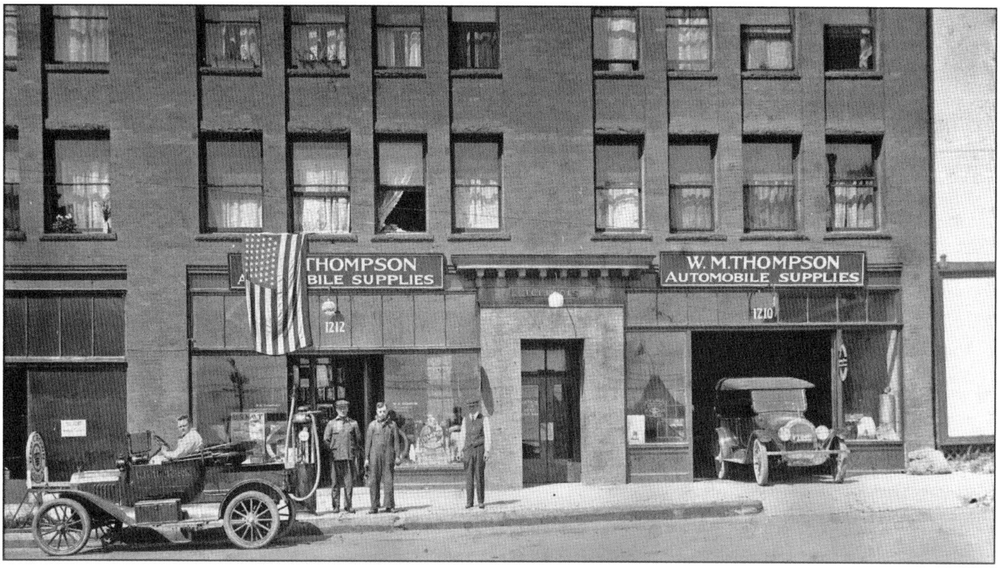

Harry R. Manley and Robert B. Thompson, along with Robert's brother William, entered the field of automobile sales in 1913, and within two years, the firm had become the Ford agency in Tacoma. Sometime after constructing a new building on the corner of South Thirteenth and Fawcett Streets in 1918, W. B. Thompson established the automobile supplies business seen here at an unidentified date and location.

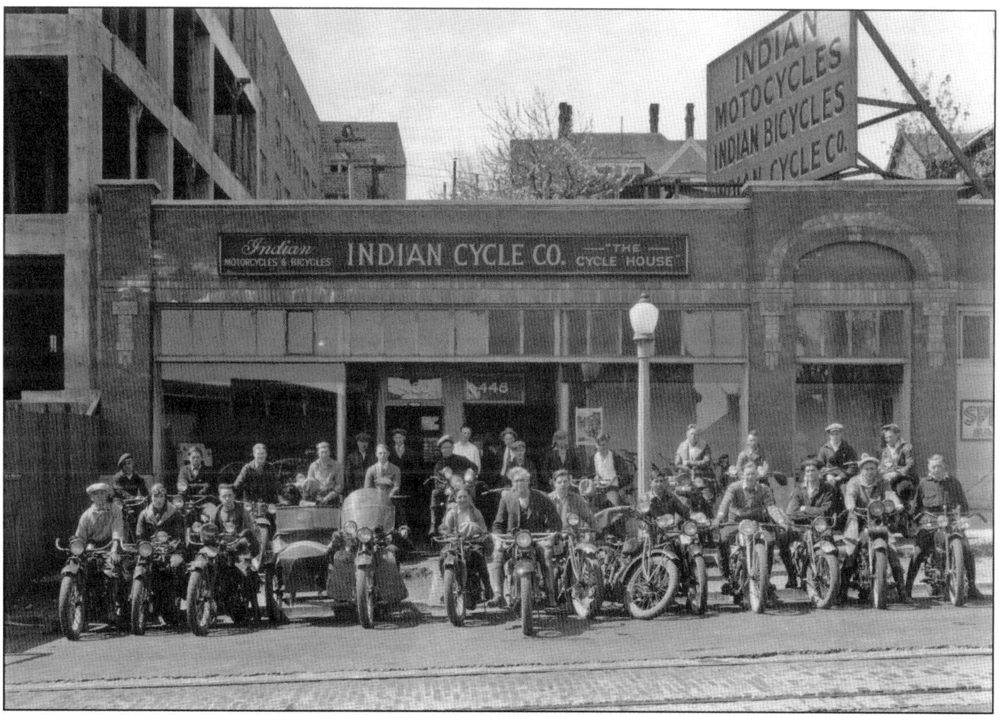

Besides automobiles, motorcycles were another form of transportation following World War I. Where this photograph was taken has yet to be determined, but it provides a good example of how popular the Indian Cycle Company was for both young and old. The company survived World War II, when its business could be found at 925 Tacoma Avenue South.

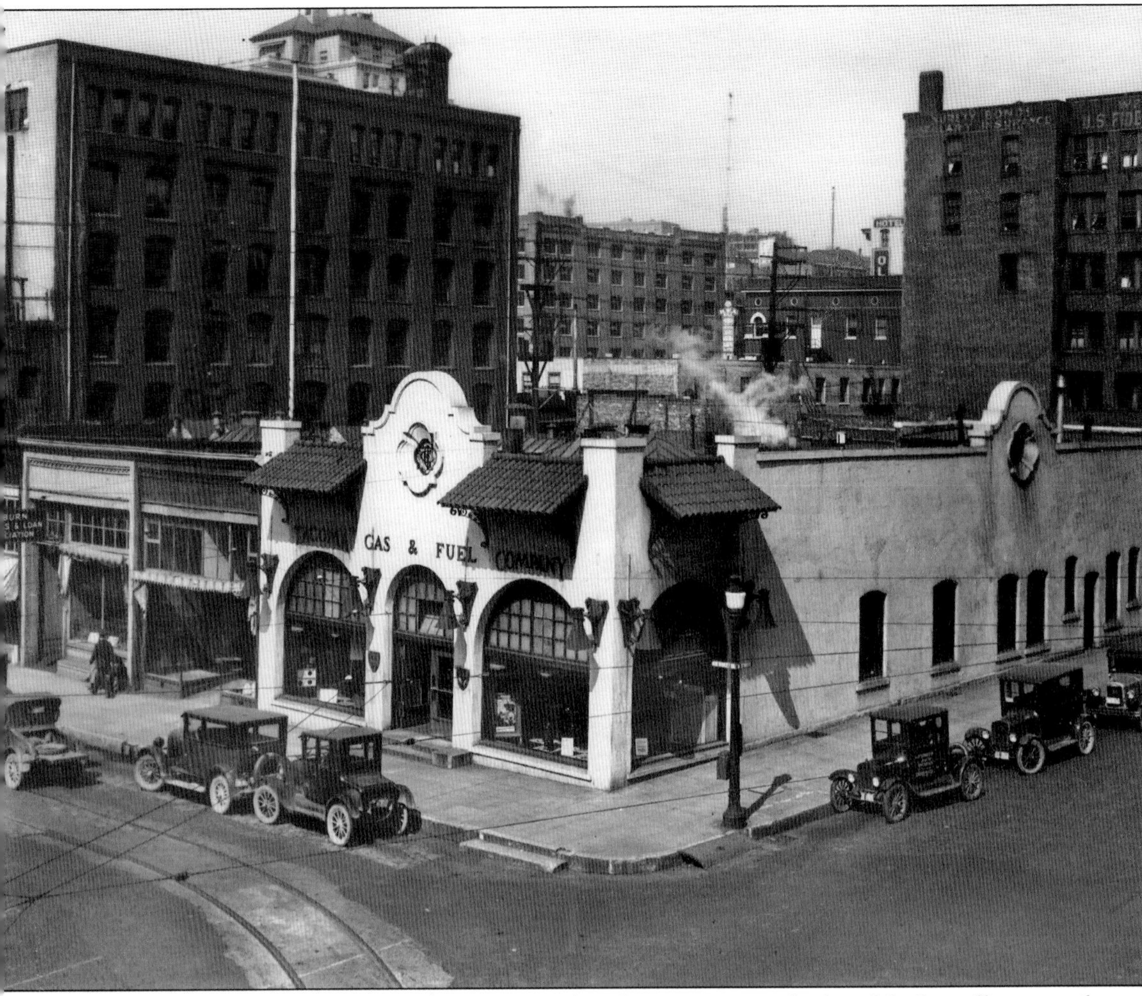

Utility infrastructures were, and continue to be, the necessities of urban life. Initially most of these services were contracted out to private companies. However, when the Tacoma Light and Water Company was unable to provide sufficient water to fight fires, voters approved a bond issue in the late 1890s enabling Tacoma to create one of the first public utilities on the West Coast. By the beginning of the 20th century, the city had created a water supply system that included drawing from the Green River. Hydroelectric power dams at La Grande and Lake Cushman enabled the city to boast about the low power rates needed for economic expansion. For unknown reasons, however, providing gas never became a part of public policy, even though gas lighting preceded electrical in many—primarily wealthy—homes and business. The Tacoma Gas Company, whose plant was located on A Street, ultimately merged with the Washington Gas and Electric Company, whose Tacoma offices, shown here in 1927, were located at the corner of South Ninth and A Streets.

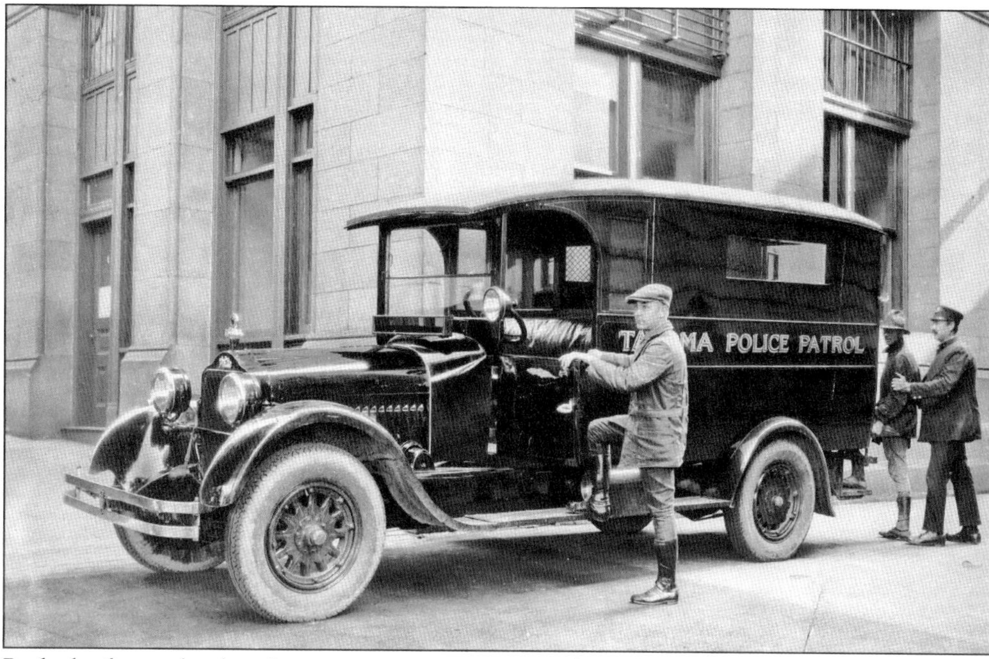

Both the fire and police departments were constants throughout the years of Tacoma's growth and development. Both agencies updated their performance as the fire engine and paddy wagon replaced the horse-drawn vehicles of the past. In this undated view, a policeman poses alongside one of the department's new patrol wagons while another escorts an alleged perpetrator into the wagon.

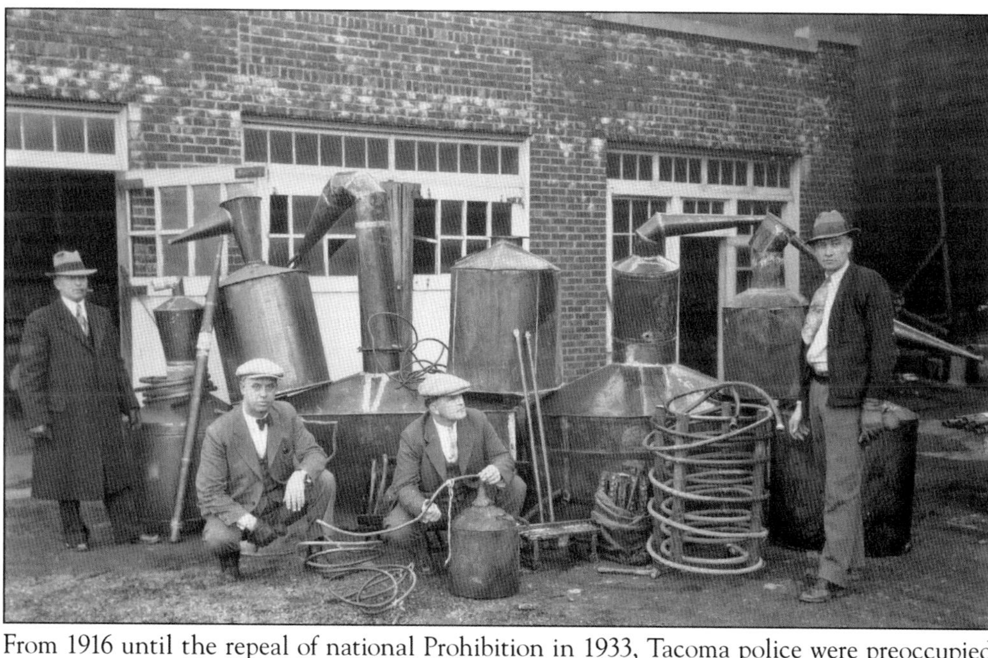

From 1916 until the repeal of national Prohibition in 1933, Tacoma police were preoccupied with catching those intent on producing outlawed moonshine. Some booze came via water on rumrunners manufactured by local boatbuilders. Stills sprouted up within the many gulches that are a part of Tacoma's urban landscape. Periodic raids yielded contraband such as this.

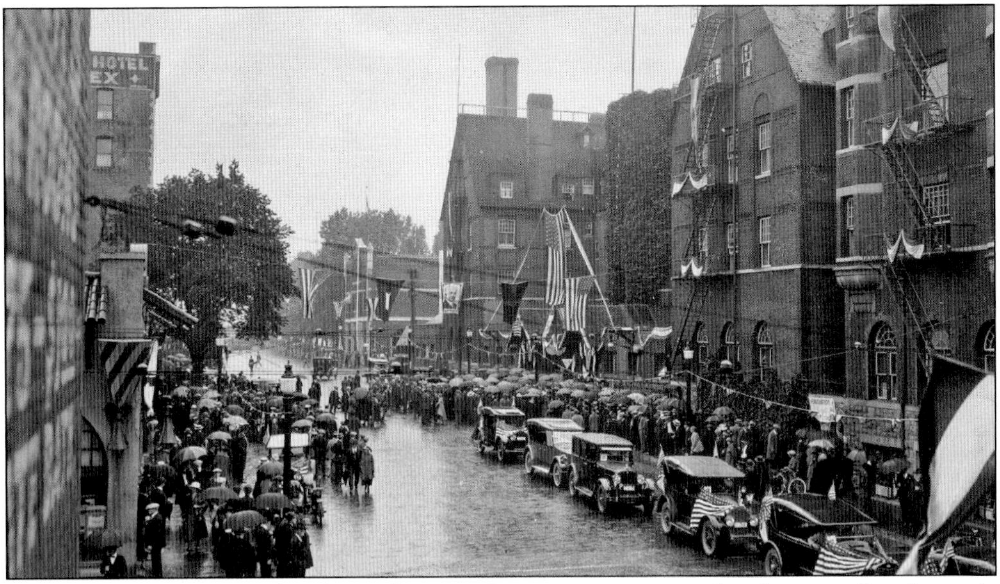

Downtown Tacoma was the place where residents came to see and to be seen. But the early technology of photography made it difficult to capture the hustle and bustle of a city alive with people. The major exceptions were parades and political rallies, events that were sometimes combined. In 1932, for example, presidential hopeful Franklin D. Roosevelt visited the city as a part of his Western campaign. His parade started at the Tacoma Hotel (above) and made its way to South Ninth Street and Broadway, where the crowds were so thick that FDR's car could hardly move. Fleet Weeks, as this one in 1935 (below), also brought out the throngs as Tacomans were able to view the latest in military hardware. This year also saw the first Daffodil Parade, a spring event that can still draw crowds downtown.

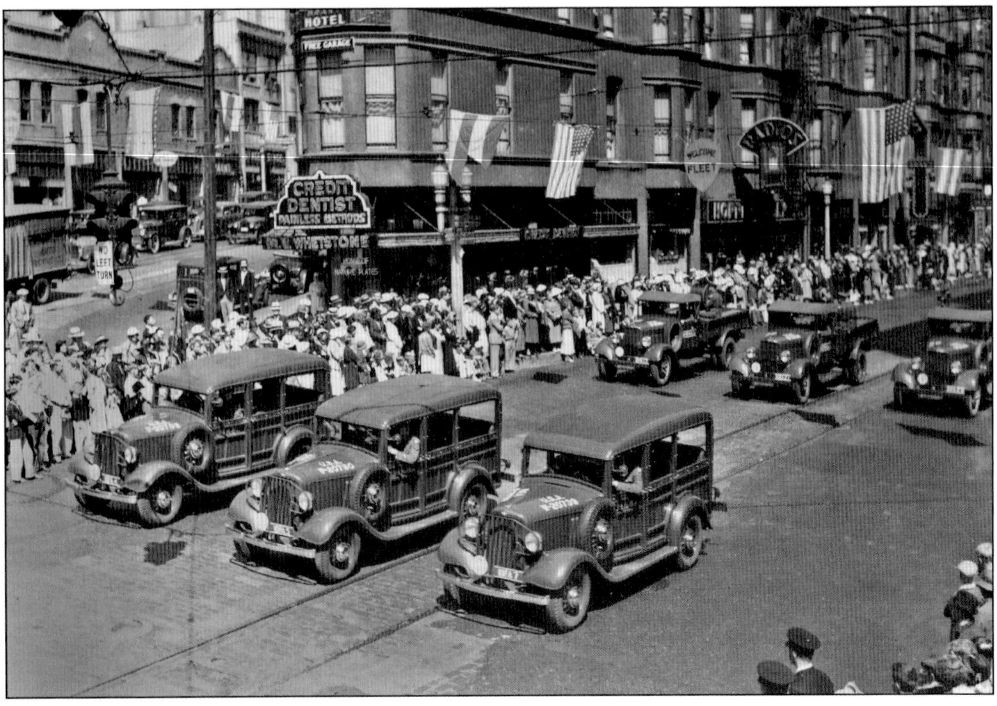

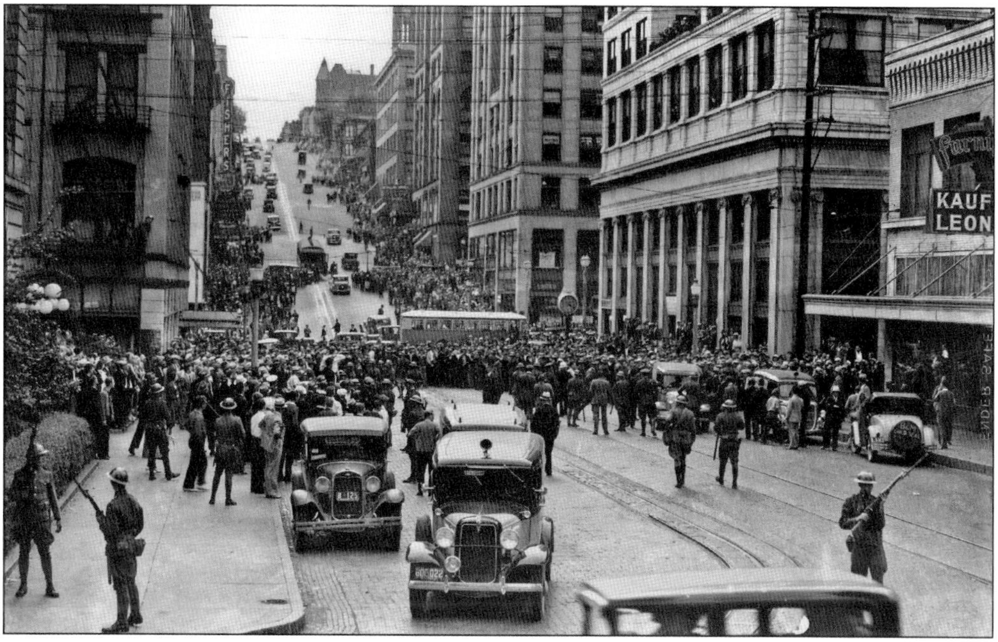

Not all crowds were pleasant events, as this 1935 Chapin Bowen photograph shows. This year witnessed labor strikes on the part of both longshoremen and lumbermen. The photographer is at the corner of South Eleventh and A Streets just before the roadway crosses the Murray Morgan Bridge leading to the port area. The Washington National Guard was called up to restore order.

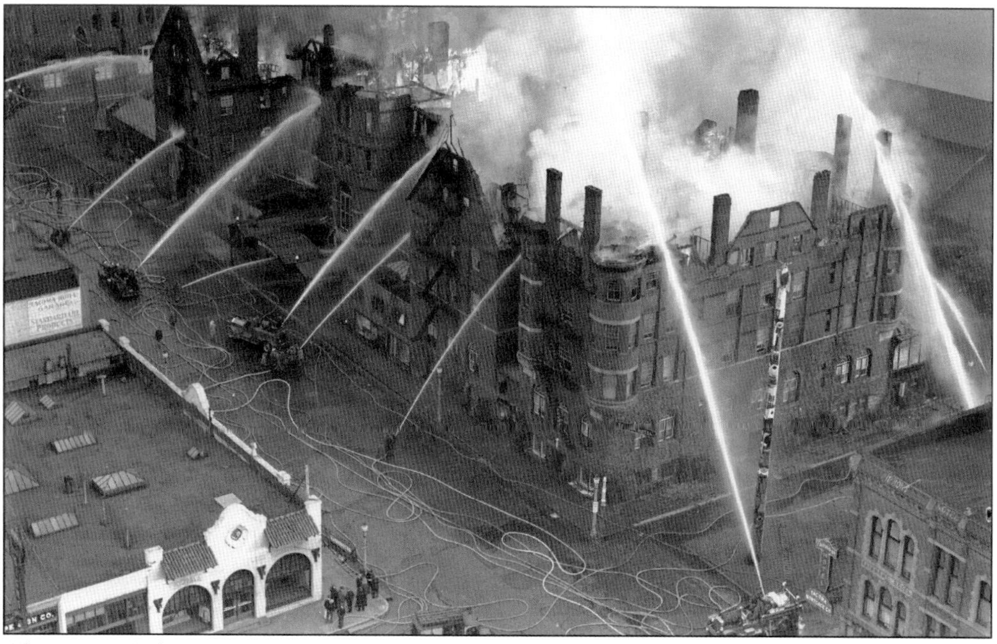

Also in 1935, the Tacoma Hotel was destroyed by fire. There is an irony to the story since the fire department's headquarters was right across South Ninth Street. Evidently hotel personnel thought they could control the fire roaring through the wood-framed structure without help. The land remained undeveloped, except as a parking lot, until 1988, when the Russell Investment Company built its headquarters here.

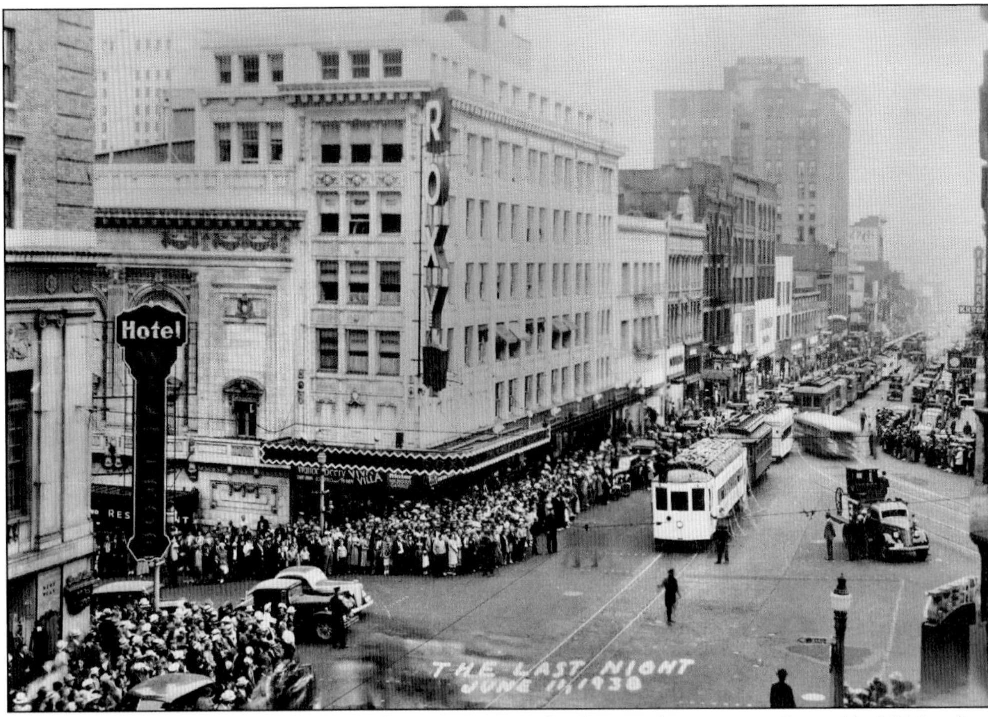

Some downtown events were nostalgic in nature. Such was the case on June 11, 1938, when Tacomans lined up (above) in front of the Pantages (now called the Roxy) Theater to take a ride for the last time on a streetcar. Ever since the end of World War I, when automobiles and delivery trucks began competing for space with the trolley, it was only a matter of time before the old mode of transportation would have to succumb to the new. What better way to celebrate the change than by having a horse-drawn trolley pose beside a new motor coach (below)? Ripping up the track began immediately, with most of it shipped as scrap metal to Japan.

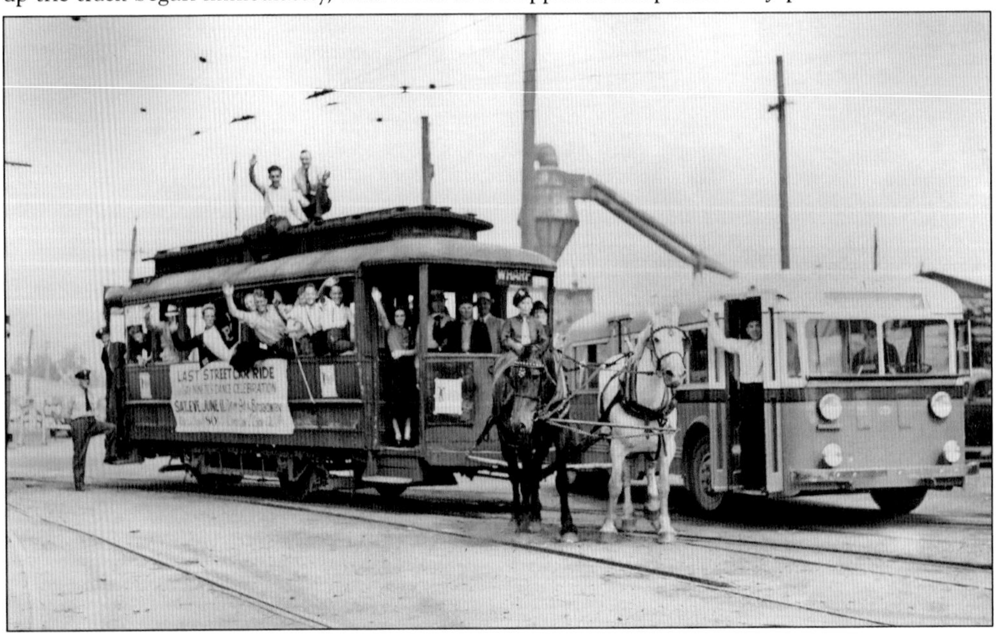

Japanese migration to the Pacific states of California, Oregon, and Washington was well established by the beginning of the 20th century. In Pierce County, many farmed in the Puyallup Valley and brought their produce to the Tacoma public markets. Others worked in lumber mills such as the Dickman Lumber Company located on Commencement Bay. With time, a Japanese commercial and residential neighborhood evolved within Tacoma's downtown. The area between South Thirteenth and Fifteenth Streets and Broadway was the commercial area, with the Tokyo Café (at right) one of the establishments that advertised in a 1919 brochure. Below, an undated photograph taken northward from the corner of South Fifteenth and Broadway shows some of the other Japanese businesses that lined the street.

To the visitors of this City Beautiful we extend a cordial welcome

TOKYO CAFE

Cor. 13th and Broadway

We serve Chinese and American Dishes

Open From 6 A. M. to 2 A. M.

Merchant's Lunch, 35c
Upstairs, 11 a. m. to 5 p. m.

Dinner, 35c Up
Downstairs, 11 a. m. to 8 p. m.

"To Satisfy is our aim"

All-Wool Bunting and Cotton

Flags

All Sizes and Kinds for Decorating Your Home, Office, Store or Automobile
Spear Head Flags for Parades and for the Children

Souvenir Goods

Pennants, Photographs, Photo Postcards, Tacoma View Folders. Beautiful Books on Mount Tacoma

Kodaks

Films, Developing, Printing and Enlarging

P. K. PIRRET & CO.

910 BROADWAY

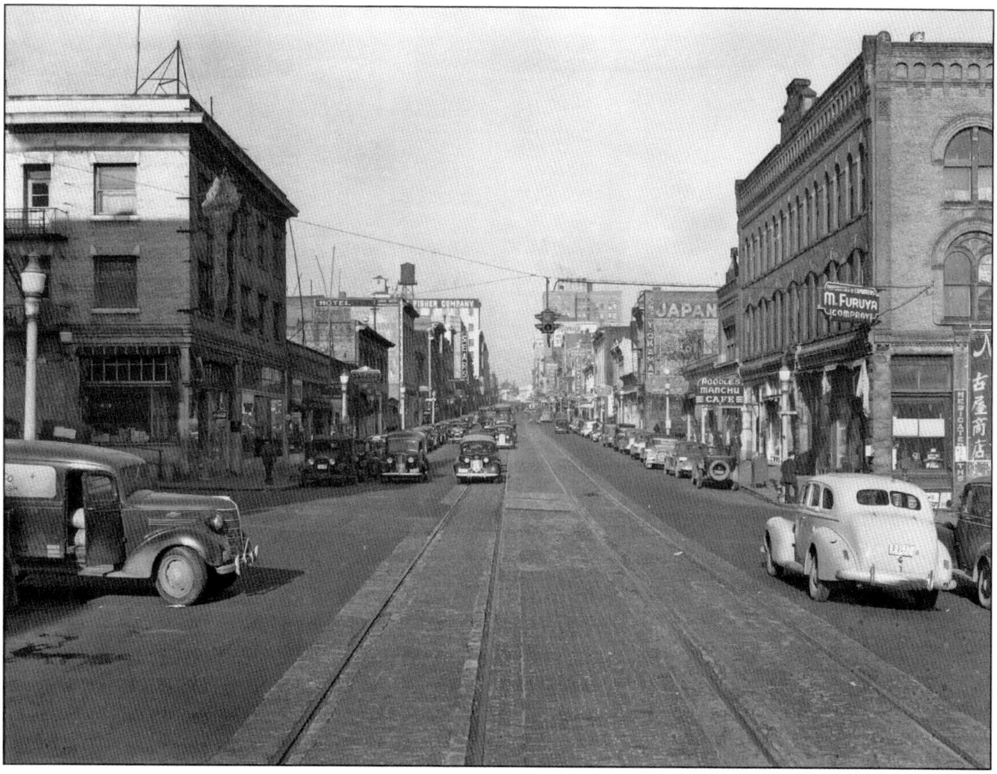

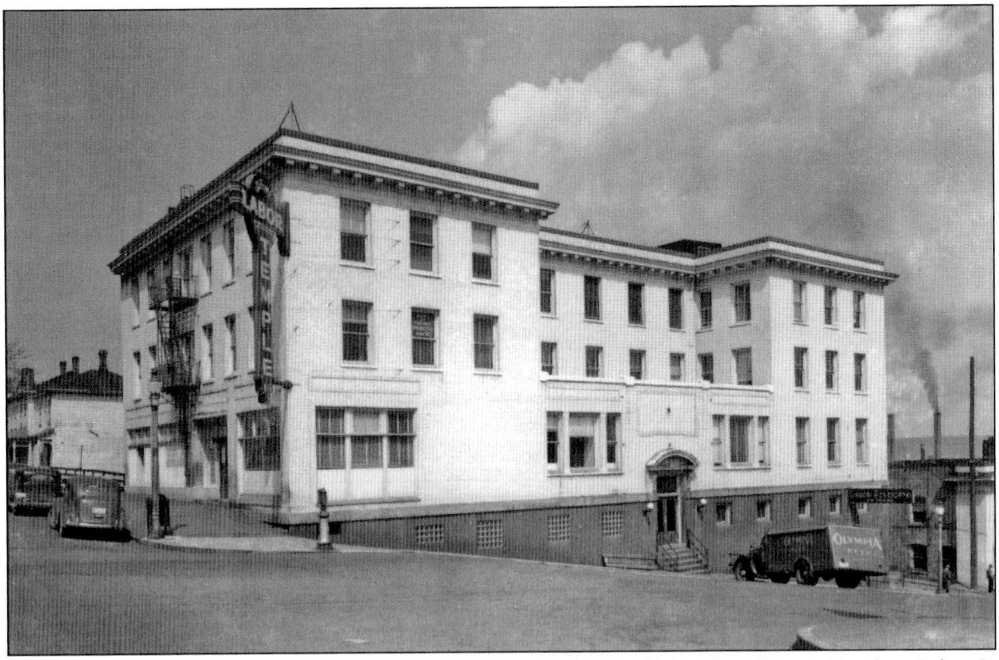

The Hiroshimaya Hotel was built in 1914 and located at 1355 Market Street. Realtor John S. Baker funded the building that architect Roland Borhek designed for a tenant who could not legally own property in the United States because of his Asian heritage. When Chapin Bowen took this photograph sometime in 1942, the building was home to the Central Labor Council. (Courtesy of Tacoma Public Library.)

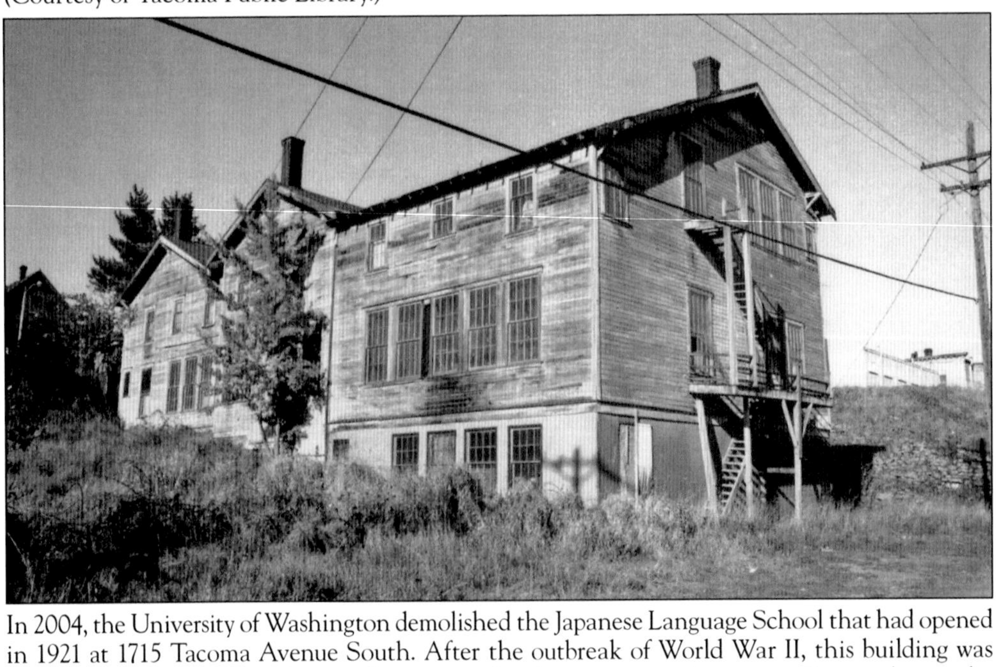

In 2004, the University of Washington demolished the Japanese Language School that had opened in 1921 at 1715 Tacoma Avenue South. After the outbreak of World War II, this building was the "processing center" for Tacoma Japanese ordered to concentration camps. Even as late as the 1970s, the school contained possessions of those forced to leave Tacoma. (Courtesy of Tacoma Public Library.)

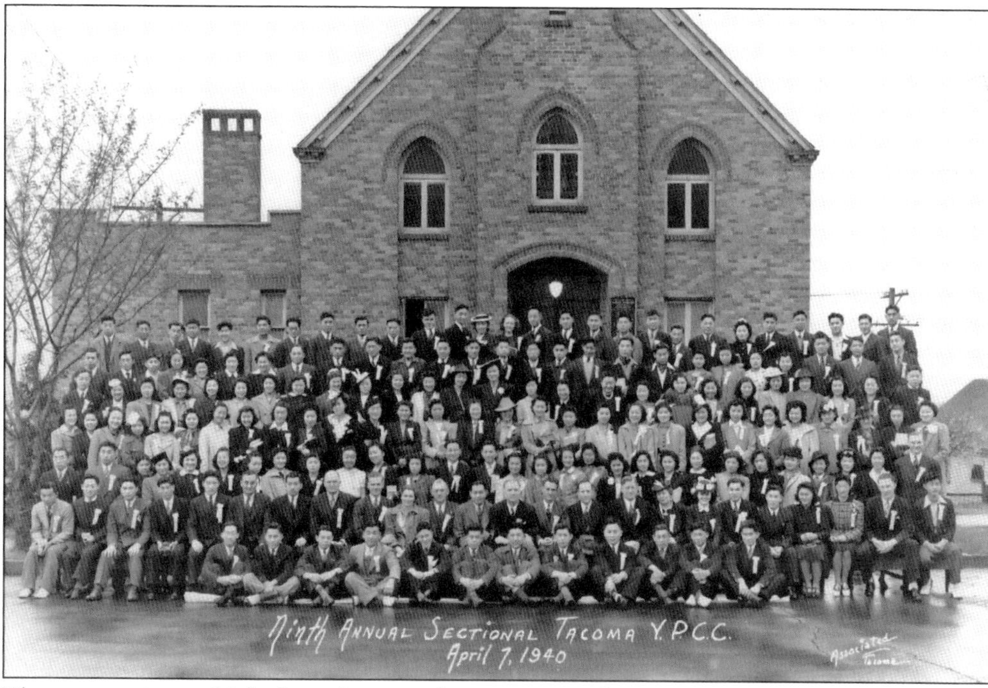

The community established a wide array of institutions and activities to engage both the first- and second-generation Japanese. Dancing to the big bands and baseball were favorite pastimes for the young, and even though the sport was segregated at this time, competing against other Japanese teams in Washington and Oregon provided a way to socialize beyond the boundaries of Tacoma. Churches were also a means to congregate. The Japanese Methodist Episcopal Church (above) at 1901 Fawcett Avenue was dedicated in 1929 and photographed here in 1940. The Japanese Buddhist Church was built in 1930 at 1717 Fawcett Avenue. The photographer did not provide a description as to the reason for the group portrait taken in 1949, but it appears to be a funeral. (Both courtesy of Tacoma Public Library.)

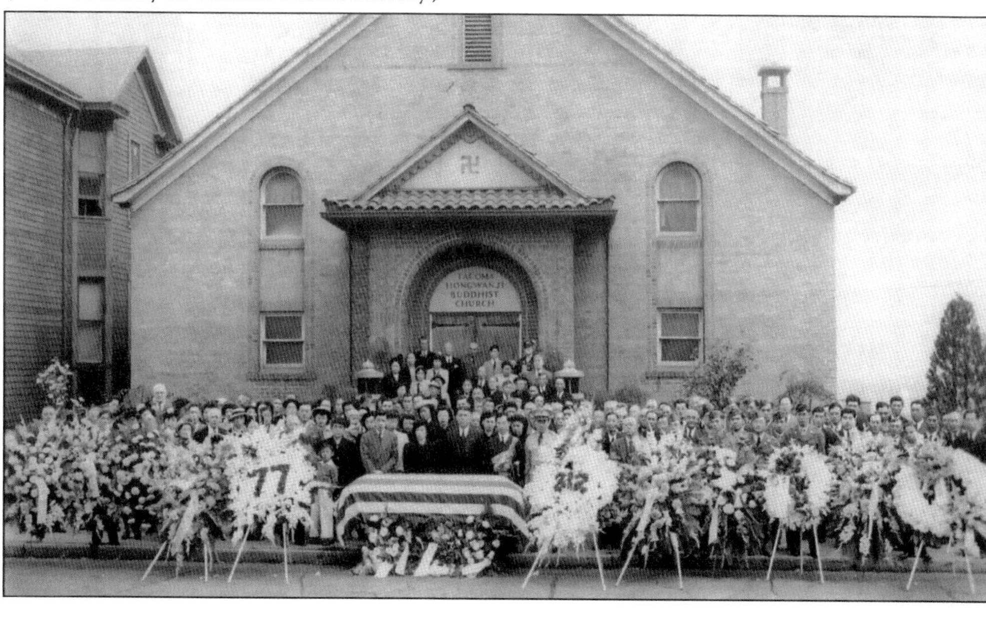

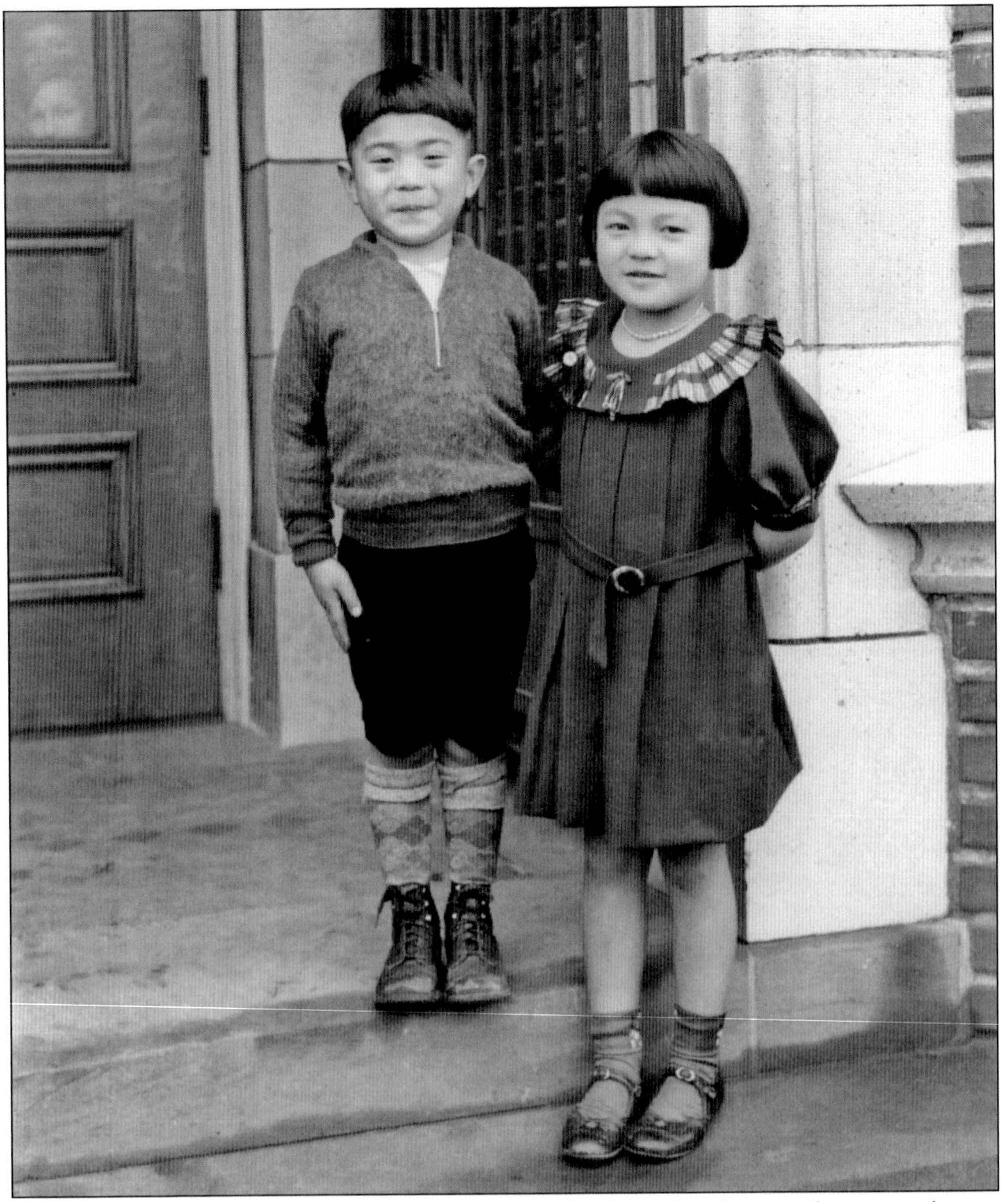

In 1934, Hisasha and Ruby Kumasaka posed for a Richards Studio photographer. According to an October 31, 1934, *Tacoma Times* article, the two children had each received $10,000 from Sweny Smith, an 80-year-old logger who had recently died. The children's family, who lived at 1706 Broadway, had befriended the Norwegian and had taken care of him in their home. Sweny was impressed with the Kumasakas and considered the two youngsters as his grandchildren. Just before he died, he informed the family of his will located in a bank safety deposit box. It was then the children learned that there was enough money to fund their future. One can wonder what happened to the children and these funds come 1942. By then, Ruby would have been 15 and Hisasha 13. President Roosevelt's Executive Order 9066 mandated the entire family's placement in a concentration camp located east of West Coast cities. As the family gathered at the Japanese Language School before being shipped to the Puyallup Fair Grounds, their future was completely unknown. (Courtesy of Tacoma Public Library.)

Five

1941–1965

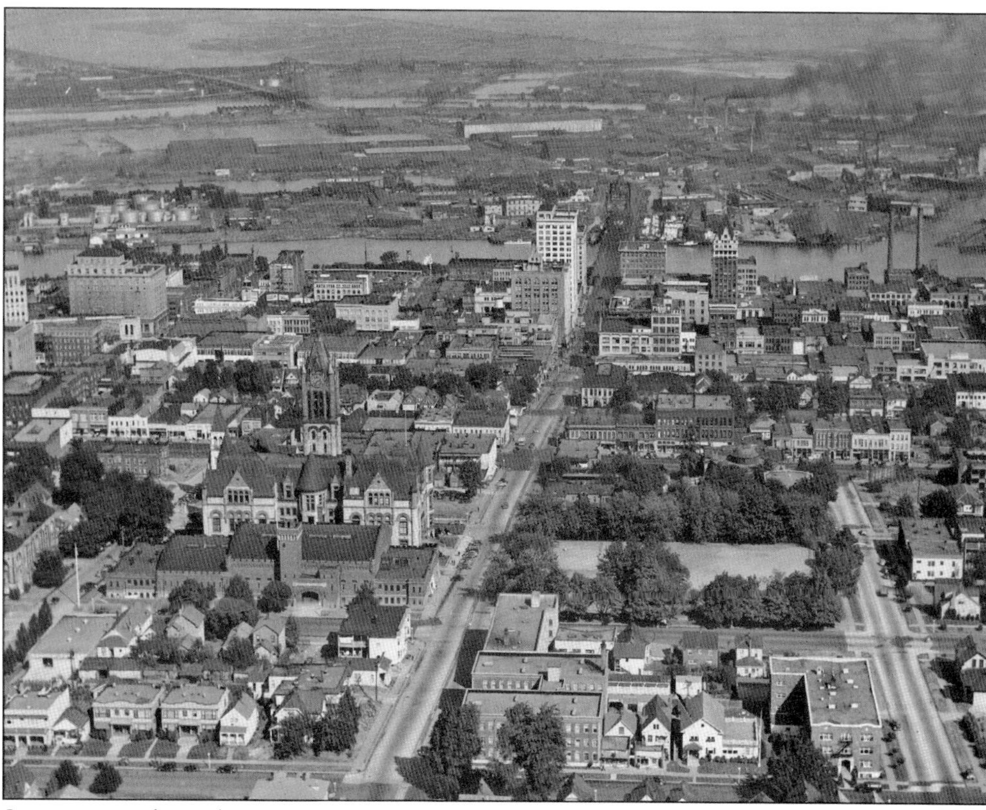

Sometime in the early 1940s, a photographer from the firm of Johnson and Kemp flew over the central business district and took this picture looking east along South Eleventh Street toward the tide flats. The view portrays downtown Tacoma just before America entered World War II on December 7, 1941. Within five years, this urban landscape would begin to change. (Courtesy of Thomas R. Stenger.)

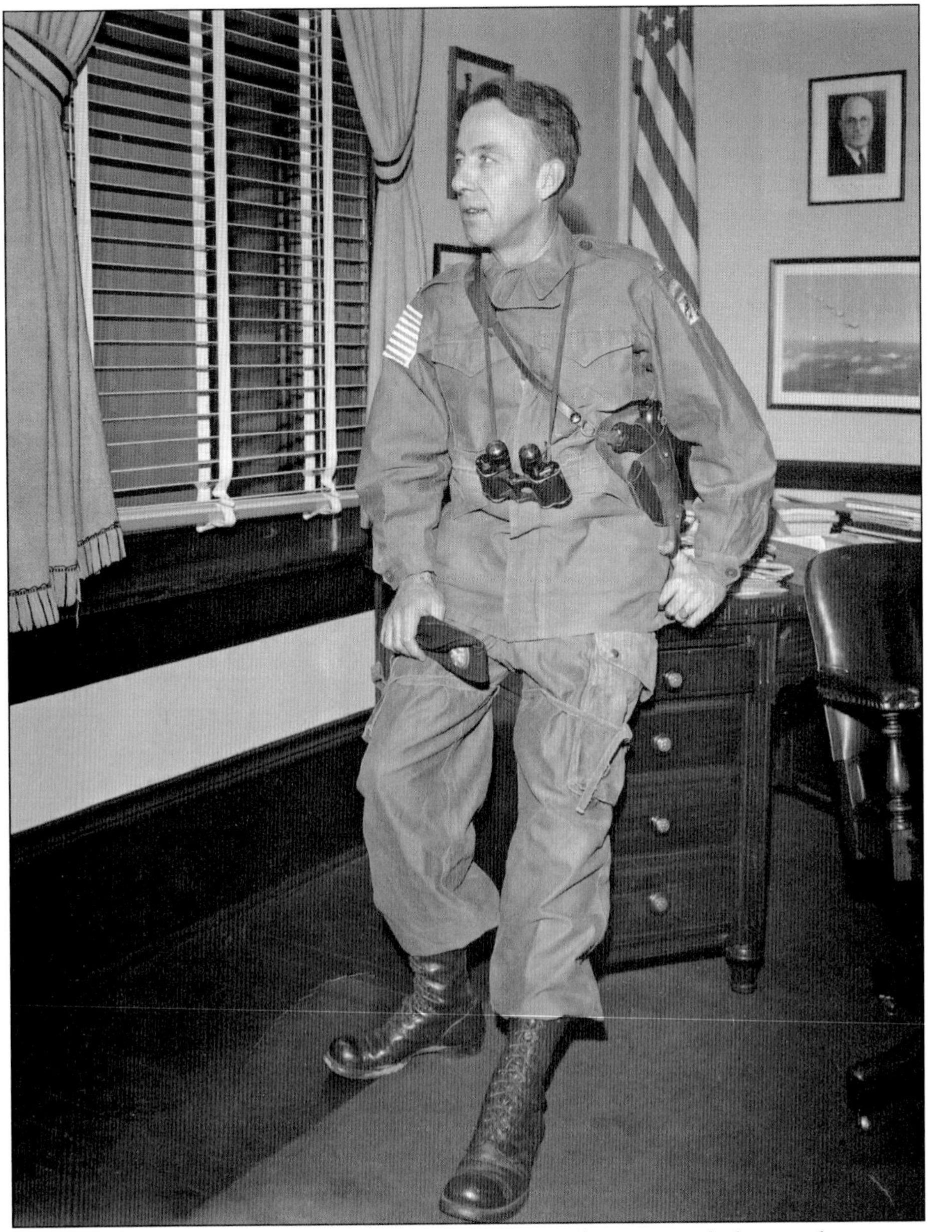

Harry P. Cain was Tacoma's mayor at war's onset. A man of many moods, he was the inspiration for much that happened in the way of urban development until his enlistment in the army in 1943. He publicly opposed Pres. Franklin D. Roosevelt's order leading to the creation of Japanese concentration camps in the West. In order to ensure that Tacoma would not be considered off-limits to the military men on leave from Fort Lewis, he sponsored an anti-vice campaign designed to rid the underworld from the bars and houses of prostitution along Pacific Avenue. With an eye to the future, he supported the spending of local funds to construct what is now the Sea-Tac International Airport. He could also be called the city's first urban planner because he convinced New Dealers that Tacoma should be part of a pilot project to determine how cities nationwide should approach urban development after the war. This undated Turner Richards photograph shows Mayor Harry P. Cain just before he marched off to war. (Courtesy of Thomas R. Stenger.)

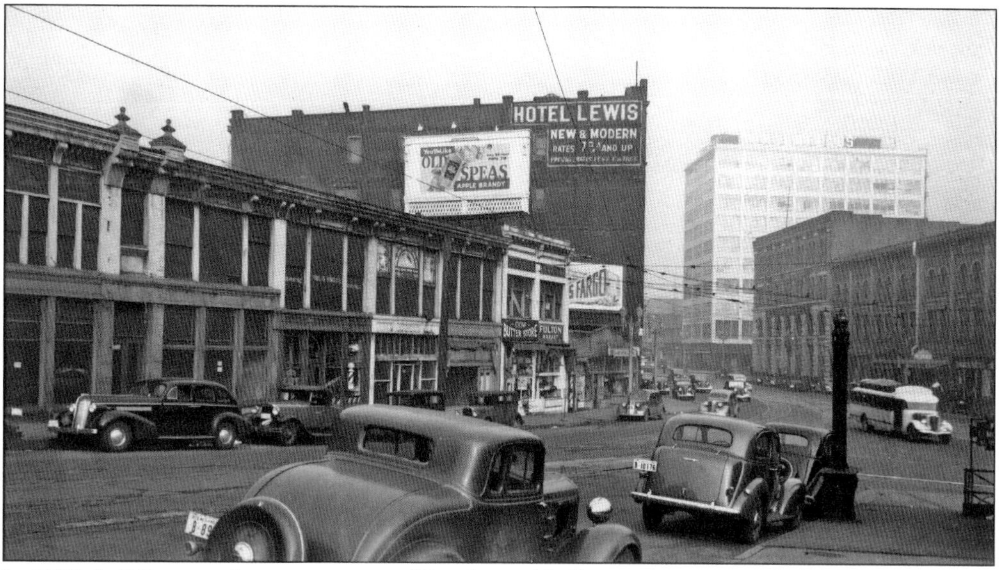

In 1938, buildings at the intersection of Pacific and Jefferson Avenues included such businesses as the Cow Butter Store that operated from here from 1901 until 1942. The Crystal Palace to its left began in 1889 as a bank. By the 1940s, however, the streetscape photographed here was, according to local newspapers, the focal point of robberies and police vice raids.

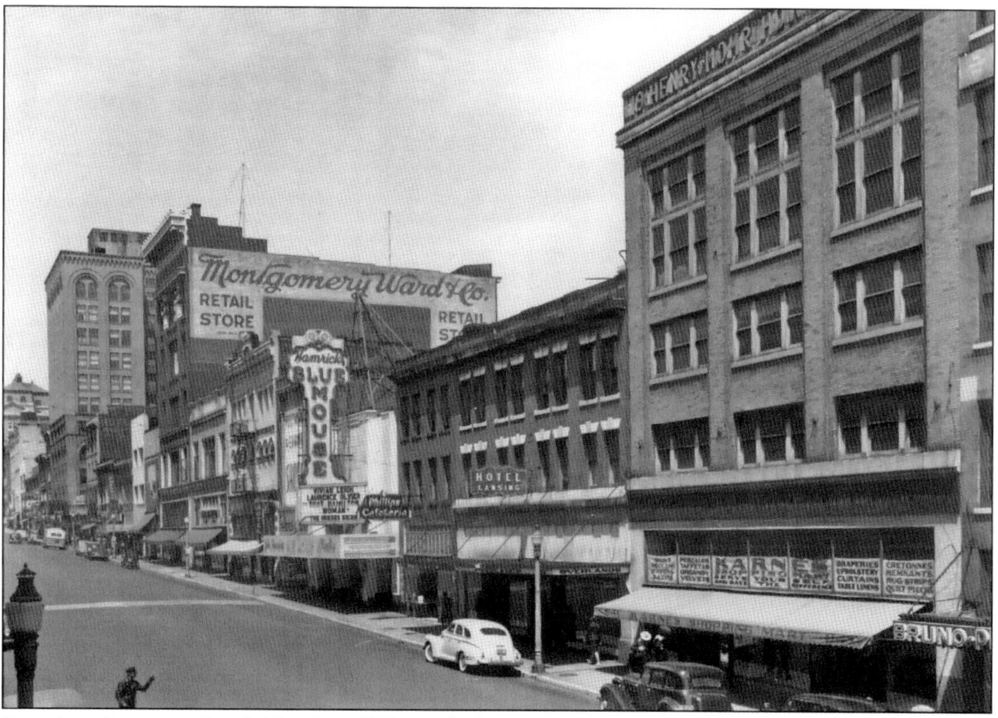

Broadway between South Ninth and Eleventh Streets was a commercial hub during the war. In this Richards Studio view taken in 1941, seen are the Henry Mohr Hardware Company (on the right) and the downtown Blue Mouse motion picture theater where Vivian Leigh and Lawrence Olivier were starring. Other businesses included the Marush Fish Market, Ted Brown Music Company, and Tacoma's Montgomery Ward Department Store. (Courtesy of Tacoma Public Library.)

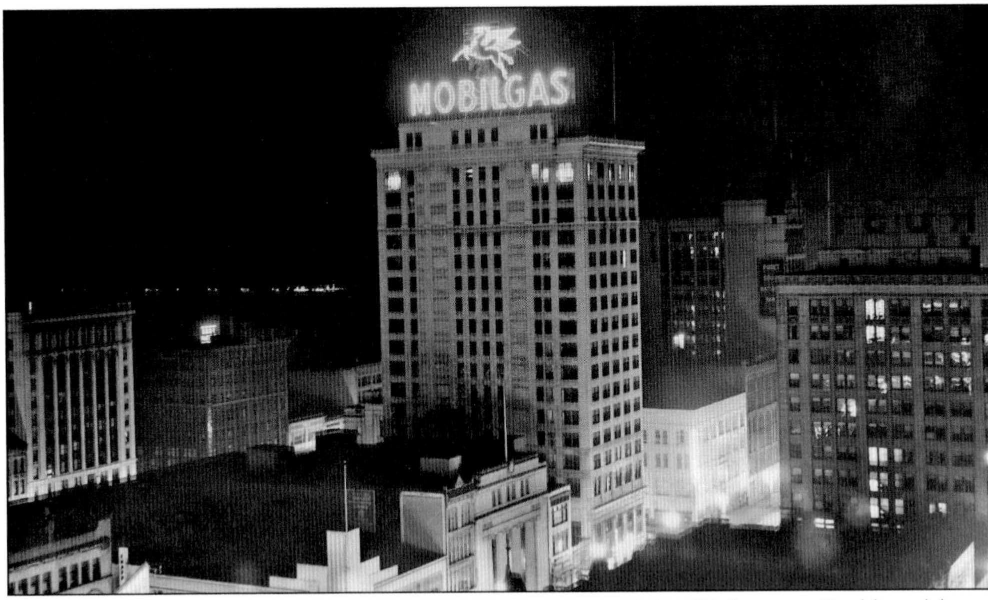

The Mobile Pegasus logo reigned supreme at night on top of the Washington Building (above) in 1946 following the end of World War II. Peoples Department Store is on its right, and the Bank of California Building is on its left. The Anderson Building, completed the day after the attack on Pearl Harbor in 1941, is seen on the lower left. During the war, it was home to the Lutheran Service Center and Knapps Business College. By 1946, Barney Elliott's Camera Shop was also located in the building, shown below in this 1949 photograph. By this time, Elliott was internationally known for his 1940 motion picture coverage of the first Tacoma Narrows Bridge collapse, film that is still seen today.

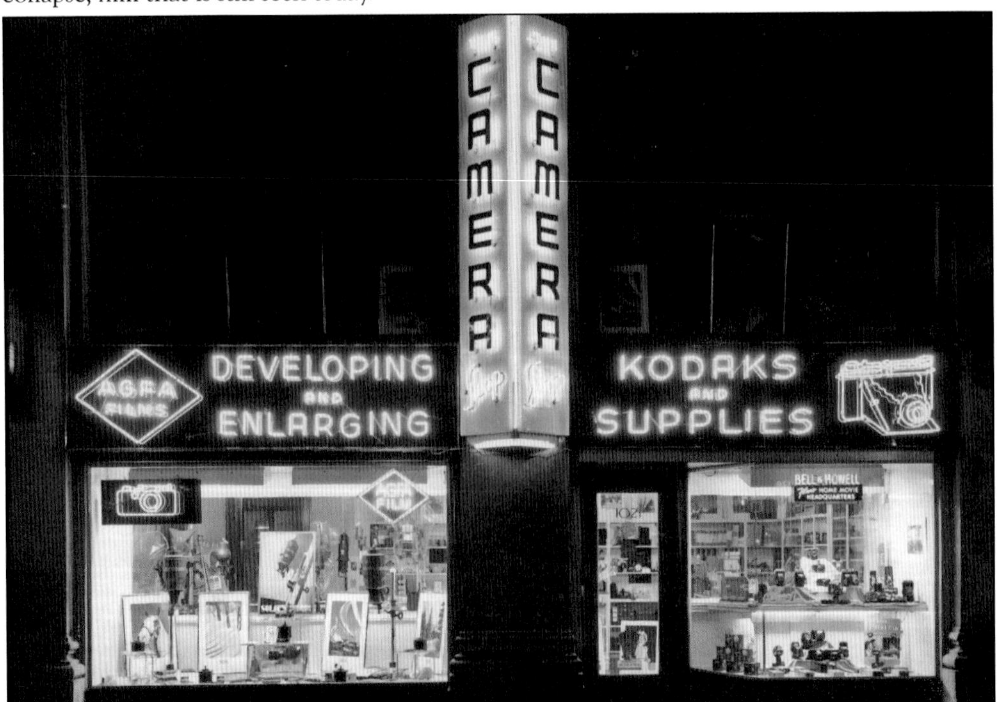

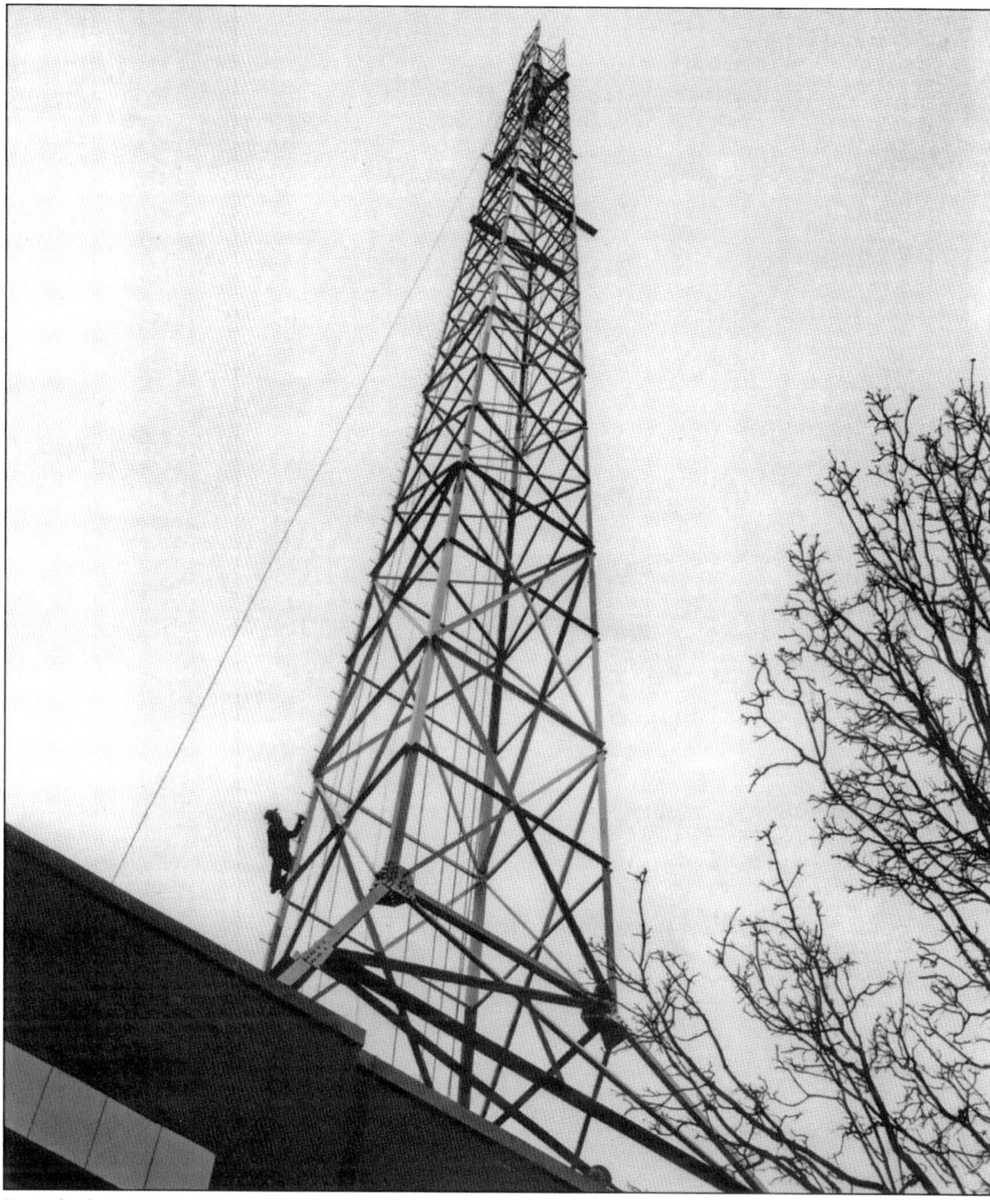

Even before America entered World War II, educators were beginning to realize that learning must transcend those subjects designed only to prepare students for a college or university education. To meet this need, school districts nationwide created the vocational school. Here students would learn how to do the many tasks that American society needed to keep the machinery of technological life running. By January 1941, the Tacoma School District was planning such a vocational school. Architect Ernest T. Mock was commissioned to design the building located on what was tennis courts at the time. War necessities delayed the completion of the Tacoma Vocational School for a time, but when it did open, its classes were available for veterans taking advantages of the GI Bill. Radio broadcasting was one course offered in 1948 after the construction of this 317-foot tower, shown while it was under construction. In 1969, the school was renamed to honor its first director, L. H. Bates. The radio tower was an urban fixture until the 1990s. (Photograph by Richards Studio; courtesy of Tacoma Public Library.)

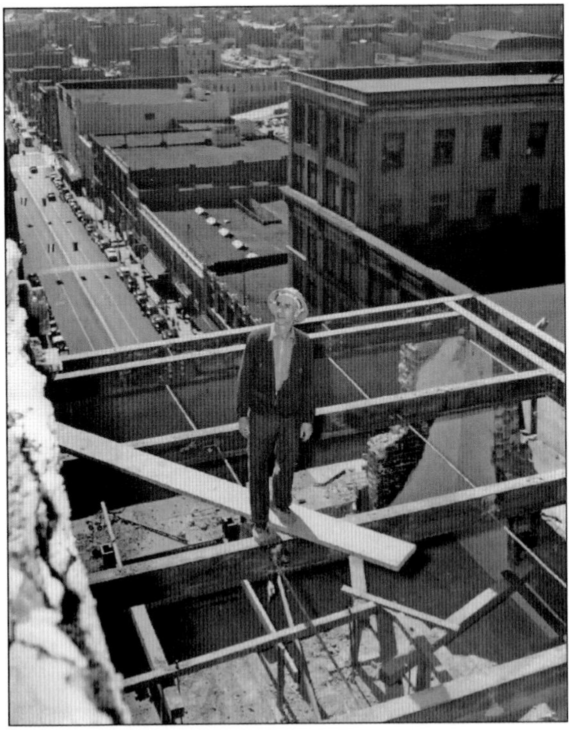

The April 1949 earthquake symbolized the beginning of the end for parts of downtown Tacoma. Artistic detailing and upper floors were removed from some buildings. With others, owners tore them down. This unidentified workman is part of a crew that is dismantling the Fidelity Building at South Eleventh Street and Broadway. (Photograph by Richards Studio; courtesy of Tacoma Public Library.)

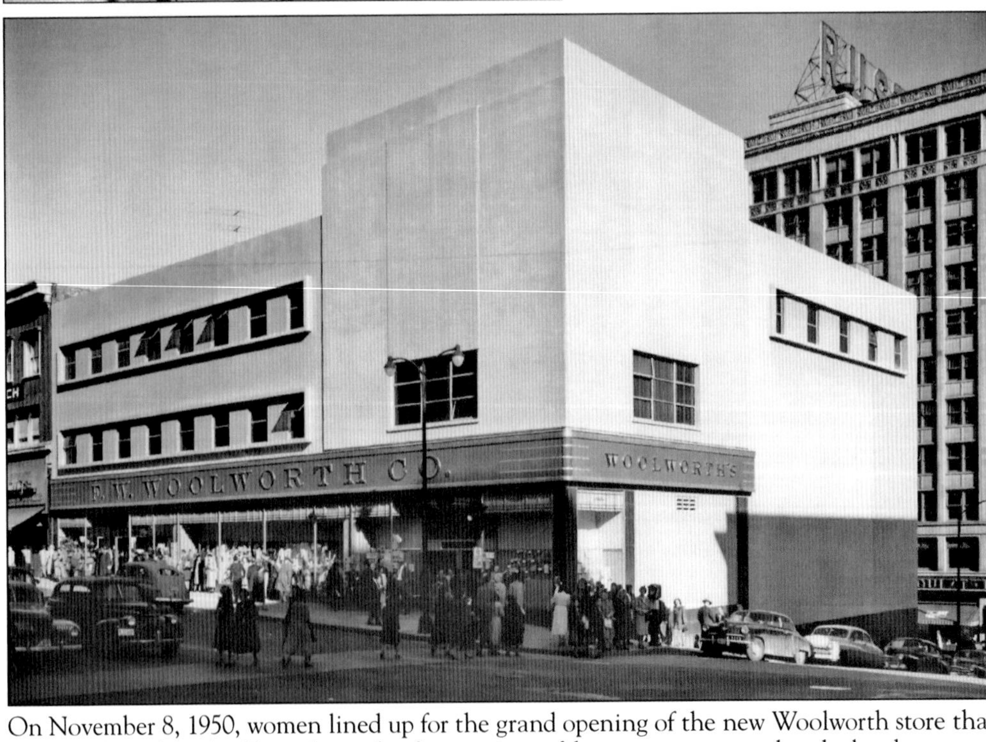

On November 8, 1950, women lined up for the grand opening of the new Woolworth store that replaced the Fidelity building. A couple of generations of downtowners remember the lunch counter. At the time it closed in 1993, Woolworth's was the only place where people who lived downtown could buy groceries. (Photograph by Richards Studio; courtesy of Tacoma Public Library.)

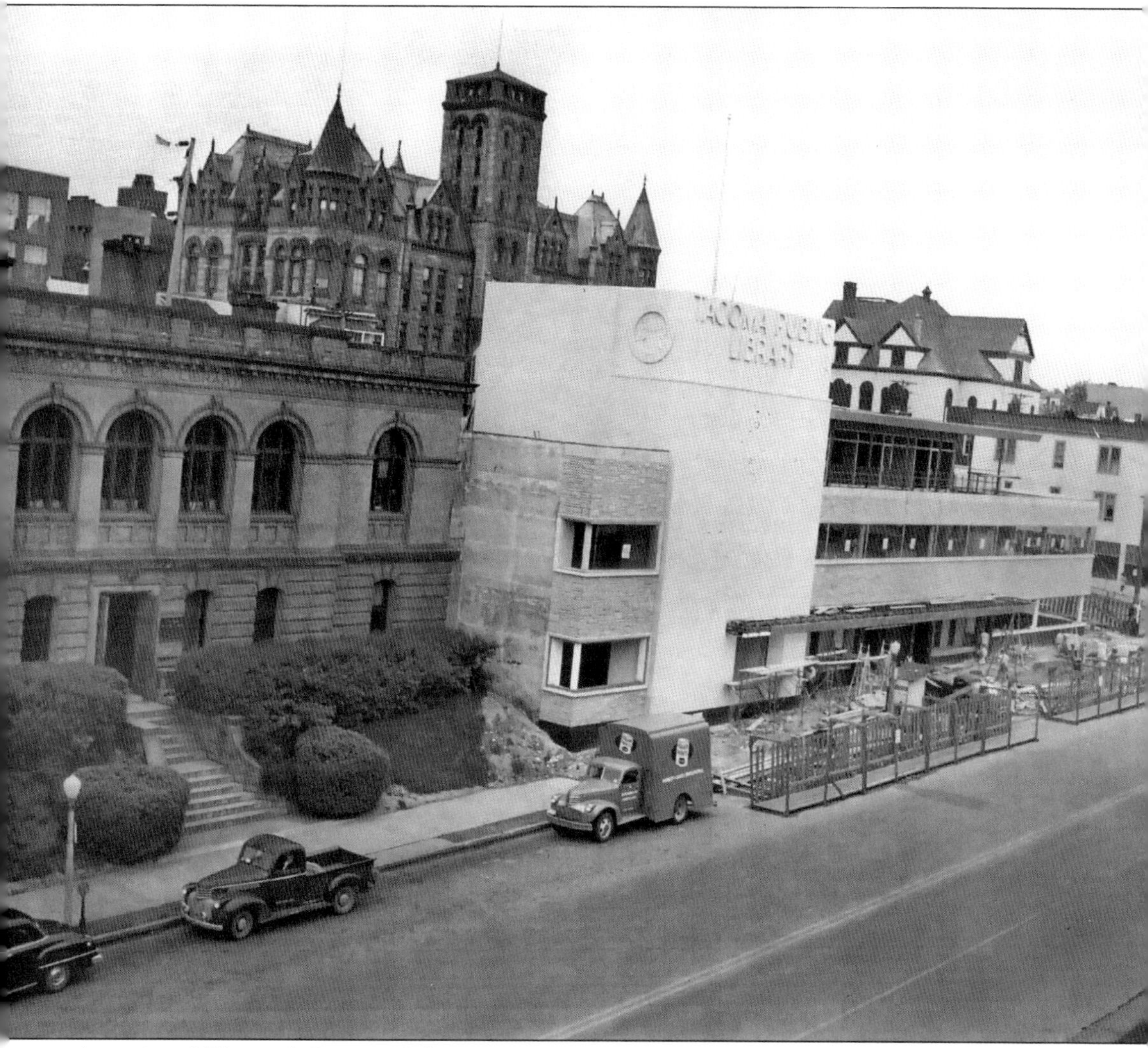

At war's end, Tacoma's Carnegie Library on Tacoma Avenue South was running out of room. How and where to expand the facility were causes of debate for the next five years. Some suggested moving it into the city hall. Others proposed a site at South Eleventh and Market Streets. According to newspaper headlines at the time, the debate was contentious. Eventually, the library board authorized an addition on to the Carnegie library and commissioned architect Silas E. Nelsen to create the design. In order to complete the project, the library board first had to acquire the commercial building that had been on the corner of South Eleventh Street and Tacoma Avenue South since the 1890s. The new building was dedicated in 1952, shortly after this photograph was taken. Behind it is the Pierce County Courthouse with one of the towers of the Tacoma armory in the distance. On the right, across South Eleventh Street, are wood-framed buildings that would soon be demolished to make way for the County-City Building. (Courtesy of Tacoma Public Library.)

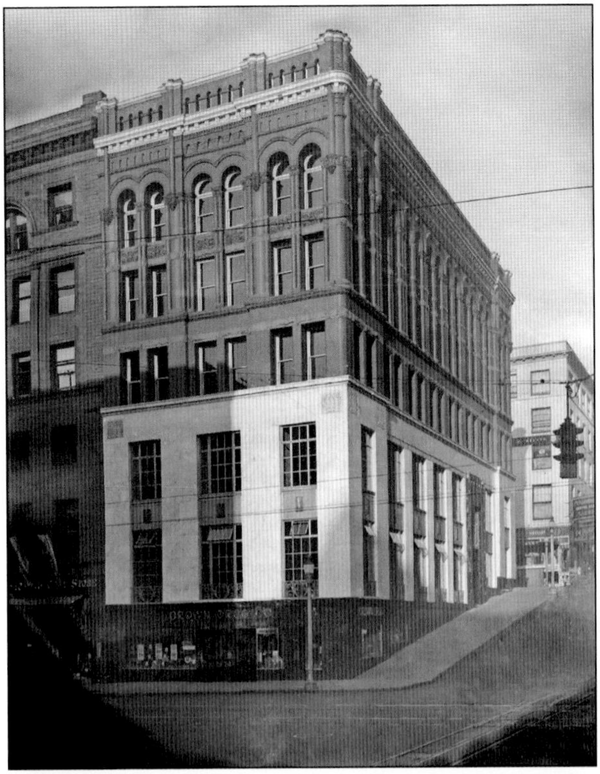

Downtown Tacoma developers were not immune to taking an existing building and modernizing it based on the design whims of the time. One of the earliest examples of this trend was the Merchants National Bank building at 1102 Pacific Avenue (at left). Here in 1922, Ernest Corner remodeled the facade by covering the original brick with pseudo-marble, a change that interested the Crown Drug Company into leasing a part of the building. Another example of this trend is the Sears, Roebuck, and Company store at South Eleventh Street and Broadway/Market Street. In this instance, there were several evolutions of building design starting in 1892 before the building reached the 1936 version that many downtown shoppers still remember (below). Sears remained at this location until 1981. (Below photograph by Richards Studio; courtesy of Tacoma Public Library.)

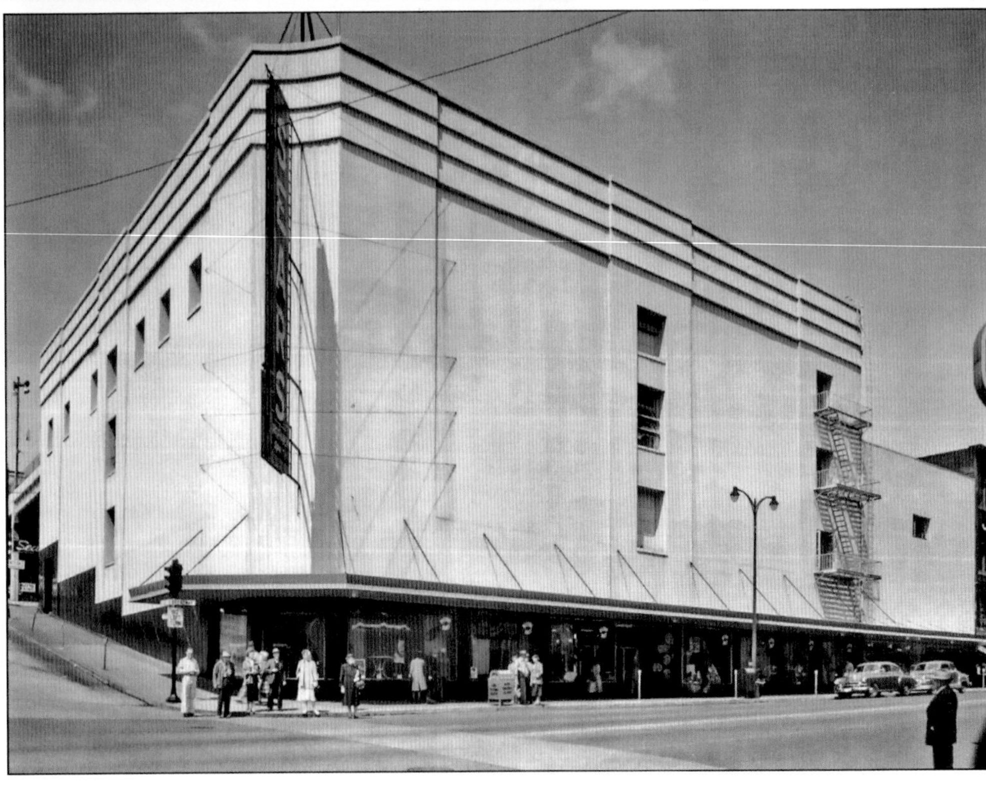

Public transportation is the glue that holds a city together. In Tacoma for almost 50 years, streetcars performed the duty. Cable cars, such as the one shown at right, carried people up the steep South Eleventh Street and down South Thirteenth Street. After buses replaced the streetcar in the 1930s, and the Tacoma Railway and Power Company removed all the rails and sold it as scrap to Japan, the old carbarn at the foot of South Thirteenth Street became home to the bus fleet. Private companies continued to run the local bus service until 1979, when voters approved the creation of Pierce County Transit. In the early 1970s, before public transportation really became public, photographer Ron Karabaich took the view below from South Eleventh Street standing near where an earlier cameraman captured the cable car.

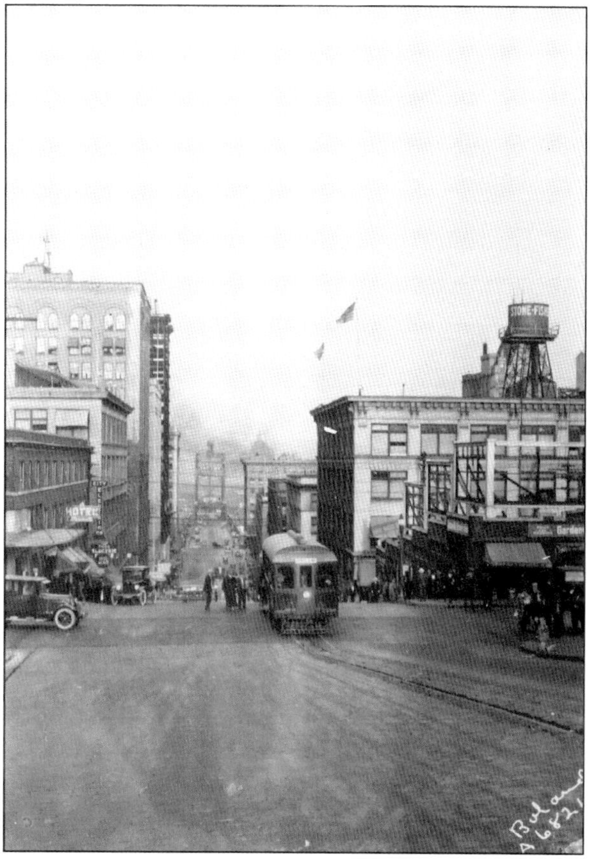

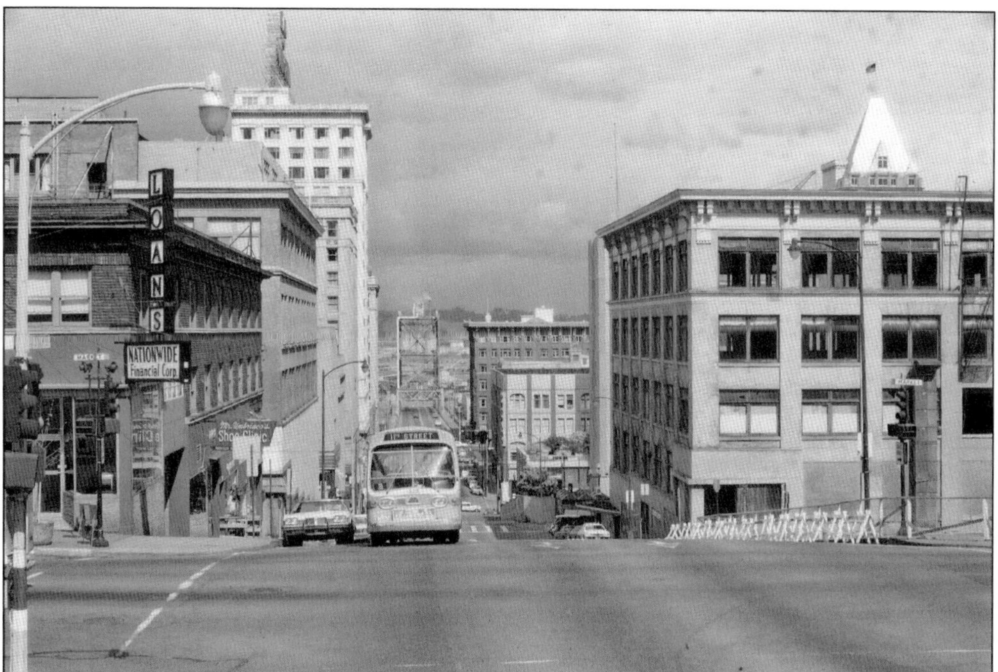

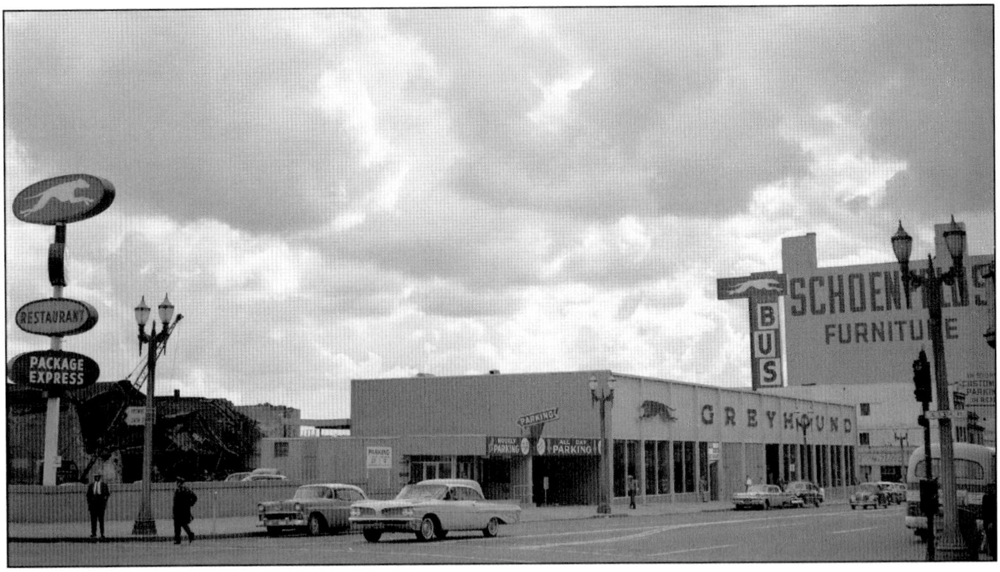

Interurban and suburban bus service began as early as 1912, when Tacoma Auto Stage constructed its depot at the corner of South Eighth Street and Pacific Avenue. In 1929, travelers could also go to the Central Bus Terminal—then home to the North Coast Stage Lines—at South Fourteenth Street and Pacific Avenue. This location might have also been the first depot for Greyhound buses following the company's incorporation the same year. The Trailways National Bus System followed suit in 1936. After World War II, the two major companies established depots at opposite ends of downtown Tacoma. In 1955, Trailways (above) dedicated its depot located in the building formerly used by Tacoma Auto Stage. Four years later, Greyhound opened its new depot and Post House Restaurant at 1319 Pacific Avenue.

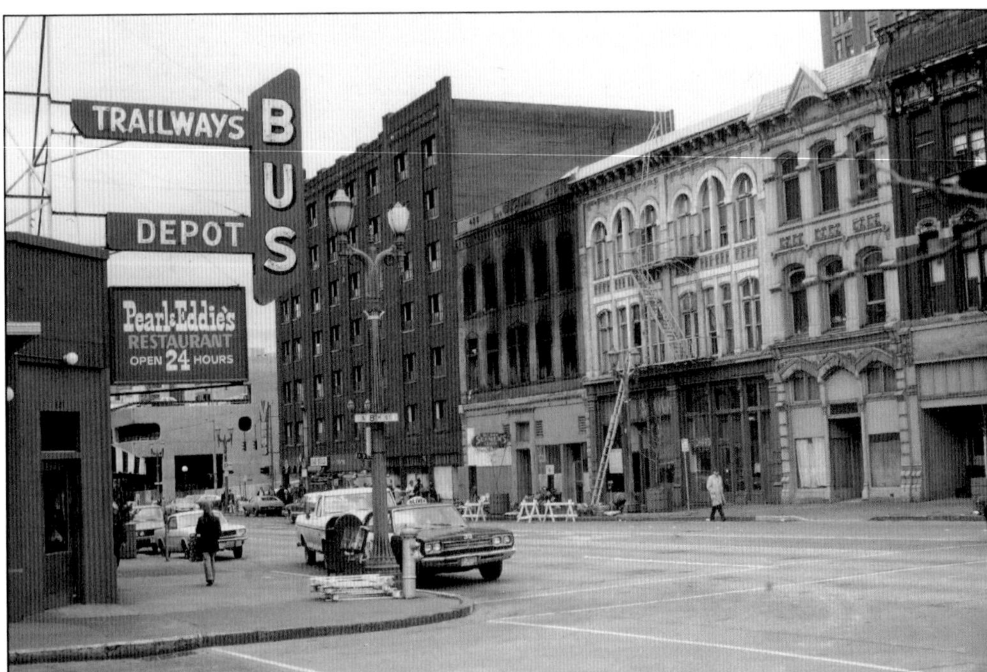

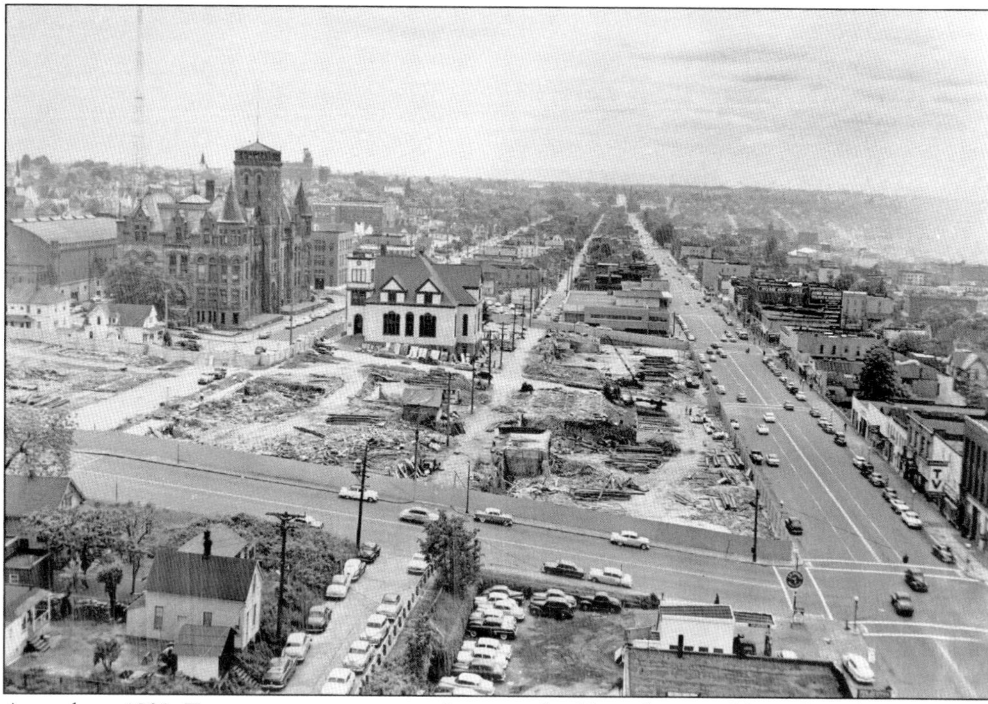

As early as 1939, Tacomans were arguing for a new building that would combine both city and county functions under one roof. Ten years later, voters approved the bond issue needed to construct what is still known as the County-City Building, located at 930 Tacoma Avenue South. Another 10 years passed as officials decided upon both location and architect A. Gordon Lumm. By 1955, the demolition of buildings on the site had begun (above), and in April 1959, the facility was dedicated. Originally the new public building shared the urban landscape with the old Pierce County Courthouse (below). However, within months after an unidentified photographer took this view, demolition of the older building had begun.

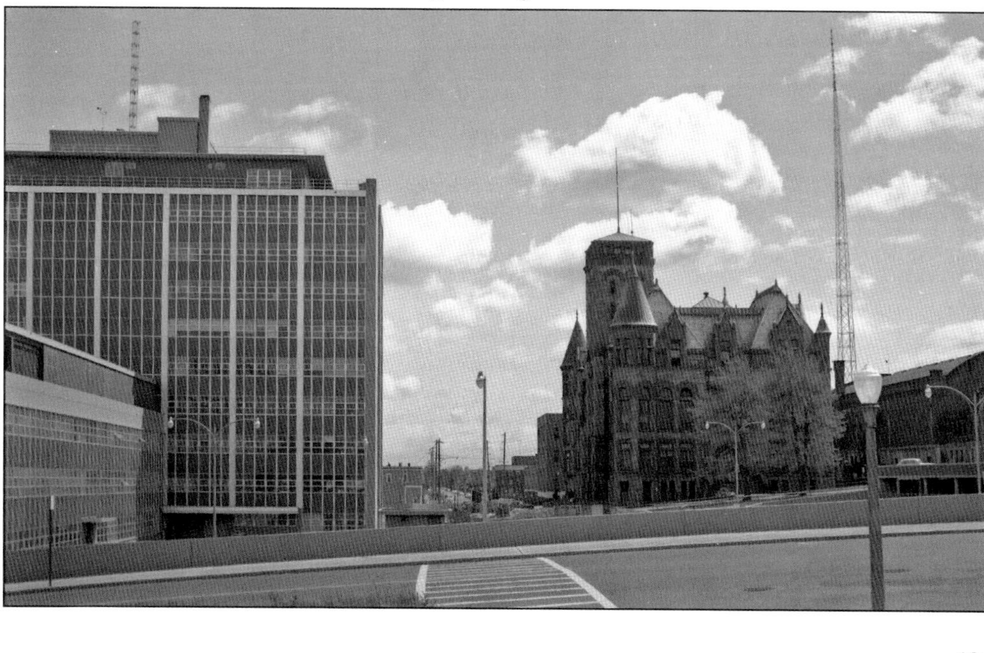

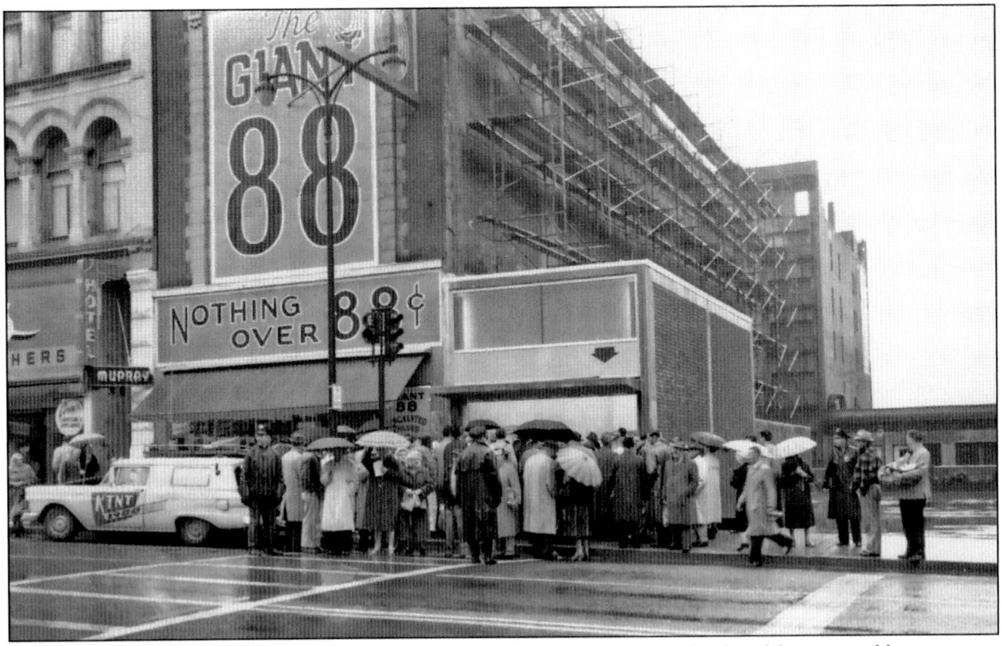

With the loss of the cable cars, Tacoma planners were faced with the dilemma of how to get pedestrians up and down the steep downtown streets. Their solution was a series of escalades, or moving sidewalks. A small rain-drenched crowd gathered on Broadway in February 1961 to witness the dedication of the first completed structure. (Photograph by Richards Studio; courtesy of Tacoma Public Library.)

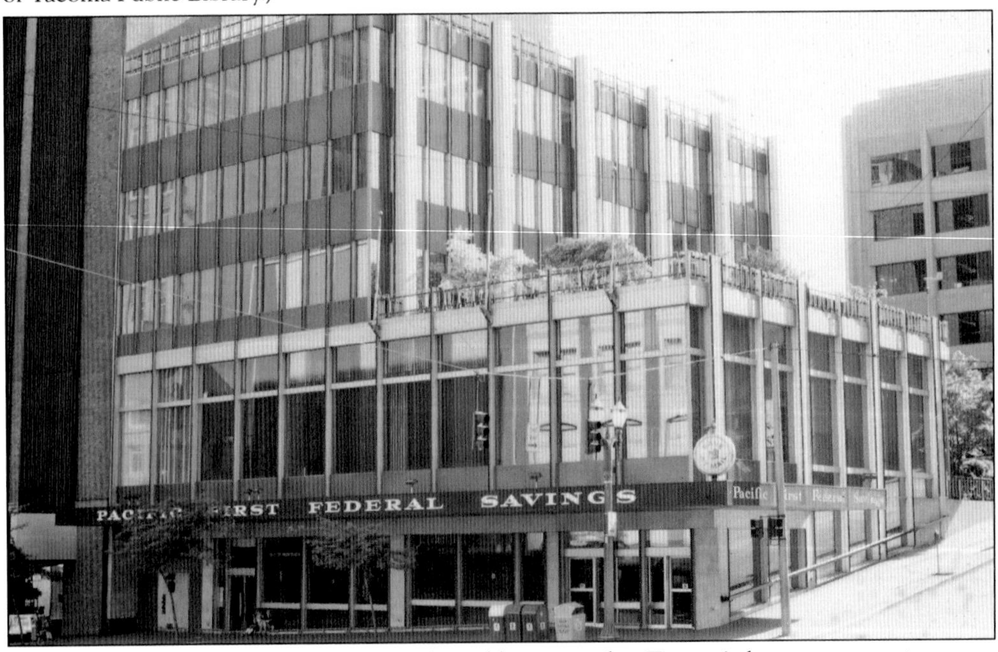

By the 1960s, modern buildings began to replace older ones within Tacoma's downtown, creating a new architecture and urban scale. One was the Pacific First Federal offices completed in 1964 and located at 1102 Pacific Avenue. It replaced the Crown Drug high-rise shown earlier in this chapter. Before the year was out, additional changes continued to transform the central business district.

Six

1965–2000

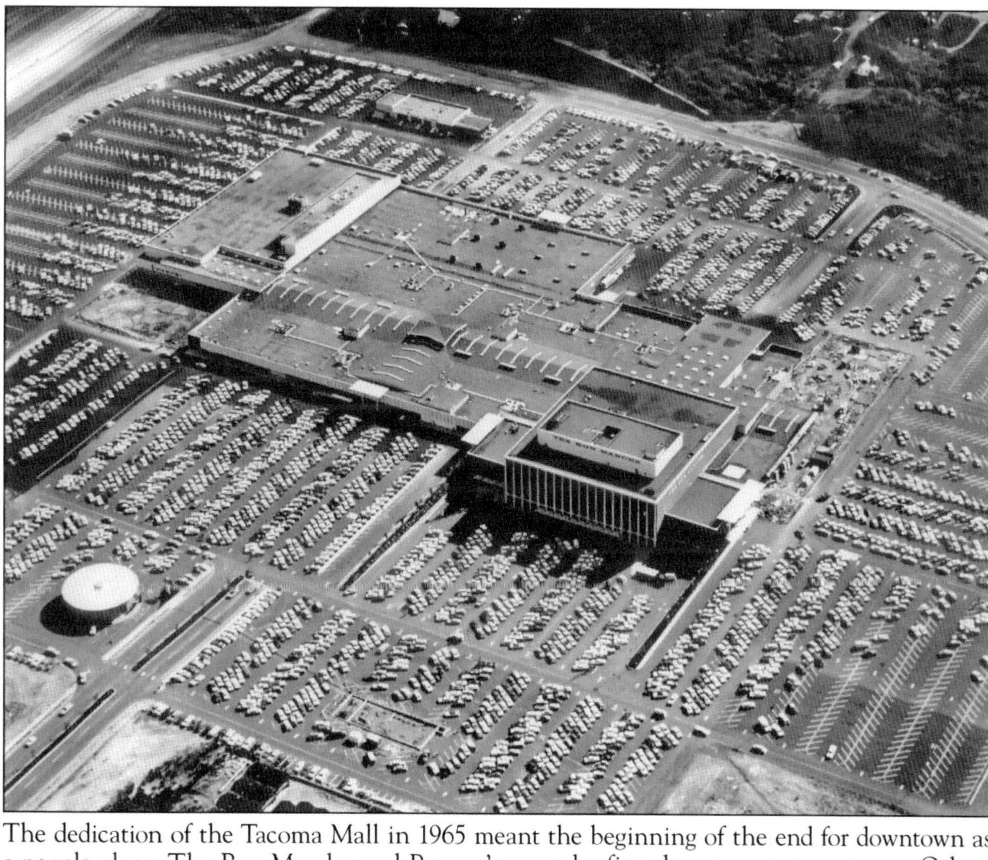

The dedication of the Tacoma Mall in 1965 meant the beginning of the end for downtown as a people place. The Bon Marche and Penney's were the first department stores to go. Others followed, each assured that unlimited parking spaces would lure the shopper to this new paradise. (Photograph by Richards Studio; courtesy of Tacoma Public Library.)

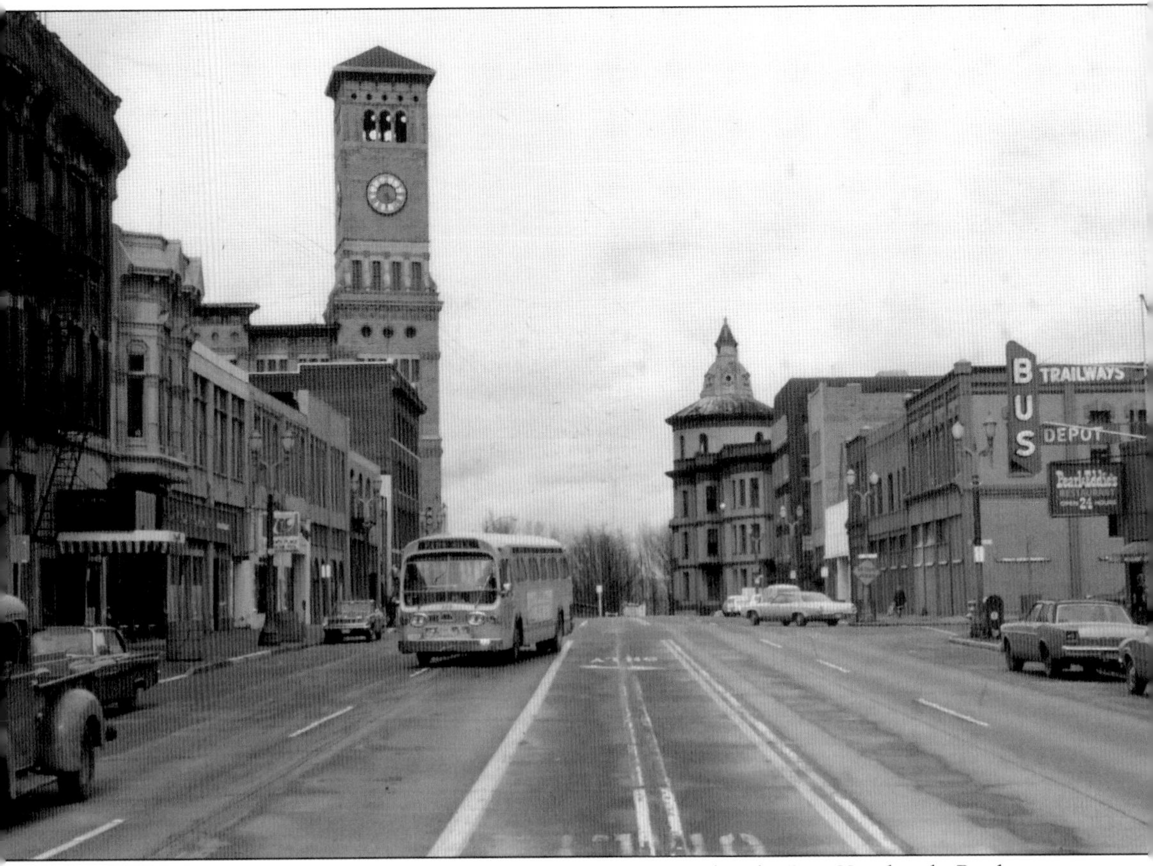

Upper Pacific Avenue seems alone in this mid-1970s view taken by Ron Karabaich. By this time, city hall offices had been moved to the County-City Building. The Northern Pacific Headquarters building, in the distant right in this view, had not seen a railroad official since the 1920s, when the company moved to Seattle. After that, the building was used by the city and then left vacant and open to vandals. However, not all was quiet along the street where buildings date back to the 1880s. Both Johnson-Cox printing company and the Richards Photo Studio—whose photographs ultimately found their way to the Tacoma Public Library—maintained their businesses among the buildings on the left side of Pacific Avenue. By this time, too, architect Alan Liddle had acquired the Bradley Block at 701 Pacific (to the rear on the right) and began the successful effort to designate this part of Tacoma as a National Register Historic District.

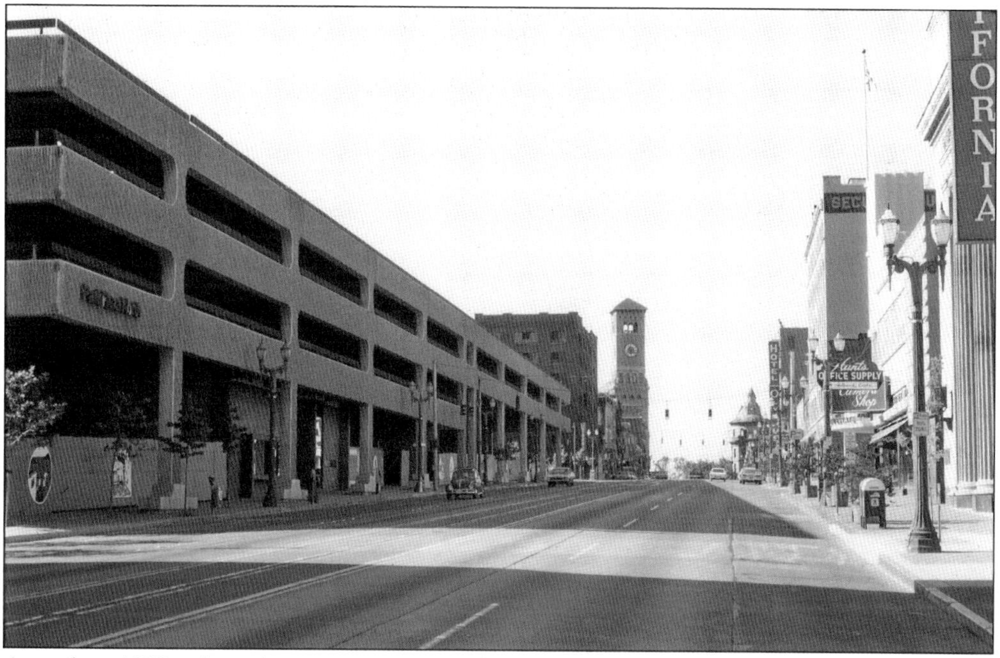

As early as 1958, urban planners were urging the City of Tacoma to build parking garages in the downtown area as one of the first steps toward urban renewal. Another 10 years were to pass before ground was broken on the Park Plaza North facility that consumed most of the city block between South Ninth and Eleventh Streets along Pacific Avenue. At the same time, Park Plaza South was begun, encompassing an area between South Eleventh and Thirteenth Streets. An earlier generation of business blocks was razed in order to build these concrete structures. Both facilities were completed in 1970. These two views show the garages about five years later: above, northward toward the Old City Hall; below, southward toward the Rust building.

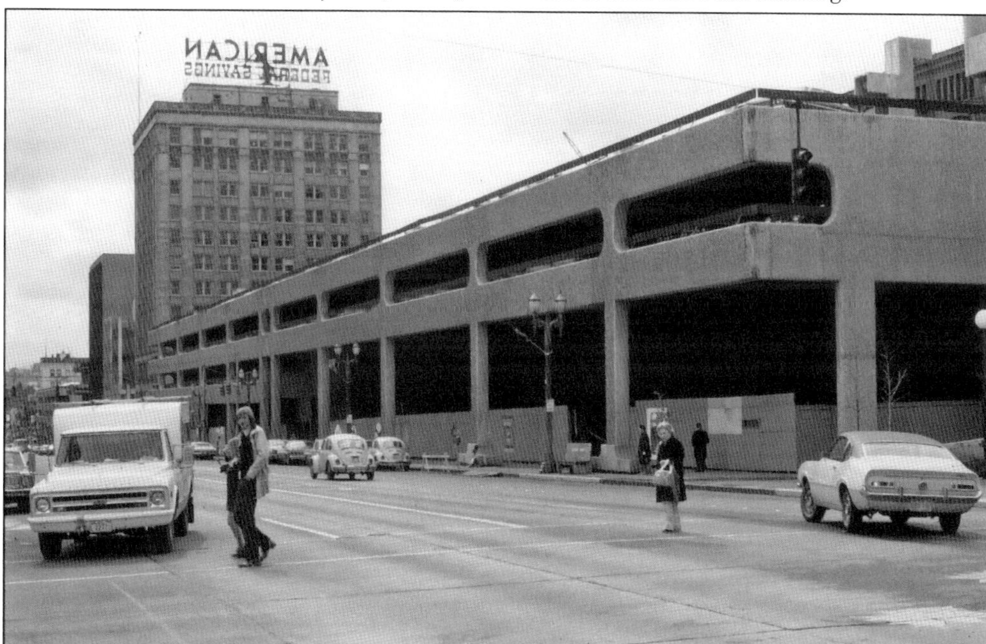

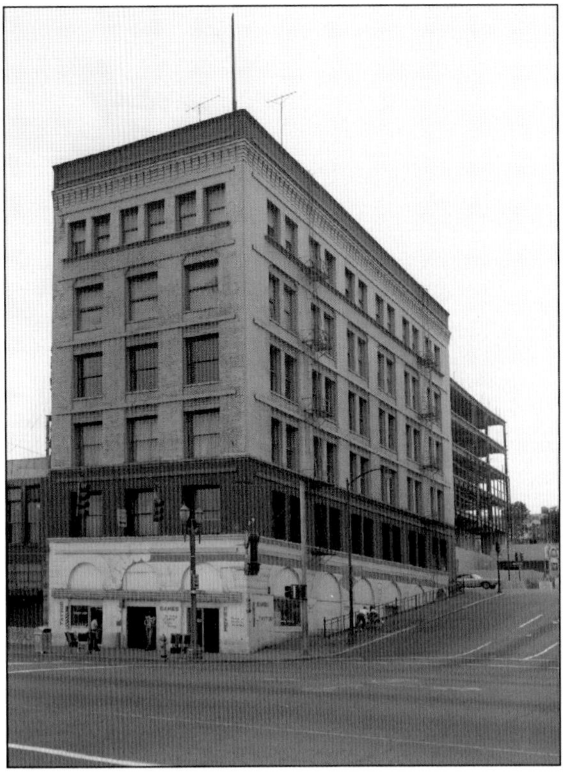

A Lower Pacific Avenue Historic District did not survive the plans of developers. The district extended southward along Pacific Avenue and included the Burnham and Root Luzon building, then called the Fun Circus (at left). Southward along Pacific Avenue from South Thirteenth to South Fifteenth Streets was a collection of commercial spaces ranging in date from 1883 to 1909, built by such Tacoma notables as John S. Baker, Samuel Wolf, David Levin, Endras Ouimette, and Frederick Olds (below). By World War II's end, however, the block was notorious as a sea of vice-related activities. In 1986, the city council concluded that the way to clean up Lower Pacific Avenue was to demolish the buildings. All but the Luzon building, that is: it continues to await someone who can restore it to its past grandeur.

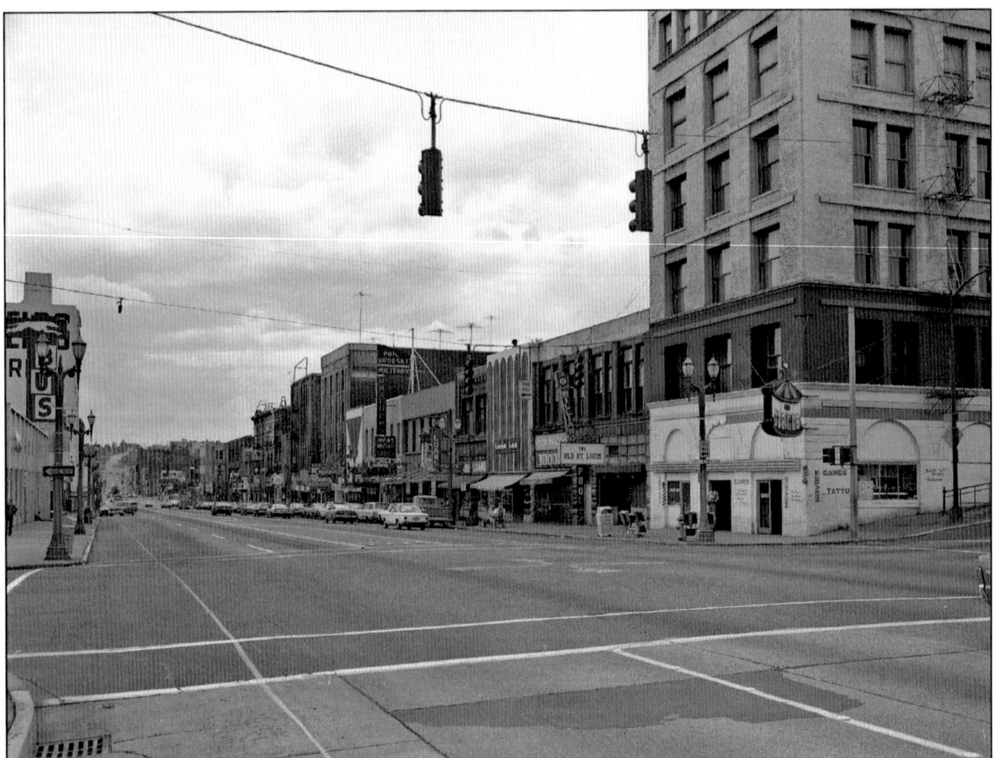

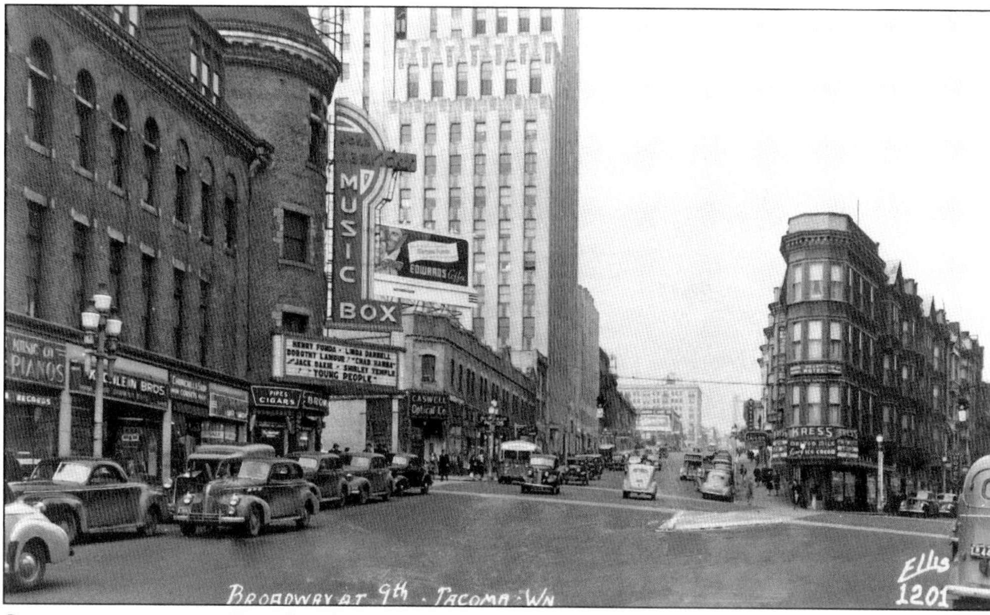

Sometime prior to 1963, ? Ellis photographed northward from South Ninth Street and Broadway, showing—with one exception—a streetscape that is familiar to most Tacomans today (above). To the right are the Bostwick Block and the Medical Arts building. To the left is the Tacoma Theater, whose presence inspired the emergence of additional palaces of entertainment throughout the years. To its south, the Colonial Theater opened its doors. To its west on South Ninth Street was (and is) the Rialto (1918). In 1963, during a showing of Alfred Hitchcock's *The Birds*, the Tacoma Theater was destroyed by fire, leaving a void in the Theater District concept. Across South Ninth Street, the Bostwick Block (below) continues to remind Tacomans of a former time when this intersection drew hundreds of people waiting to be entertained.

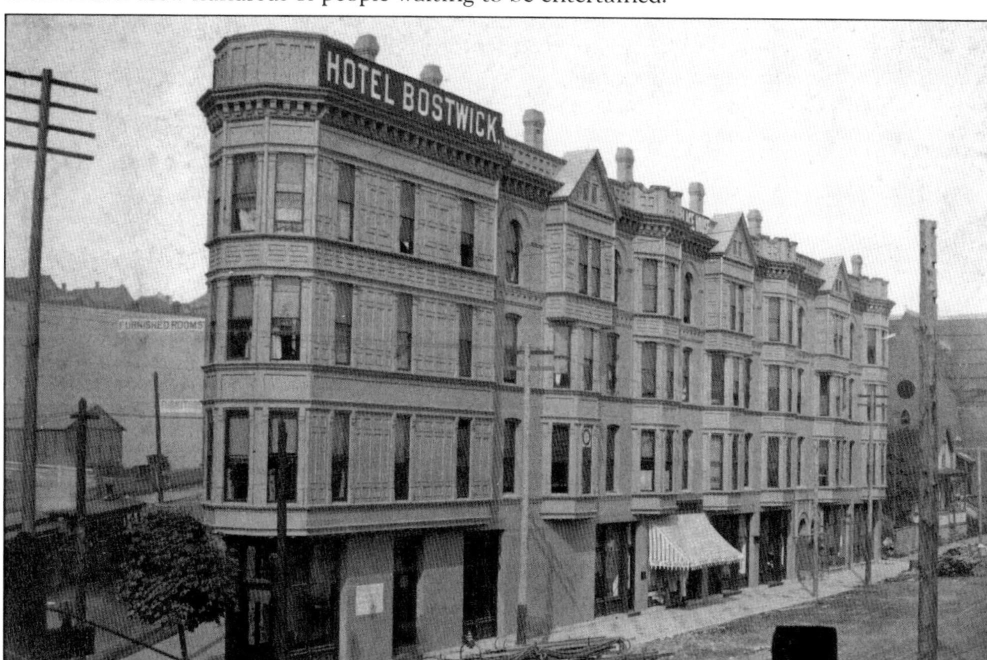

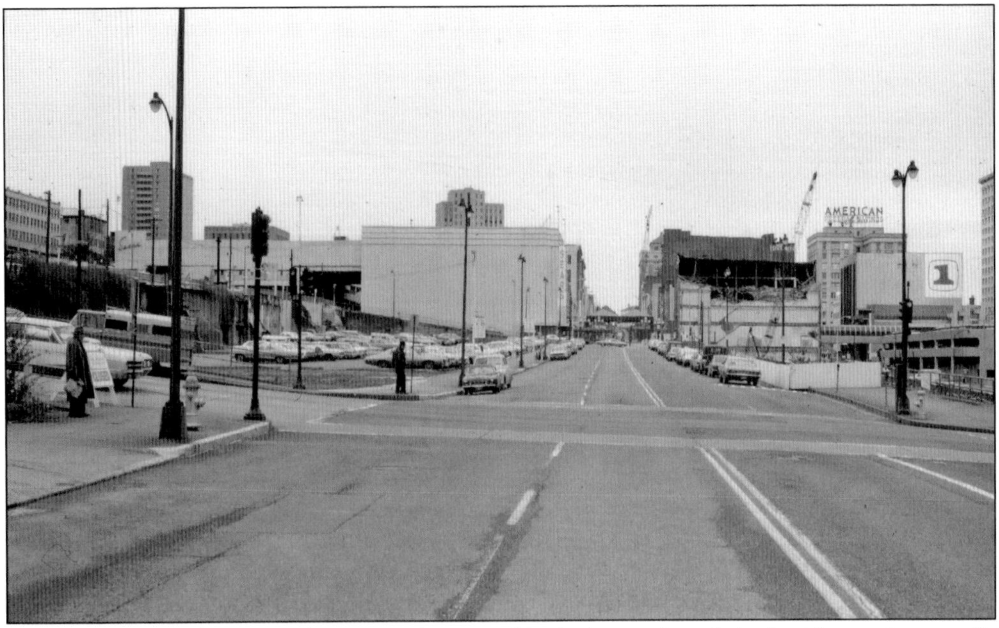

Urban renewal led to some downtown business blocks being demolished with no clear, easily documented reason. In this mid-1970s view, photographer Ron Karabaich looked northward from South Fifteenth Street along Broadway. As shown previously, the buildings that were once here were the commercial district for the pre–World War II Japanese community.

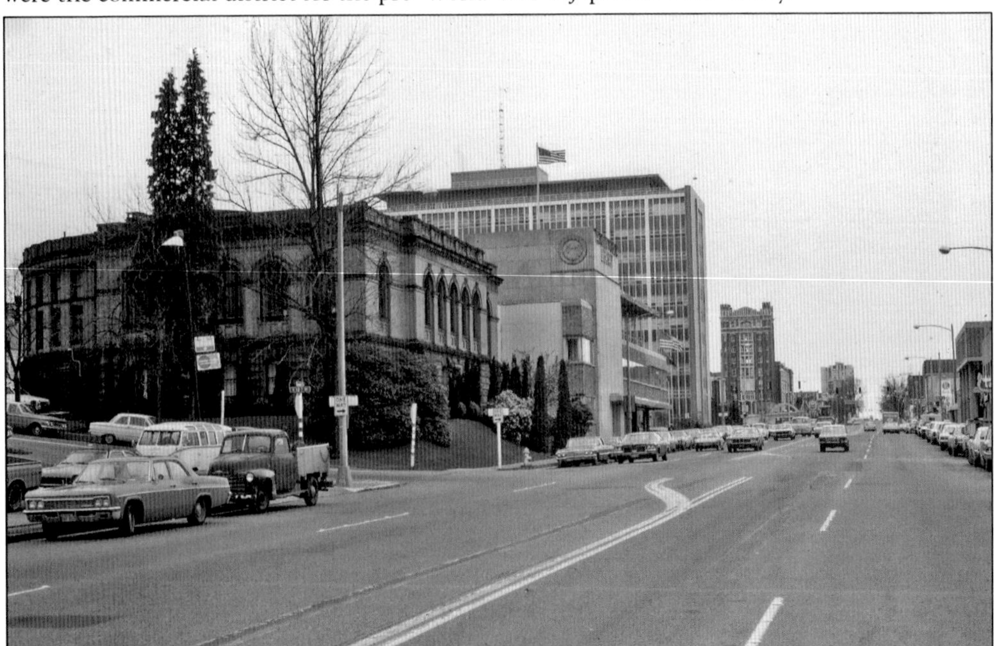

When looking northward from Tacoma Avenue South and South Twelfth Street, Tacomans in the mid-1970s would see, from left to right, the Tacoma Public Library, the County-City Building, and Central School, now the administrative headquarters for the Tacoma School District. Hidden from view are the golden arches of Tacoma's first McDonald's restaurant, one of the few places where juries on lunch break can go.

Urban renewal planning in Tacoma began around 1958 when local merchant associations and city agencies developed a series of studies and reports designed to determine what would be best for the future of the central business district. The passenger escalades and parking garages shown previously were two aspects of this program. After the Tacoma Mall began to lure department stores and other commercial establishment out of downtown, planners decided to create a Broadway Mall. From South Ninth to South Fifteenth Streets, traffic was blocked so that shoppers would not be hindered in their quest for merchandise. Street furniture, including shelters, was a part of the design, as shown in these two mid-1970 photographs. At right, the Winthrop Hotel serves as a backdrop for the southern anchor of the mall. Woolworths (below) remained downtown until 1993.

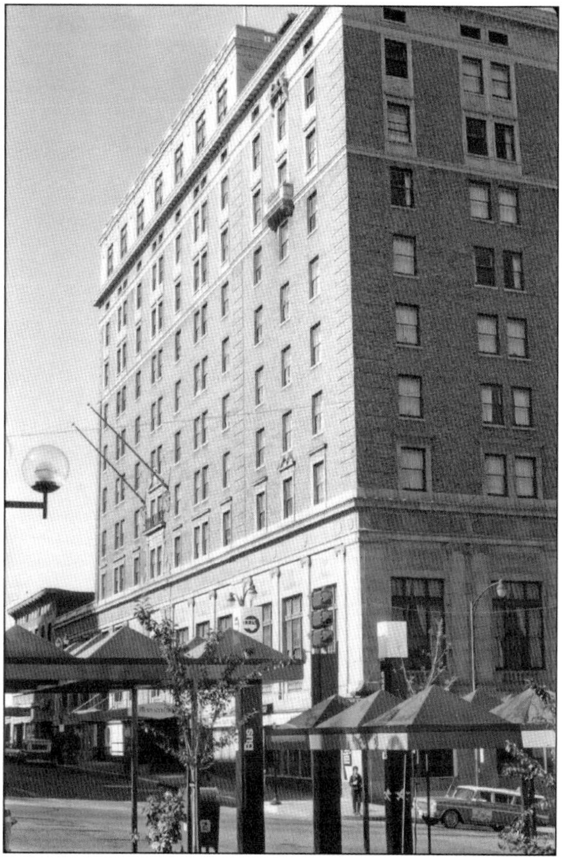

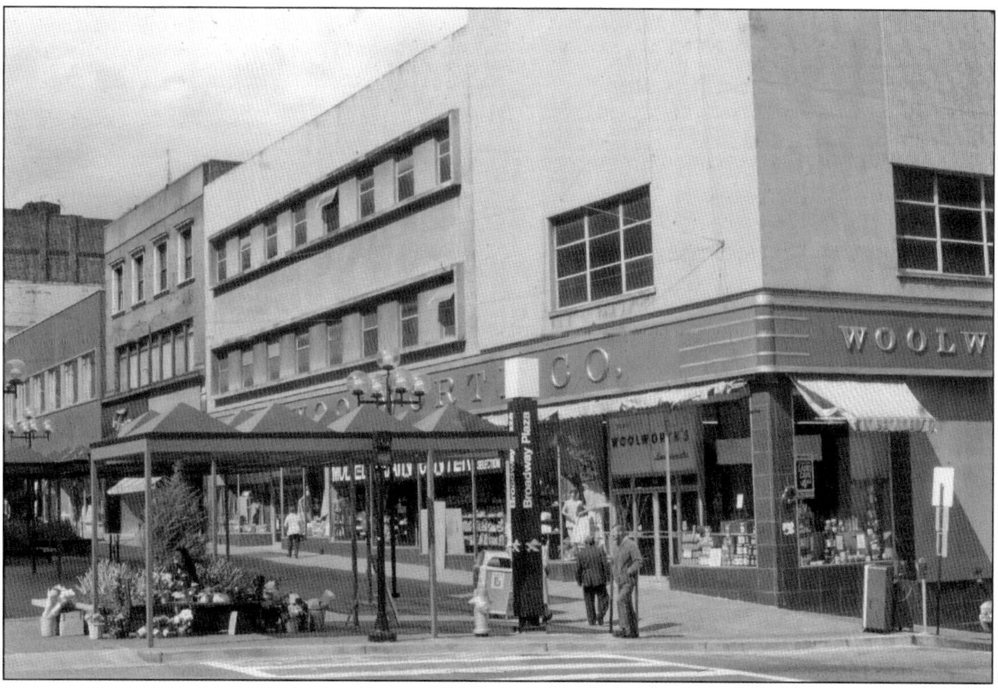

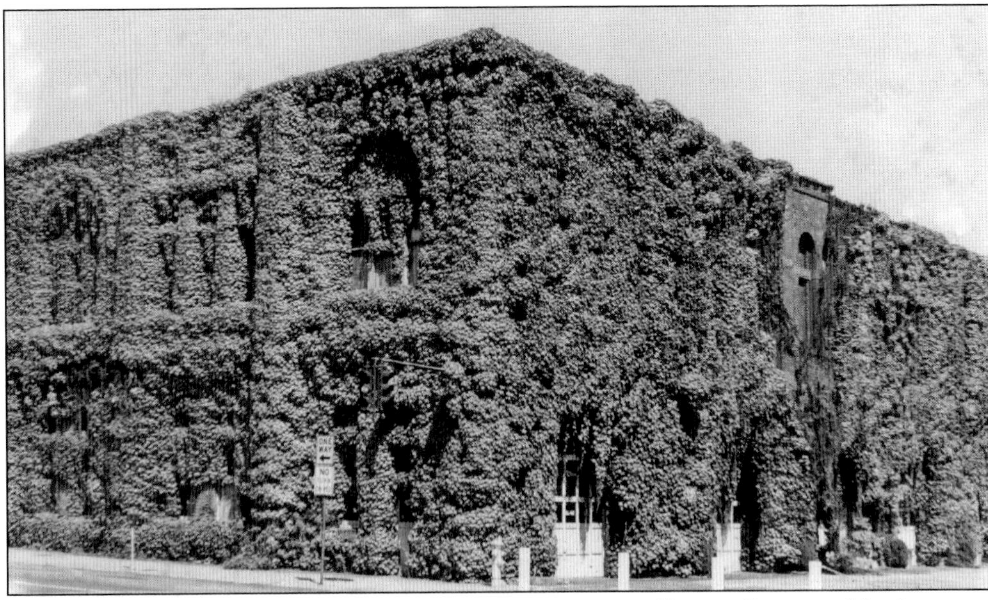

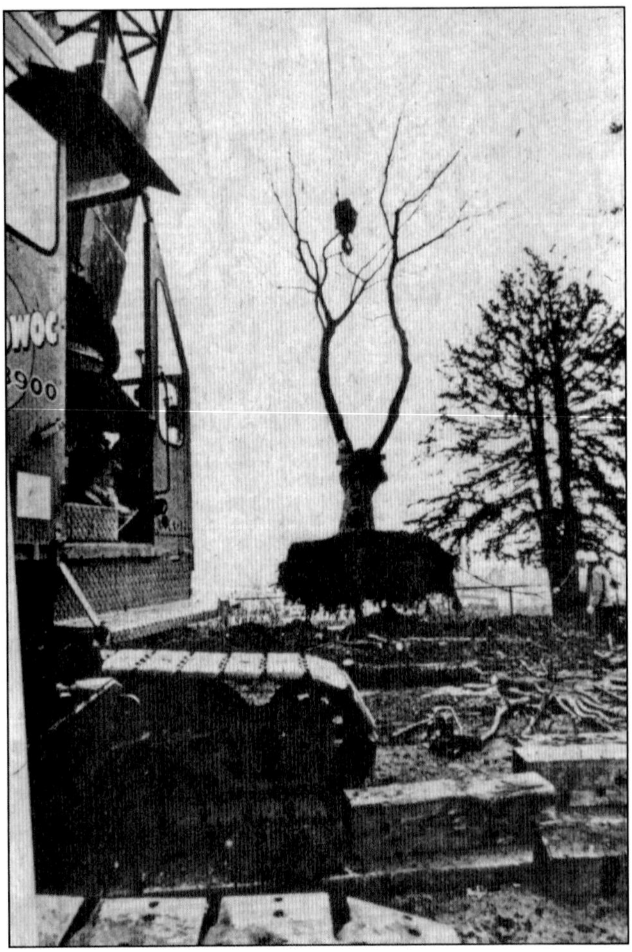

Engine Company No. 6 on A Street remained as headquarters for the Tacoma Fire Department until 1968. During its years of operation, this building witnessed the technological changes from horse to fire truck. By August 1973, when Ron Karabaich took this photograph, the station was wrapped in ivy and awaiting the wrecker's ball.

Firemen's Park, located just north of the firehouse, received a similar fate as plans were laid to construct a freeway underneath this historic open space. Gary Reese, creator of the Northwest Room at the Tacoma Public Library, however, discovered that some of the plantings were memorial trees. These were successfully moved to another city park so as to ensure their preservation.

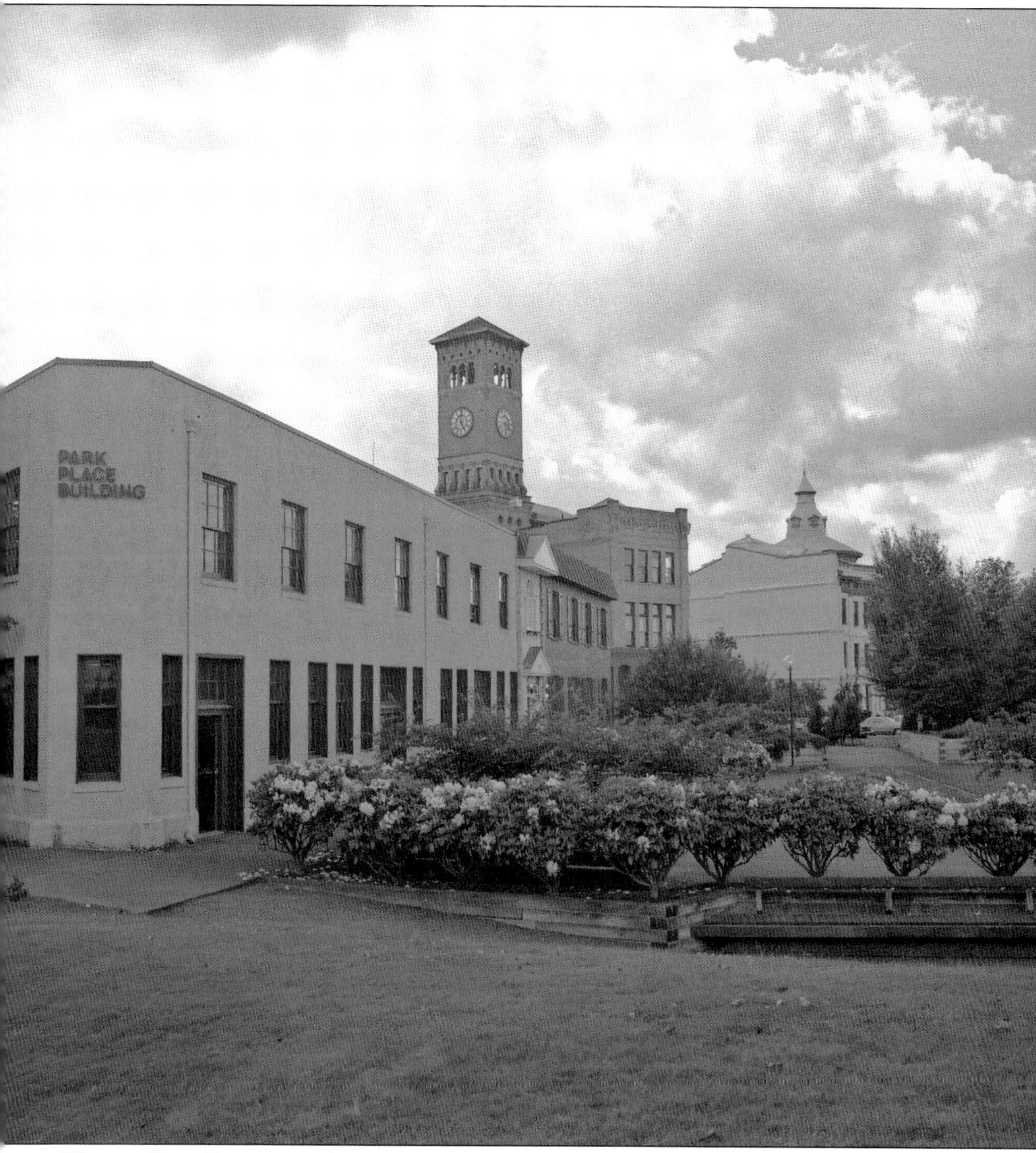

There still is a Firemen's Park at its original site today, although many Tacomans are not aware of its link to the past. In this Ron Karabaich view, taken in the 1970s, a part of the new park is in the foreground where South A turns onto South Eighth Street. Out of view to the right, the city created a space for the restored Tacoma Totem Pole that was originally at the end of South Tenth Street. The city hall (now called the Old City Hall), along with the Northern Pacific Headquarters building, serves as a backdrop in this view. By the time this photograph was taken, developers were planning that both of these buildings be restored and adapted to commercial uses. While the original interurban station seen in the foreground had outlived its usefulness as a transportation mode, it too was re-created into commercial offices.

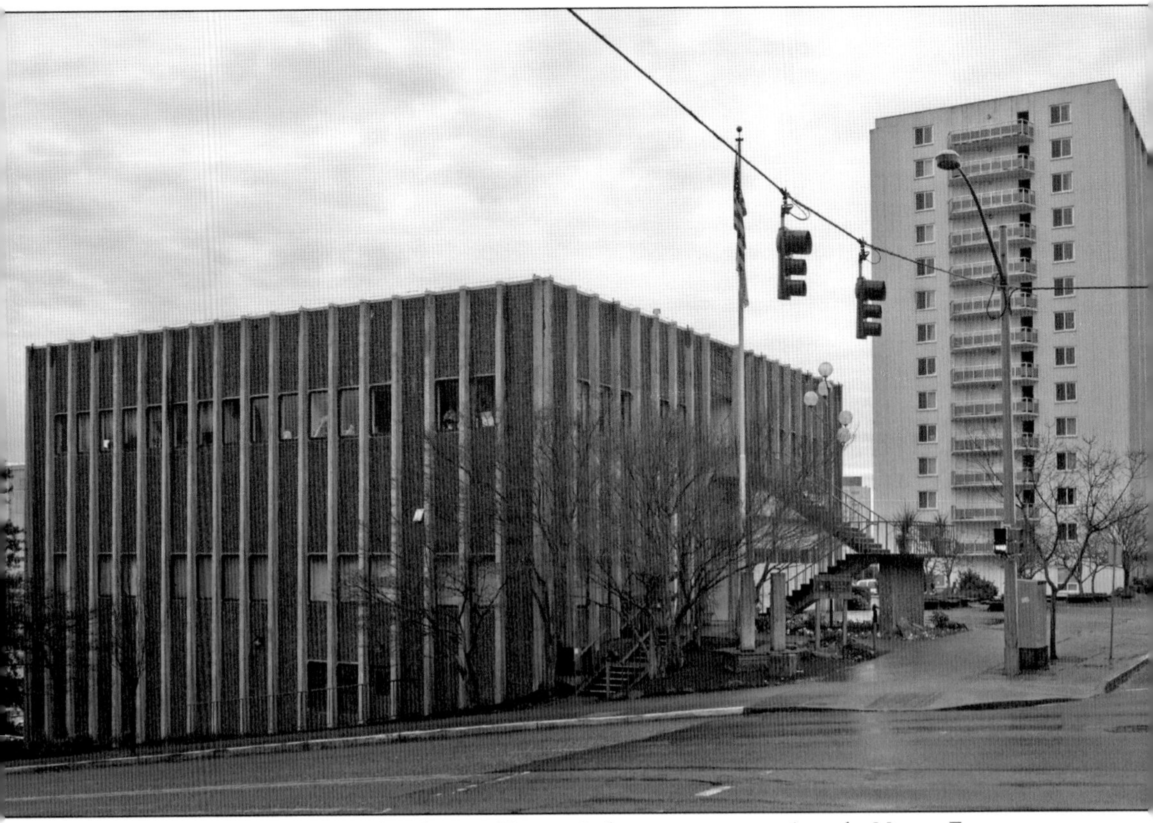

Fawcett Avenue, so named to honor Tacoma's four-time mayor Angelo Vance Fawcett, was never one of the city's busiest in terms of commercial activity. Early on, Tacomans would have found the local telephone company offices, the Sampson Hotel, and the World War II USO club building along the street. But most of the street south of the central downtown core was housing, specifically for the Japanese. In 1960, the 1888 Gottlieb Jaeger building was located at 901 Fawcett Avenue, a typical wood-framed structure with housing above and businesses below. Within eight years, architect Robert B. Price had designed a new headquarters building for the Tacoma Fire Department. This photograph, taken by Ron Karabaich in 2009, shows both the station and the Harbor View Manor located immediately to the south. The First Baptist Church, whose sanctuary was at 902 Market Street a little over a block away, built this high-rise retirement facility.

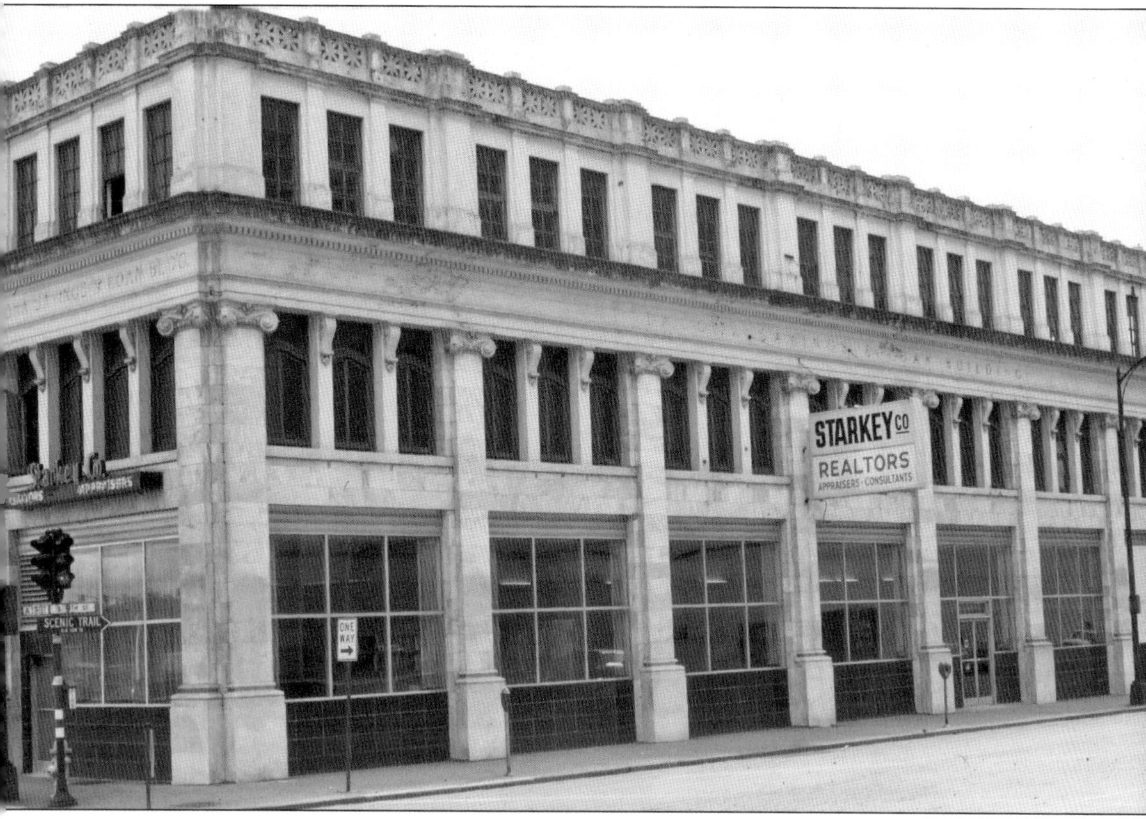

Savings and loan institutions were a part of Tacoma's history from the very beginning. These facilities enabled many working-class families to place savings into an account for future use and enabled thousands of local residents to build and own their homes. The Pacific Building and Loan and the Tacoma Savings and Loan Associations were two of the city's earliest such institutions, and both had their offices in this building at 100 South Ninth Street at various times. The building itself was the inspiration of Edward Bowes, who retained the architectural firm of Heath and Twitchell to design a monument to the real estate industry. In 1908, when the building was completed, Bowes was working on behalf of the Union Pacific Railroad Company on a suburban development called Regents Park. Tacomans now know this local community as Fircrest. People nationwide remember its developer as Major Bowes of the original *Amateur Hour* on radio.

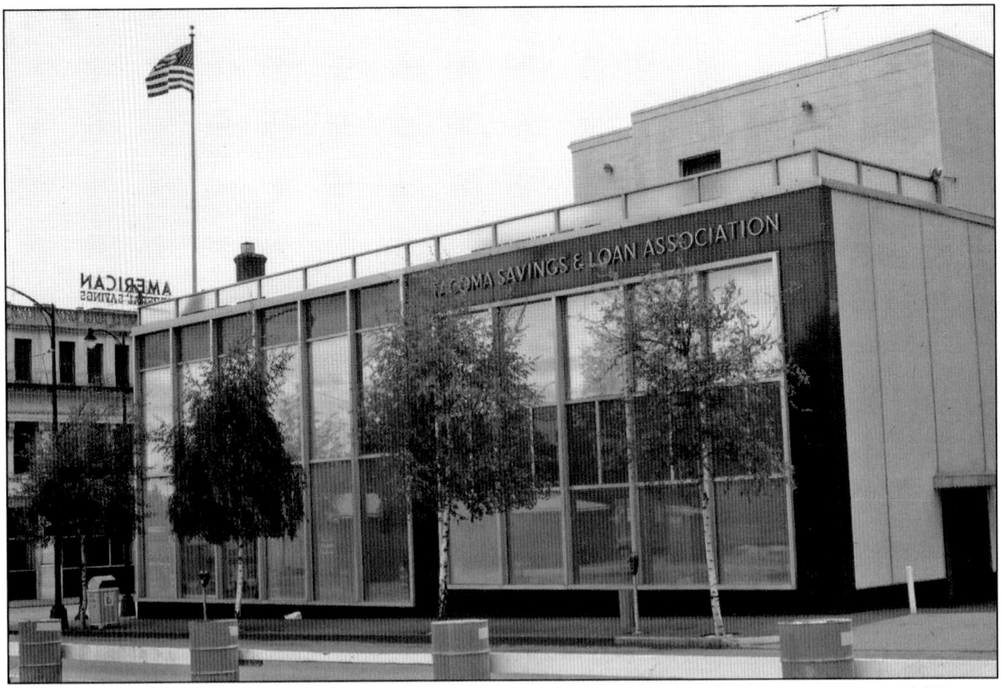

The Tacoma Savings and Loan Association was founded in 1899 so that a depositor could "write your own future" when it came to home loans. In 1956, the company moved to 101 South Ninth Street across the road from its earlier quarters. This was the third building on this site where the Uhlman Block had early been replaced by the Tacoma Gas company years before.

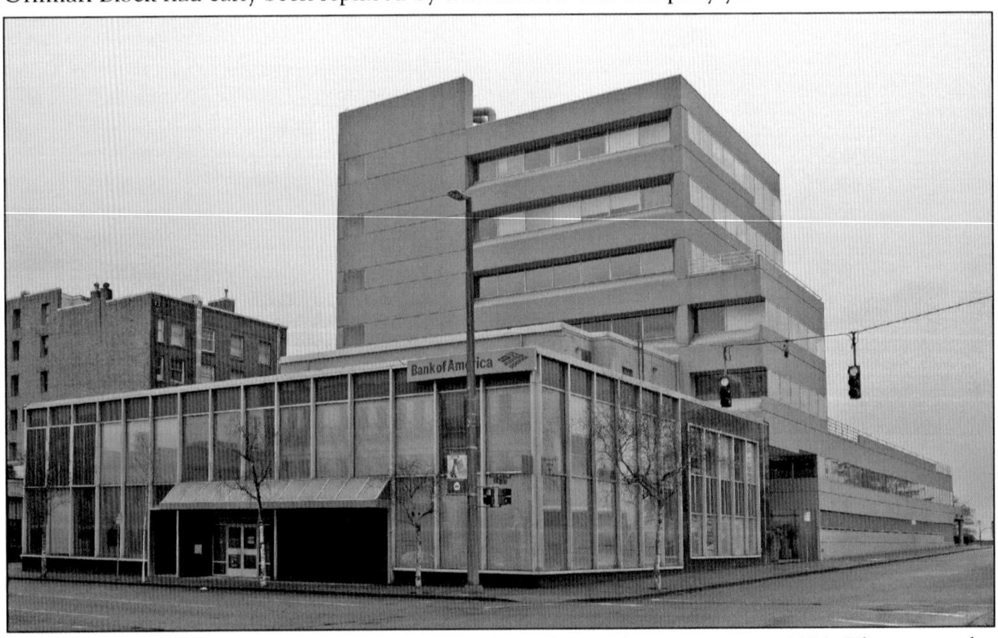

The site of the Tacoma Savings and Loan building changed once again in 1979. This time, the association built a seven-story headquarters and parking garage that was attached to the original structure. Other users here include the firm of Morton and McGoldrick, an attorney firm in existence since the late 1930s. Ron Karabaich photographed the complex in 2009.

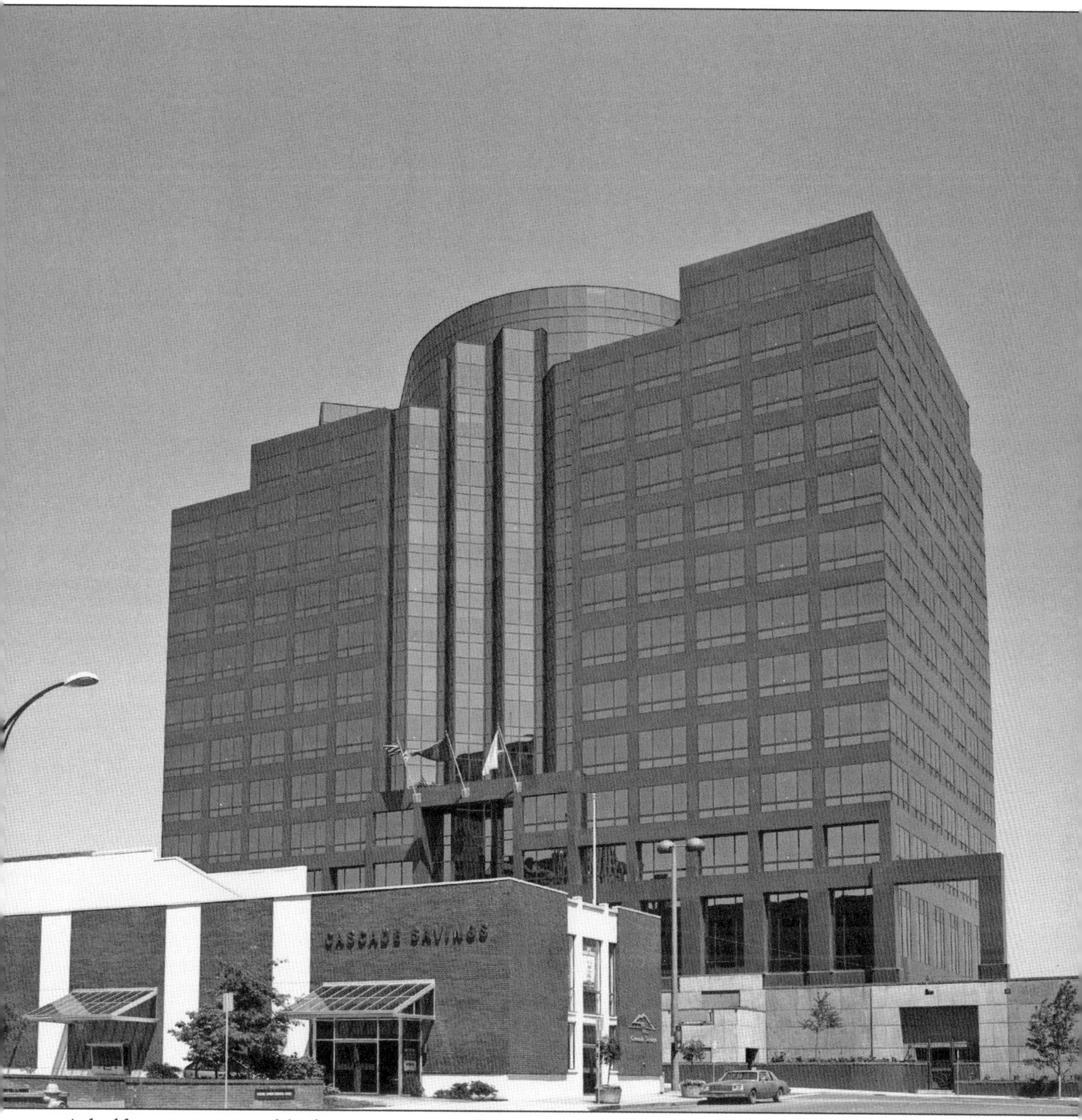

A half-century passed before a use, apart from a parking lot, was found for the former Tacoma Hotel on A Street. In the 1980s, however, the Russell Investment firm decided to build its world headquarters in downtown Tacoma. According to the company Web site, the building was custom designed by George and Jane Russell "to reflect both the urban and natural environments." It was "deliberately oriented on the property so that every floor has direct views of Mount Rainier." Frank Russell had started a brokerage firm in 1936. His grandson, George, entered the firm in 1958 and began an expansion that included strategic pension fund consulting. By 1969, the Russell firm moved from managing money to "managing money managers" and expanded its field of operations by establishing offices in New York; Toronto, Canada; and Tokyo, Japan. Ron Karabaich photographed the headquarters building sometime after 1988, the year it was dedicated.

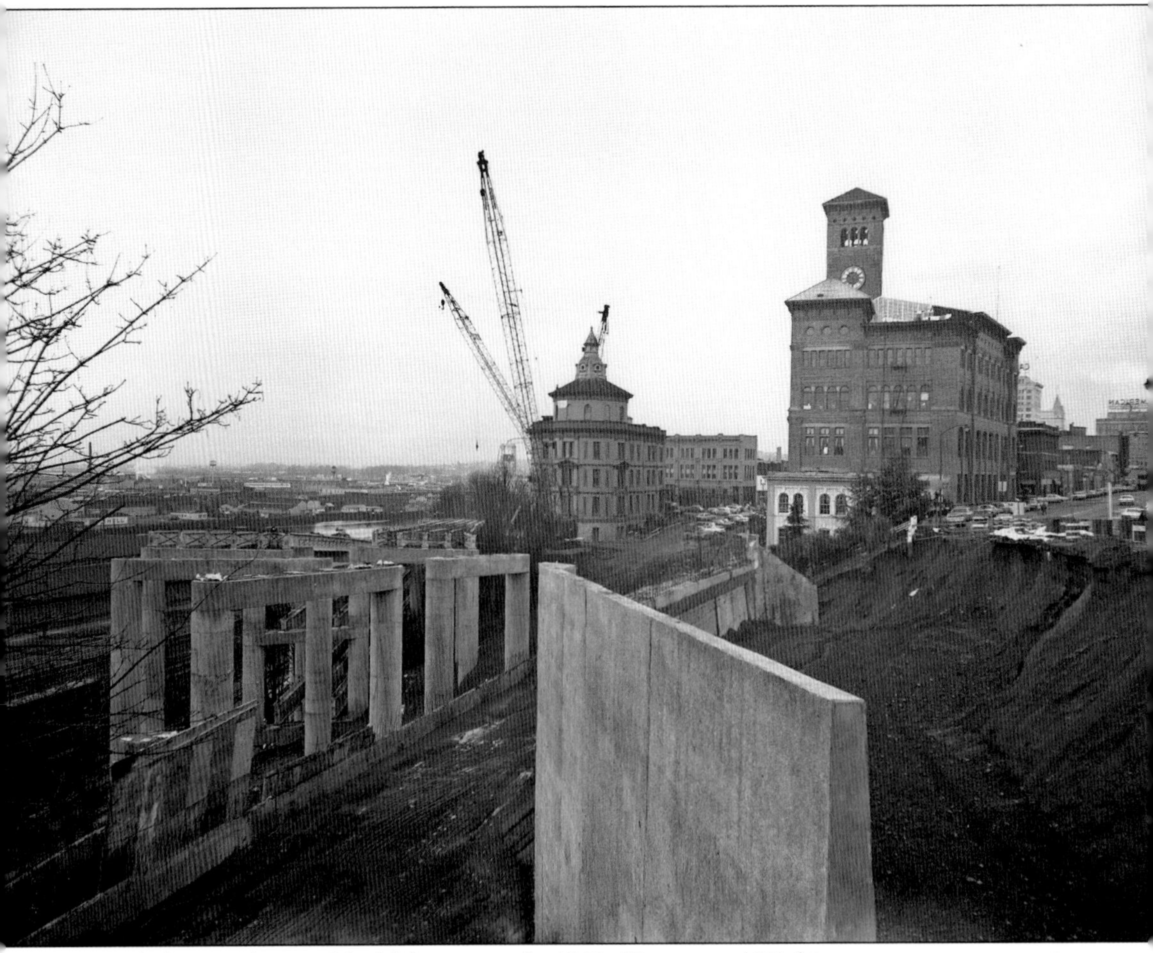

With the completion of the I-5 freeway in the 1960s, Tacoma and Washington state transportation engineers began to consider additional links to the national system, including one that would lead to a shoreline boulevard extending along Commencement Bay northward from downtown to Old Tacoma and Ruston Way. The original road design called for the demolition of both the city hall and Northern Pacific Headquarters buildings. The plan created a public outcry that led ultimately to the creation of the Tacoma Landmark Preservation Commission in 1975. City engineers redesigned the road to bypass the two important downtown structures. Even so, the final plan did not prevent the demolition of historic Engine House No. 6 and Firemen's Park on South A Street. When the shoreline route was completed in 1975, the city council named it to honor Gilbert M. Schuster, public works director at the time. Ron Karabaich took this photograph in 1974 when the road was under construction.

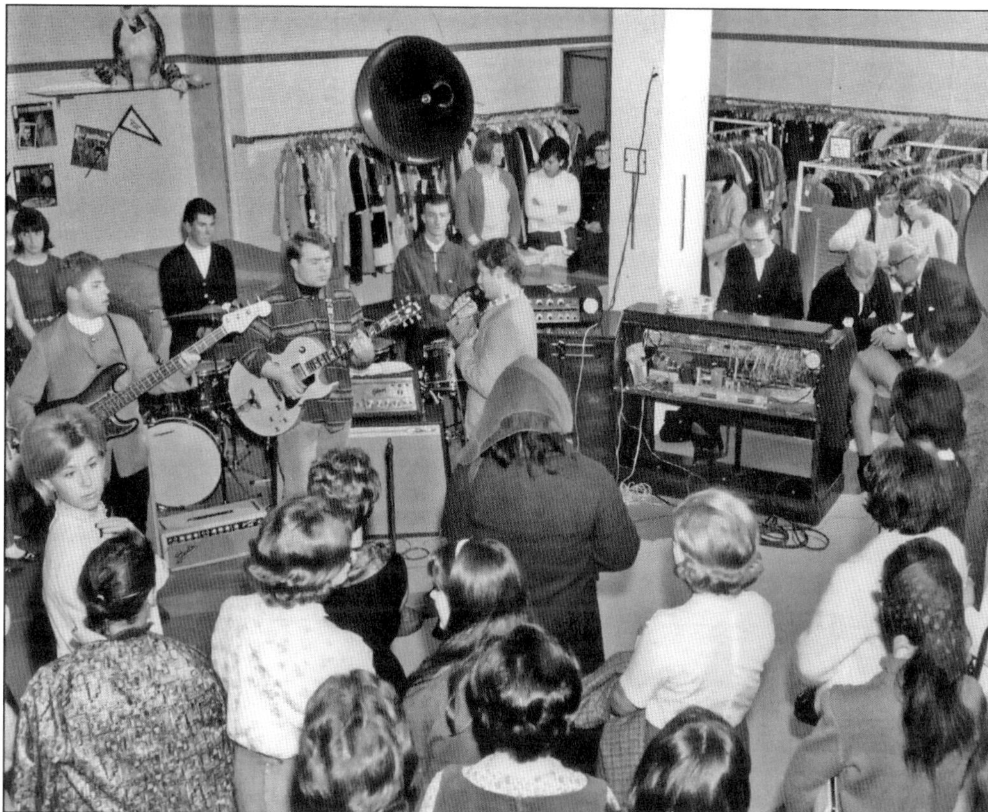

In 1965, Peoples Department Store celebrated its 77th anniversary. To lure teenagers to the Junior World Department, managers featured this unidentified rock band. Australian disc jockey Rhett Hamilton Walker, heard daily on KOL radio, is shown in the center of this photograph. Peoples remained in operation downtown until 1983. (Photograph by Richards Studio; courtesy of Tacoma Public Library.)

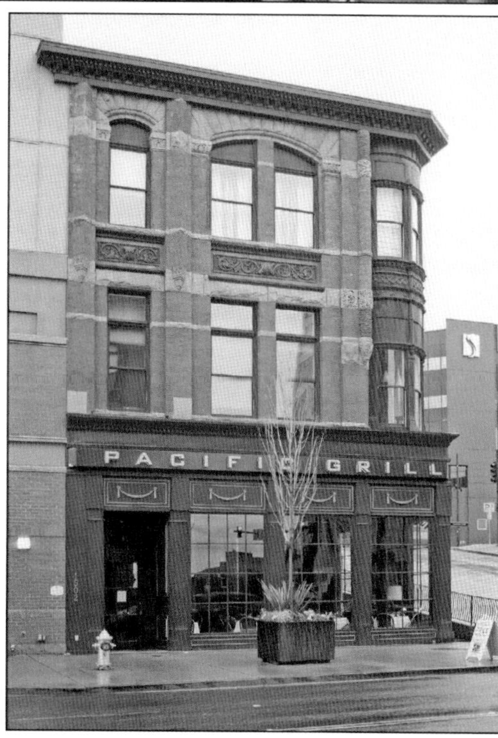

The Waddell building at 1502 Pacific Avenue is a modern-day example as to how an 1890 structure can be rehabilitated and put into a productive use even if its neighbors are more modern in design. Seen here in 2009, it originally had a corner turret that probably was removed following the 1949 earthquake. (Photograph by Ron Karabaich.)

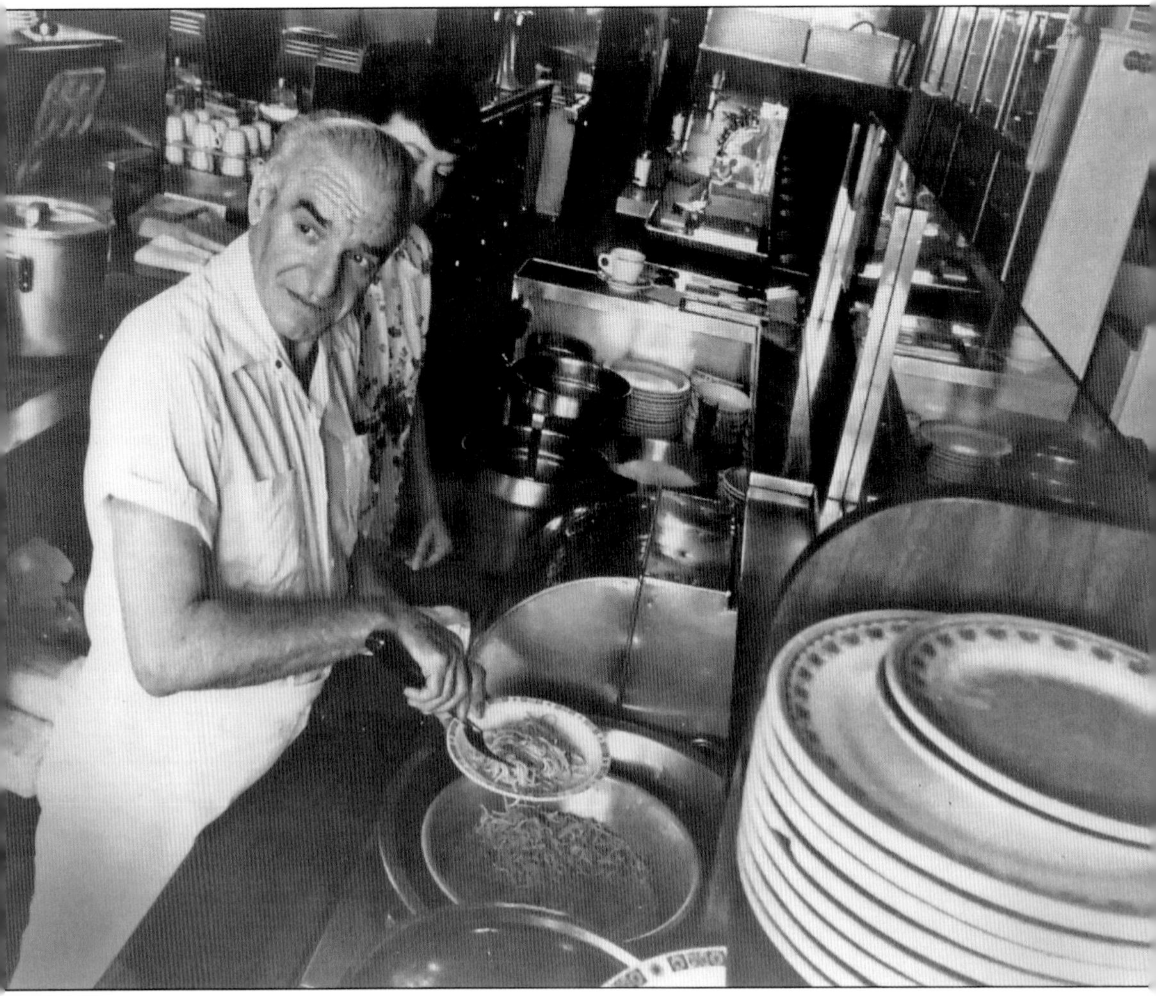

Fr. Peter Hylebos built the Hotel Grand at 1514 Pacific Avenue in about 1907. Japanese pioneer Kyuhachi Nishii was the first to operate a restaurant at this location. By 1921, Vittorio "Bimbo" Perniconi and John Teglia had opened a lunch counter in the building. Originally called the Avenue Café, by 1953, the name had changed to Bimbos. From this time on until the City of Tacoma acquired the site in 2001, the Italian restaurant lured generations of Tacomans wanting to savor the sauces. In this 1976 view, then owner Reno Rosi—nephew to the original Bimbo—prepares a spaghetti dish for a willing customer. When the city acquired the business, it also obtained rights to all the sauce recipes, and periodically the question arises as to what is to become of these epicurean delights. One such respondent in a *News Tribune* poll in 2007 suggested that a giant bronze pot statue be placed in a downtown park with the recipes embossed on the sides. (Courtesy of Tacoma Public Library.)

The Union Station forms the background for this view of an undated Daffodil Parade. In parade views shown previously, people were crammed along the streets. By the time this picture was taken, however, people were bringing their automobiles along, probably creating a traffic jam once the bands and floats went by.

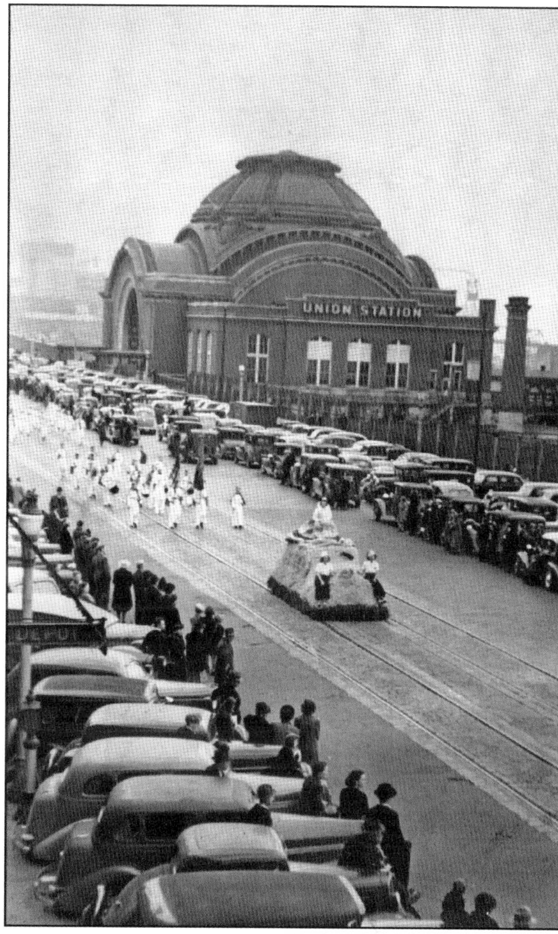

Even though Daffodil Parades still pass by it, today the Union Station is home to federal courts, not passengers. The station is shown here in the distance in a 2009 photograph by Ron Karabaich. To its south in 1991, the Austin, Texas, architectural firm of Moore-Anderson designed the Washington State History Museum—dedicated in 1996—to reflect the same style as the former train depot.

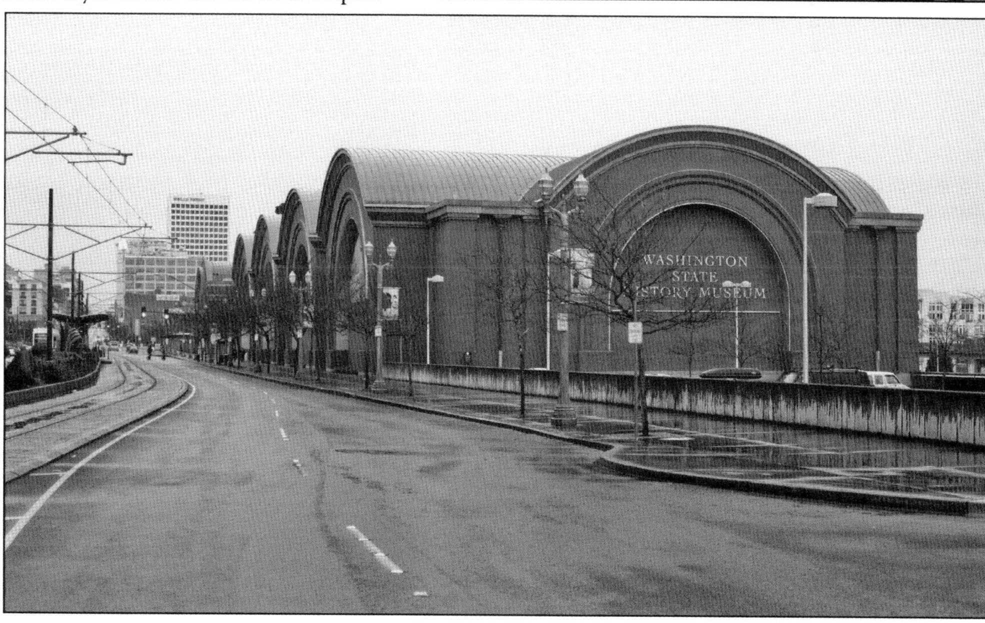

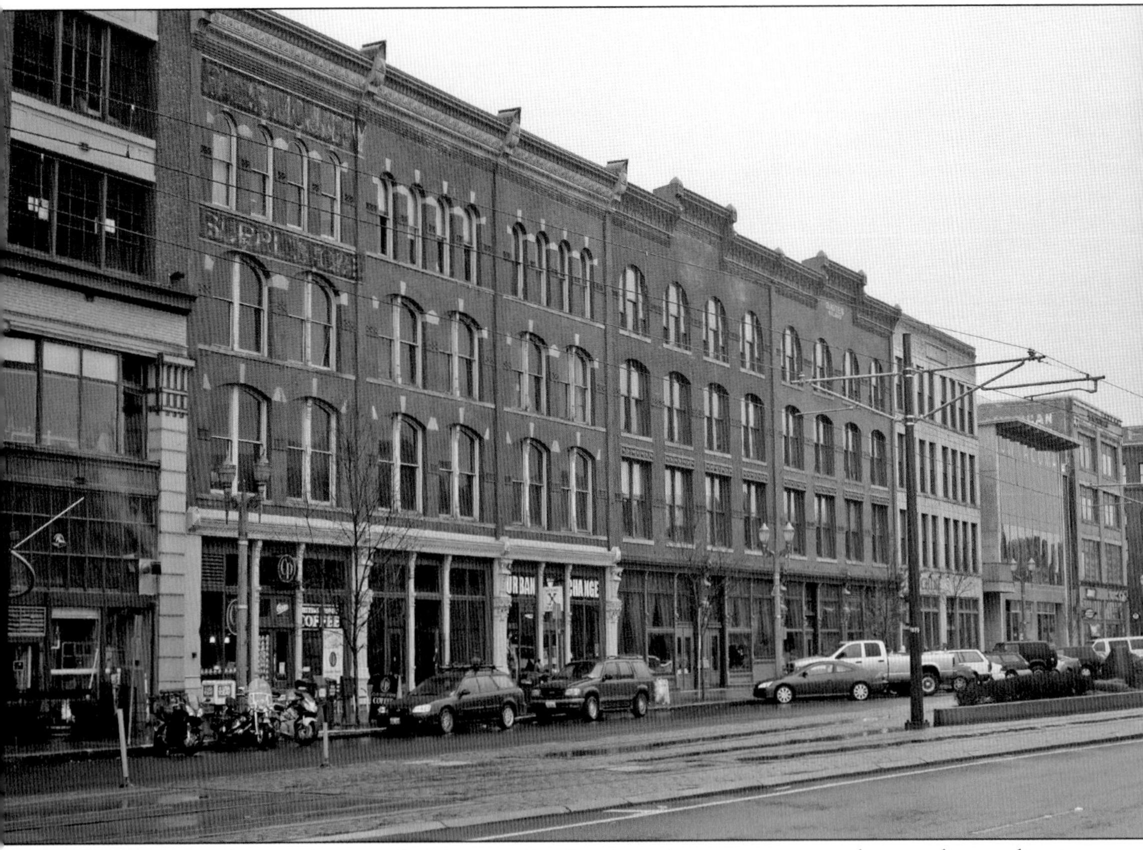

The Union Station is part of a historic district that also encompasses the warehouse district located to the west across Pacific Avenue. Preserving these buildings, once home to grocery and other commercial outlets, has always been a challenge for city planners and developers alike. What saved this part of Tacoma's urban landscape was the University of Washington's decision to transform the buildings into a campus. University of Washington Tacoma was the product of a 1990 legislative decision to expand educational opportunities beyond the school in Seattle. At first, classrooms and library were housed in the Perkins Building on South A Street. In order for it to remain downtown, Tacoma planners convinced the university that the warehouse district would make an ideal campus. According to one Web site, "The somewhat unorthodox choice to renovate some of Tacoma's oldest remaining industrial structures for campus classrooms and offices, instead of razing the buildings and erecting new ones, has since been heralded for its foresight." (Photograph by Ron Karabaich.)

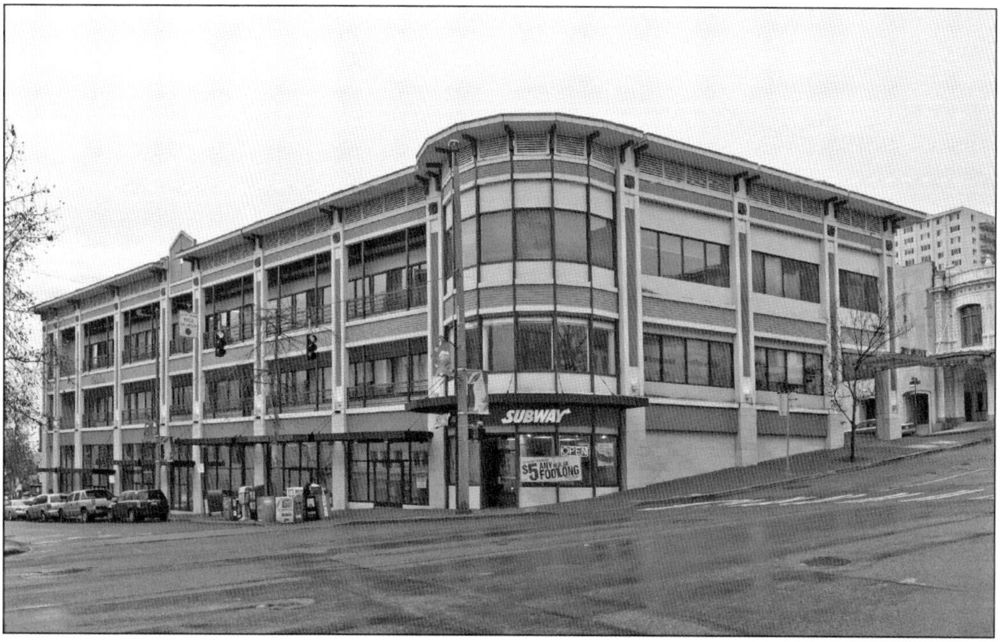

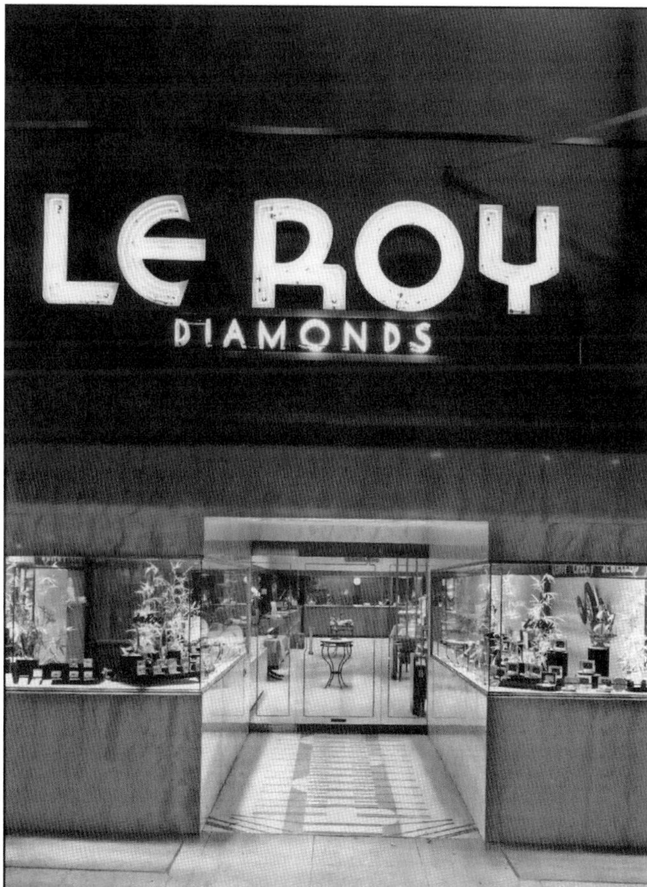

Following the Tacoma Theater fire in 1963, Henry Rhodes commissioned the local architectural firm of Lea, Pearson, and Richards to design the Broadway Terrace building (above) for the site, one that was ready for occupation a year later. Mierow's Jewelers, Sherman Clay and Company—whose specialty was in musical instruments—and Fraser's Gift Shop were the first to occupy the commercial spaces. LeRoy Jewelers, established by Irving Farber and Jack Slotnick in 1941, was settling into its new home in 1966 (at right). Known as the "Diamond Store of Tacoma," it was first located in the Fidelity building prior to various locations on Broadway. When Irving died in 1965, his wife, Hazel, moved the store to this location at 919 Broadway. (Above photograph by Ron Karabaich; below courtesy of Tacoma Public Library.)

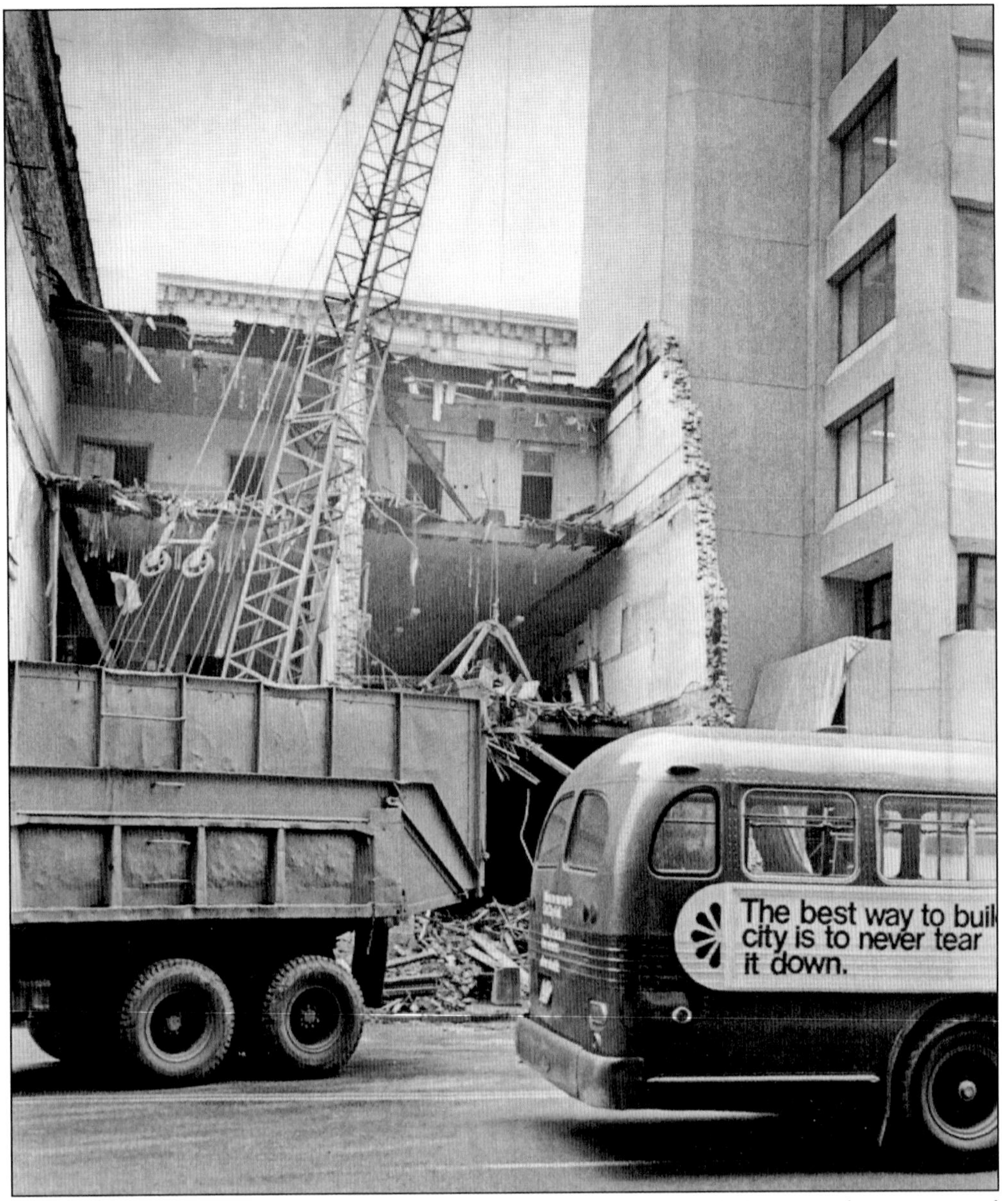

Tacoma's approach to urban renewal in the 1960s and 1970s often led to mixed messages and therefore mixed planning goals, as this photograph illustrates. Here an unidentified *Tacoma News Tribune* photographer was able to capture, sometime in the mid-1970s, the two conflicting moods that represented the need to both save old buildings and to rebuild for the future. "There seemed to be a difference of opinion between the message on this downtown shuttle bus and what was happening to the building in the background," said the Associated Press when sending the image along to its subscribers. The photographer took the view near South Eleventh Street and Broadway where, according to the AP release, the United Mutual Savings Bank was preparing this site for a minipark. There were also additional instances of planning conflict, especially in terms of transportation. For example, were the new freeway routes designed to bring people downtown or to allow the driver to avoid Tacoma's central business district? The question has yet to be answered.

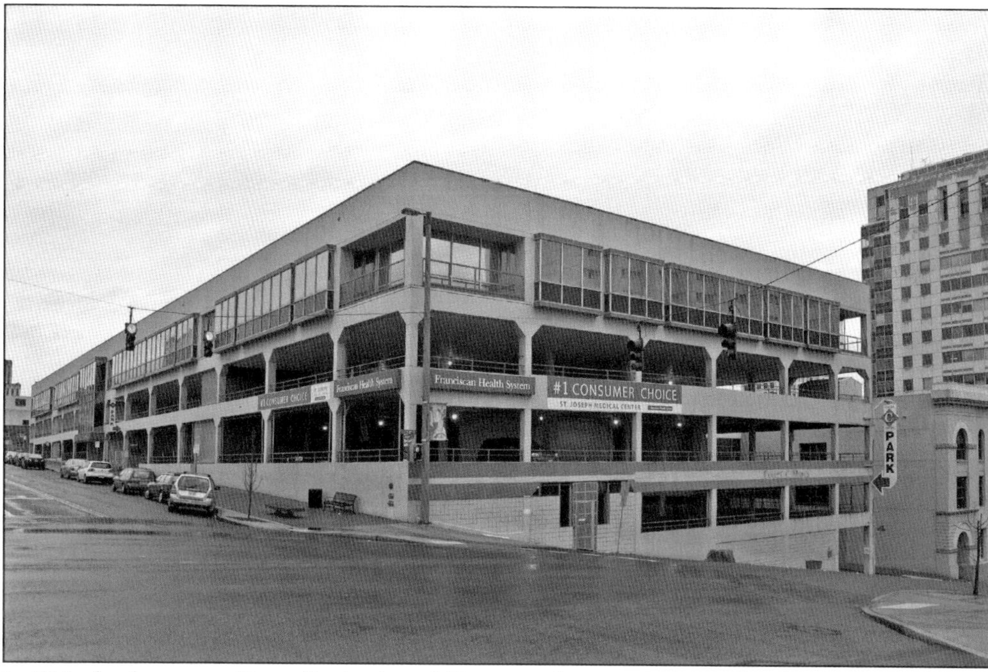

In 1981, the downtown Sears, Roebuck, and Company department store closed its doors and moved to the Tacoma Mall, and once again the building—originally constructed in 1892—received another face-lift (above). Cornerstone, a Weyerhaeuser development firm, removed all vestiges of the building's past, and in 1982, Hillhaven moved its corporate offices into the reconstructed building. Ted B. Hill had incorporated his firm of health care providers in 1955. Two years later, the Tacoma YMCA (below) opened a new recreation facility across from the old Sears building on the corner of South Thirteenth and Market Streets. The organization had departed from its former facility, shown previously, in 1975, but by 1984 realized that downtown still needed a YMCA. (Both photographs by Ron Karabaich.)

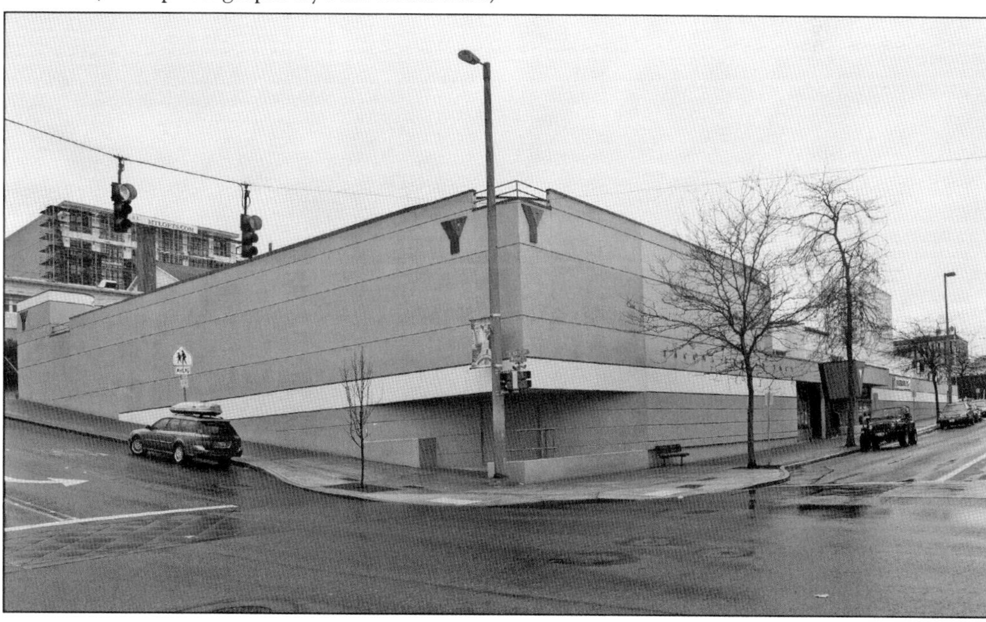

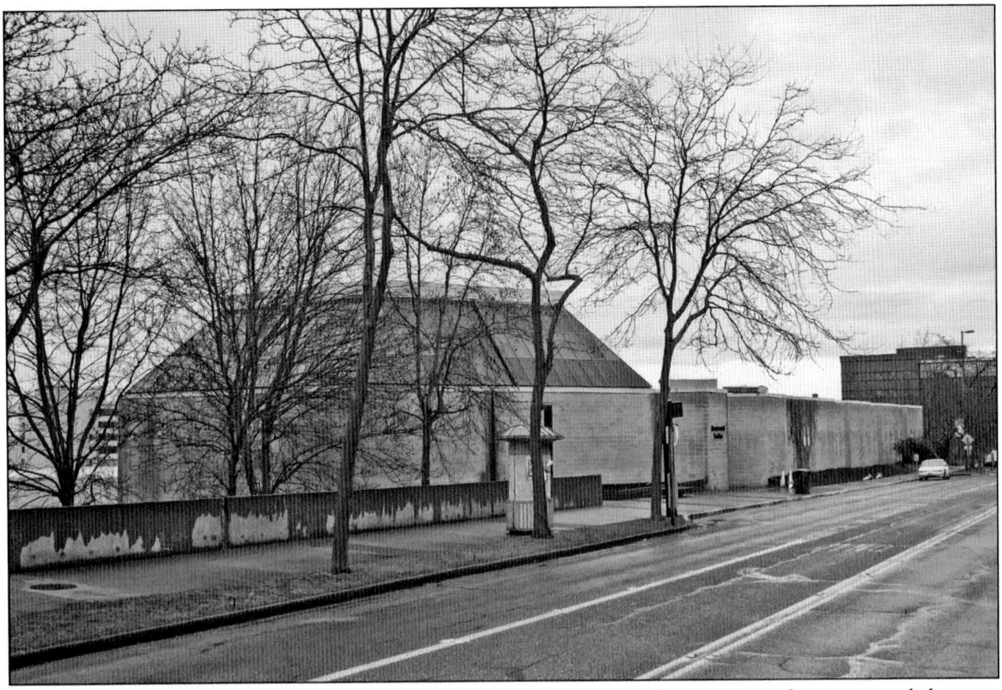

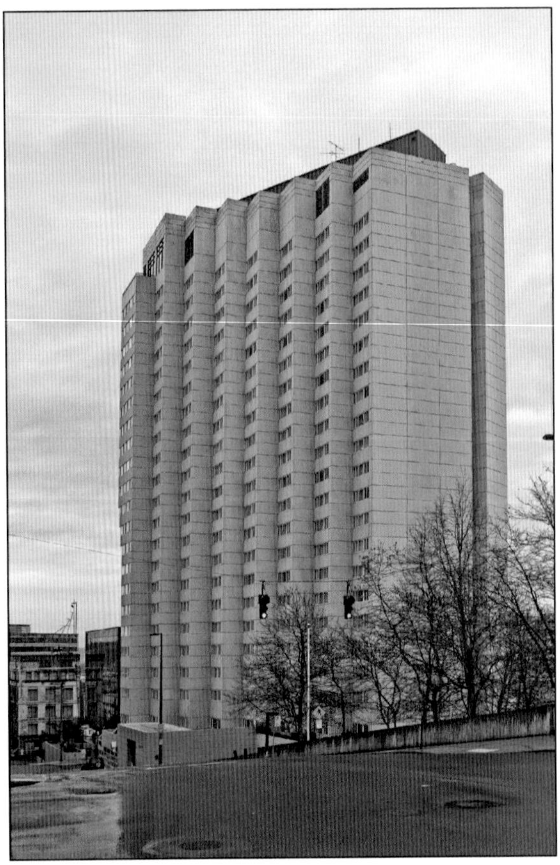

Part of Tacoma's urban renewal dream was the creation of a convention center and the construction of a major hotel that would lure people downtown, much as the Tacoma Hotel had done decades ago. In 1974, Robert Price designed the Bicentennial Pavilion, so named because its scheduled completion date in 1976 was to be part of the commemoration of the founding of the United States. Located at 1313 Market Street, it became Tacoma's first downtown convention center. In 1982, city officials gathered for the ground-breaking for a new Sheraton Hotel (now called the Hotel Murano) that would be adjacent to the pavilion. Reporters lauded the grandeur of the Presidential Suite, one that George Herbert Walker Bush occupied in 1988, then Ronald Reagan's vice president. (Both photographs by Ron Karabaich.)

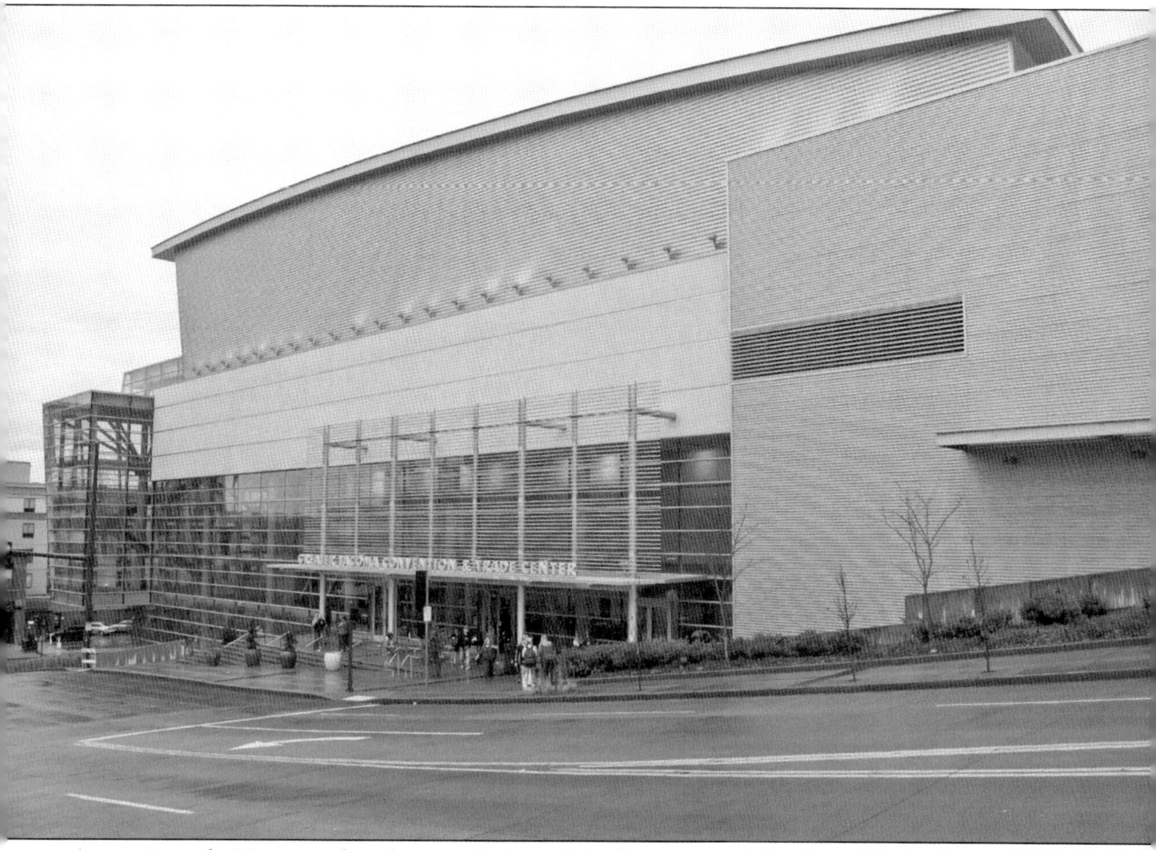

Approximately 20 years after the completion of the Bicentennial Pavilion, Tacoma's economic planners concluded that downtown needed a new convention center so as to attract a new and larger generation of conference goers. The concept was a massive one that involved the purchase and demolition of the older commercial properties situated around South Fifteenth Street and Broadway southward to where Pacific Avenue meets Jefferson Avenue. Many of the buildings had been constructed between the 1880s and the early years of the 20th century and included a wide array of restaurants and hotels that planners concluded did not fit into the concept of Tacoma as a new, modern, and computer-wired city. By 2001, the Tacoma architectural firm of Merritt and Pardini had provided the initial design for what is called the Greater Tacoma Convention and Trade Center, a facility completed in 2004 and pictured in 2009. (Photograph by Ron Karabaich.)

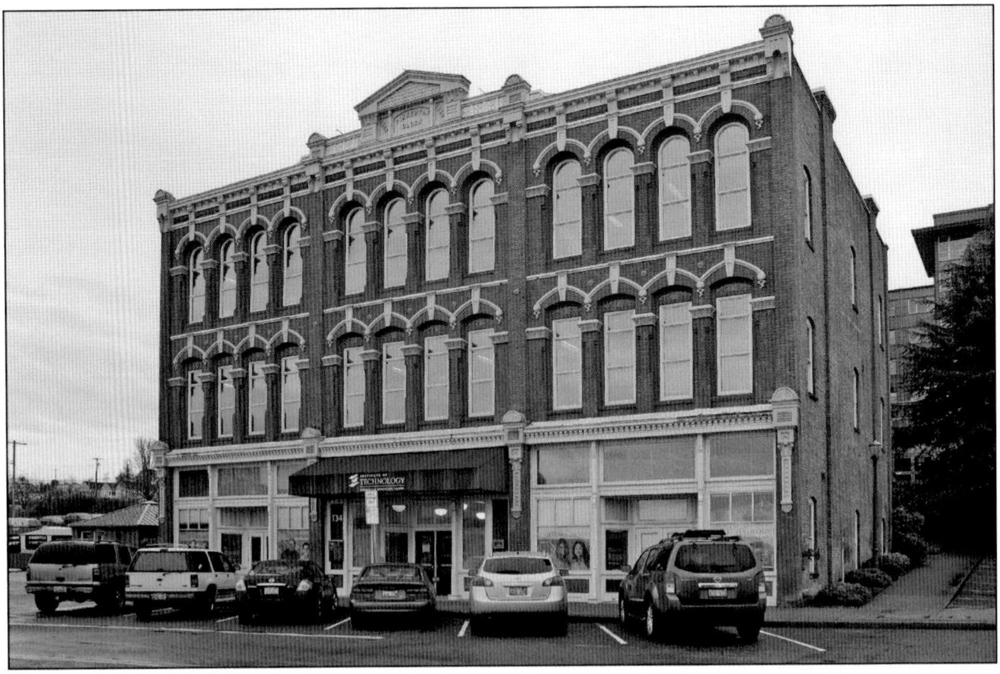

South of the new convention center and close to the University of Washington Tacoma campus are two buildings that have survived all the changes surrounding them. One is the Massasoit Hotel at 1702 Broadway (above in 2009). Upon its completion in 1887, Col. John W. Pinkerton named it after a New England hotel of the same name. Now restored, it houses offices. The Swiss Society constructed its hall in 1913 at 1902 South Jefferson Avenue, where it became the focal point for the organization's social events (below in 2009). In 1992, however, ownership was transferred to the University of Washington. Even so, two years later, the Swiss had become a favorite watering hole and music venue for college students and other Tacomans alike. (Both photographs by Ron Karabaich.)

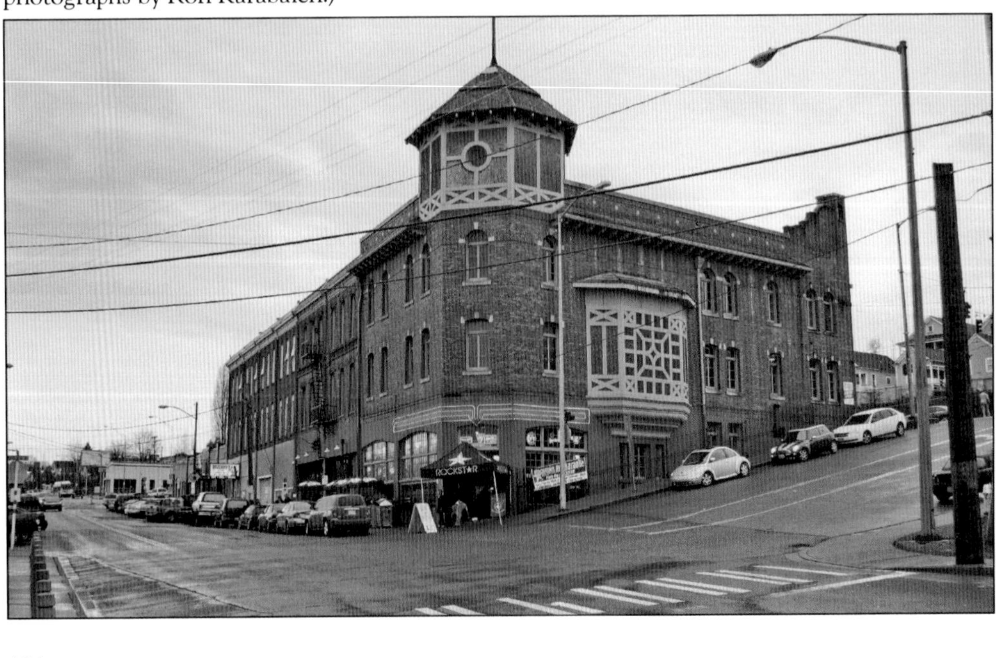

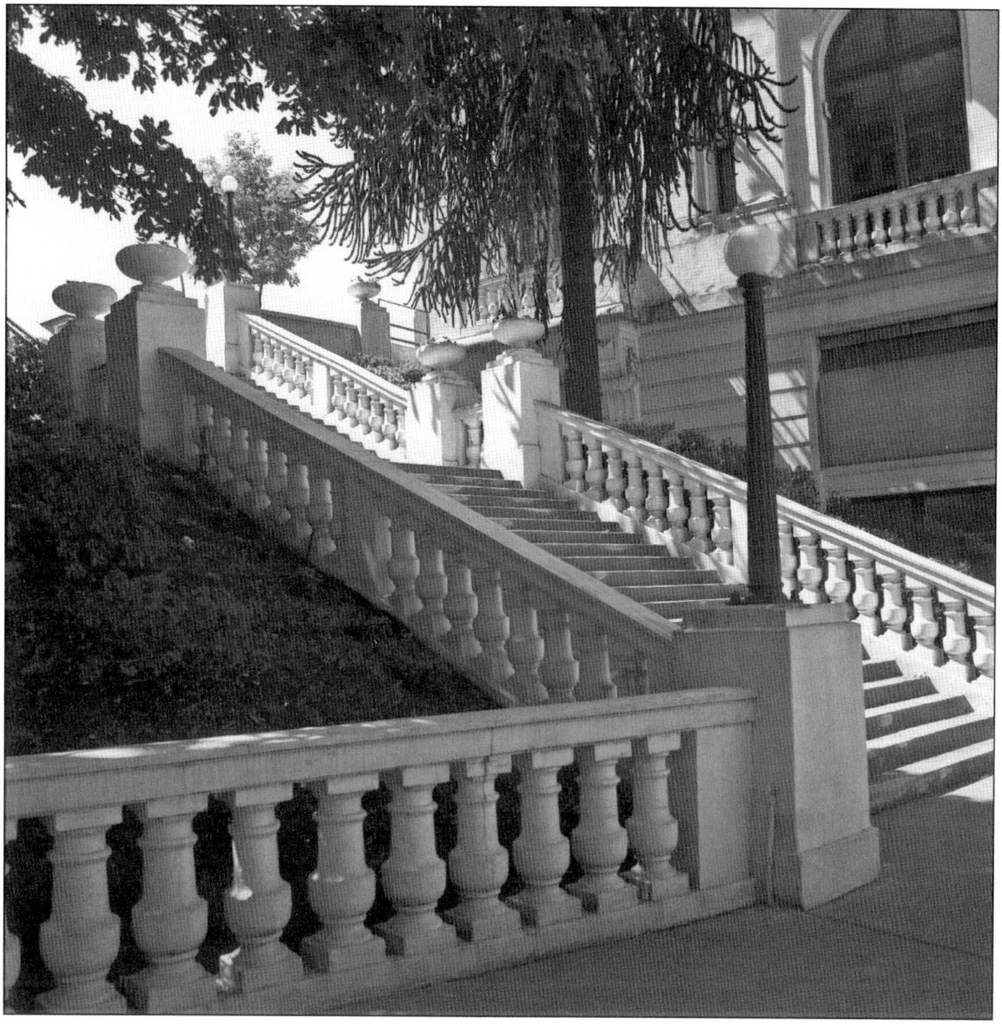

For generations, Tacomans have witnessed the birth, growth, death, and change that are a part of all cities in the United States. Born in 1873 as an infant of the Northern Pacific Railroad, the city sprouted in the 1880s when a building boom created many buildings still seen today. Before automobile transportation and commercial malls fractured Tacoma's downtown fabric, it was truly a people place. Everyone living in the city had to ride the streetcars from their respective neighborhoods to shop, eat, bank, watch government in action, or be entertained. But no city is ever a static place. Throughout Tacoma's history, buildings were constructed and demolished with new ones placed upon the old. Amid this ever-constant change, however, the past has survived thanks to those citizens who have insisted that the present is not interesting without a little bit of the past. The Spanish Stairs, originally built as a fire escape for the Elks Temple but still surviving today as a landmark, serve as a symbol of this Tacoma urban spirit. (Courtesy of Ron Karabaich.)